Job Search Guide

BE YOUR OWN CAREER COACH

Jan Tegze

© Copyright 2022 Jan Tegze

Edited by Sarah Lane.
Proofread by Katerina Nenkova.
Cover and book design by Euan Monaghan.

Published in 2022 by Net Image, s.r.o.,
Kumpoštova 7, Brno, 612 00, Czech Republic

ISBN 978-80-908069-1-7

Table of Contents

DISCLAIMER

Any opinions represented in this book are personal and belong solely to the author and do not represent those of people, institutions, or organizations that the author may or may not be associated with in a professional or personal capacity unless so explicitly stated. Any opinions are not intended to malign any religion, ethnic, group, organization, company, or individual.

This book is published for informational and educational purposes only. The publisher and/or the author make no representations or warranties with respect to the accuracy or completeness of the contents of this work and specifically disclaim all warranties, including, without limitation, warranties of fitness for a particular purpose. No warranty may be created or extended by sales or promotional materials. The advice and strategies contained herein may not be suitable for every situation. Publication of this book does not create a consultant-client relationship.

When you access this book or e-book, you agree that the author and/or publisher of this book shall not be liable to you for any loss or injury caused by procuring, compiling, or delivering the information gained from the book. In no event will the author and/or publisher of the book be liable to anyone for any action taken on the basis of such information or for any incidental, consequential, special, or similar damages. The author and/or publisher of this book expressly disclaim any and all liability for any direct, indirect, incidental, consequential, or special damages arising out of or in any way connected with the buying and reading of this book and/or any information contained in this book. The author and/or publisher of the book disclaim all responsibility for any loss, injury, claim, liability, or damage of any kind resulting from, arising out of, or any way related to any information and content of this book. The information contained in this book or e-book is strictly for educational purposes. Therefore, if you wish to apply the ideas in this book or e-book, you are taking full responsibility for your actions.

Technology and services are constantly changing; therefore, this book might contain information that, although accurate when it was written, may no longer be accurate by the time you read it. Your use of or reliance on the information in this book is at your own risk, and the author and/or publisher are not liable or responsible for any resulting damage or expense.

Every possible effort has been made to ensure that the information contained in this book is accurate at the time of going to press, and the publisher and author cannot accept responsibility for any errors or omissions.

This book is dedicated to all job seekers who never heard back after an interview or did but got useless feedback like "You are overqualified," "We found somebody with more experience," or "You were our second choice."

You all were my main motivation for writing this job search guide.

ACKNOWLEDGMENTS

This book wouldn't have been possible without all the amazing people and candidates that I met during my career who shared with me their positive stories and also their frustration about the recruitment process.

I want to thank all of the individuals who took the time to speak with me and share their experiences, both good and bad. Without their help, this book would not have been possible.

I owe an enormous debt of gratitude to those who gave me detailed and constructive comments on one or more chapters: Thomas Swan Bittencourt, Elizabeth Lembke, Trish Wyderka, Ann Wilkerson, Jee Kang, Jiří Herodek, Munira Ali, Katerina Nenkova, and many others.

Thank you all for your time and contributions!

ABOUT THE AUTHOR

Jan Tegze is an experienced international recruiter and talent acquisition leader, with more than eighteen years of experience in the recruitment industry.

He started his professional career in a recruitment agency and after that worked for several large corporations where he was responsible for global hiring initiatives. Over the years, he interviewed more than 10,000 candidates, recruited hundreds of people, and trained and coached thousands of professionals from all walks of life and seniority levels in many different countries around the world.

He is a sourcing and recruitment trainer, blogger, keynote speaker, recruitment advisor, career coach and author of several books including *Full Stack Recruiter,* which became an international bestseller in the recruitment industry.

To learn more about Jan Tegze, please visit www.jantegze.com.

INTRODUCTION

Searching for a job is tough. You spend hours tailoring your resume and cover letter, applying to dozens of positions, and crossing your fingers that you'll get at least one call back. And then, if you're lucky enough to land an interview, you have to go through the nerve-wracking process of meeting with a potential employer and trying to sell yourself as the best candidate for the job.

The book you are holding in your hands or reading on a digital screen is different from other books covering the job search process. It is based on decades of research: During my career I interviewed more than 10,000 candidates and helped find the new dream job for hundreds of them.

This guide is for *anyone* looking for a new job—not just people new to the process—regardless of whether they just finished university, have several years of experience, or are a seasoned employee.

Unlike other job search guides, which are step-by-step manuals promising that you will land a job within the next few days, this book will help you *throughout* the hiring process, including the interview and salary negotiations.

And this is perhaps the most important difference, this book is not a step-by-step manual that you need to follow to the letter, as most of the steps included in such manuals will never work for you or for your specific situation. There is no "one-size-fits-all" approach to landing a new job.

Rather than telling you what to do, I decided to share with you what is behind the curtain of the recruitment process and disclose all the things that recruiters and hiring managers are doing, things no one has told you about before.

No book in the world will guarantee you a job after you finish reading it, but after you read this job search guide and use the methods mentioned in it, your chances of landing a new job will increase.

Once you've found your new dream job, please share this book with your significant other, family, friends, colleagues, or anyone who is currently looking for a job. Give them an advantage over the other candidates.

If you have a few seconds to spare, I would appreciate any positive review on Amazon or on LinkedIn so more people can find out about my book. Many thanks for considering my request.

I hope you enjoy reading it!

—Jan

1. Ways to Find a New Job

You've been at your job for a while now and you're starting to feel stagnant. It's time for a change. But where do you even start? If you're like most people, your first stop will be the local job boards. You'll scan through the postings, looking for anything that catches your eye.

Many job seekers focus mainly on online resources when looking for a new job. Although online job boards can be a great way to find open positions, they are not the only option. There are many other job search resources that are often overlooked but can be just as effective.

For example, networking is a great way to learn about unadvertised jobs and make connections in your industry. Talking to friends, family, and acquaintances can also lead to job leads. On LinkedIn, you can connect with new people in your field and learn about opportunities that you might not have otherwise heard about.

Although checking company websites for job postings can be time-consuming, it is still a very effective way to find job openings. The good news is that many job aggregators, like Indeed.com, can help you with this process, as they scrape job postings from company websites.

By taking the time to explore all of the available job search resources, you will improve your chances of finding a position that is a good fit for you.

JOB SEARCH RESOURCES

1. Talk to the people you know

One way to find a job is to let your family and friends know that you are looking. You can also post on Facebook and share with your network what you are looking for to see if anyone knows of any openings. Asking around like this could give you insider information about jobs that may not be posted anywhere or roles that are open primarily for internal candidates.

You never know where a new opportunity will arise. Sometimes a single post on LinkedIn, Facebook, or Twitter shared by your friends is enough to help you land your next job.

2. Get referred

Some of the best opportunities are not made public. This is especially true for well-known companies, which tend to receive a high number of referrals[1]. As a result, the available positions are filled very quickly, without the company needing to employ a traditional recruiting process.

During your career, you will build a vast network of people. If you have some experience behind you, you can reach out to this network now. Your network might include ex-colleagues, customers, or LinkedIn influencers who are familiar with your industry. Contact them via LinkedIn message/inMail to ask about any job openings they may know of.

If you have a good relationship with someone who works at a company you're interested in, ask if they can share your resume with their leadership or recruitment team. This will help start a conversation about your past projects and could even lead to internal opportunities. If you have the skills and experience that they are looking for, they may even create a new opportunity specifically for you. The worst that can happen is they say no, so it's worth asking.

Even if they don't have any job leads for you, they can still share information, advice, and encouragement during your journey.

3. Check the career pages of companies

If you have several favorite companies where you always wanted to work, the best step you can take is to check out their career websites. You'll not only see what career opportunities are currently available, but you'll also learn more about each company, its products, its values, and its culture.

To find a career page, look for sections titled *Careers* or *Jobs* on a company's home page. Career pages may also be hidden under the *About Us* link.

If you can't find the career section on the company website, you can try a simple Google search for "[Company Name] Jobs" (example: "Nike jobs") or "[Company Name] Careers" (example: "Nike Careers"). With this strategy you might also find some other job sites where a company and its competitors post job opportunities.

---

[1] Referrals are one of the main sources of all hires in many companies.

If you don't find any job opportunities on a company's career site, sign up to receive alerts about new job postings by joining the company's career network.

4.   Cold call

What is a cold call? A cold call is contacting someone with whom you've had no prior contact. In the context of recruitment, it means reaching out to a company you would like to work for, even if there are no jobs currently available.

To reach out, either call or email the human resources department/recruiters to ask if they know of any current or upcoming vacancies. Recruiters don't always post job openings on public job boards or websites like LinkedIn.

They may share job opportunities only internally or on their company career sites. So if you really want to get your foot in the door, it's worth reaching out to see if there are any openings that haven't been publicly posted.

Although this method may generate some positive results, be prepared to deal with less pleasant reactions. Some companies may appreciate your interest and initiative, but some may not have the time for it, and some may not even pick up the phone. But a cold call may get you some inside information or even increase your chances of getting noticed before a job is even advertised.

5.   Send a cold outreach message

The best way to reach out to a recruiter or HR representative is to use LinkedIn. This site is the go-to platform for professional networking. And it's no wonder— with its ability to connect you with other professionals in your field, as well as potential employers, LinkedIn is an invaluable tool for anyone looking to further their career. When it comes to reaching out to a recruiter or HR representative, LinkedIn is definitely the best way to go.

This way, they can easily see your profile and understand how you might fit into their organization. Plus, if they have any open roles that fit you, they can easily contact you via LinkedIn.

As with cold emails or voicemails, consider the length of your message. No one wants to read or hear a long message from a stranger. For this same reason, don't send your cover letter along with the first message or describe your entire career. Keep it simple and short!

If you don't have a LinkedIn profile or you prefer email, you can try to send an email to the HR/recruitment department or specific recruiter and let them know that you are interested in working for them. In this case, it's a great idea to attach your resume and a cover letter as well. You may not get a reply, but it's still worth a try.

Although it is fine to reach out to more than one recruiter from the same company at the same time, don't expect amazing results from your email inquiries. Even if you hear from them only that you need to apply via the company's career page, you've still gotten some extra attention.

Recruiters may not be able to keep your personal information (resume) in their systems because of the General Data Protection Regulation (GDPR)[2] in the European Union and other privacy laws elsewhere.

My recommendation is to first reach out on LinkedIn to connect with recruiters from the company where you want to work. This will help you expand your network and stay in touch. When they are searching for someone with your skill set, the LinkedIn algorithm may make you appear in the results in a higher place because you are already connected with them.

6. Reach out to hiring managers

If you're not a fan of recruiters, you can try to skip them and contact a hiring manager directly via LinkedIn. It can be difficult to identify who the right hiring manager is, as there are often numerous hiring managers within a company. But you can try to find the senior managers within the company who are in your location and asked them.

If you send a LinkedIn connection request to one of the company leaders, you may be more likely to have your LinkedIn profile screened by them directly rather than being rejected by a recruiter. After the hiring manager accepts your connection request, you should thank that person for accepting your LinkedIn invitation and let them know that you are interested in working for their company.

If you're applying to a large organization, you may not be able to contact the right person, which could lead to your resume being overlooked. Also apply directly via a company's career site, which will speed up the process if the hiring manager asks the recruitment team to prescreen you. Even if the recruitment team already rejected your application, a message from the hiring manager

---

[2] *The General Data Protection Regulation (GDPR) is a law that came into effect on May 25, 2018. The GDPR replaces the 1995 Data Protection Directive. It strengthens EU data protection rules by giving individuals more control over their personal data and establishing new rights for individuals.*

Employers can store your personal data without your consent if they have a legitimate reason for doing so, such as for performance monitoring or compliance with legal obligations. However, employers must ensure that your personal data is collected and processed in a fair, transparent, and lawful manner. If you have any concerns about how your personal data is being used, you can contact the employer or the data protection authority in your country.

could prompt them to reconsider you profile and move forward with your application.

Privacy laws may restrict hiring managers from contacting you directly; you may be asked to speak with the recruitment team before you are interviewed as you will need to provide your consent for them to examine your personal data. If you apply via a career page, you will be asked there to give consent.

7. Check online job boards

Today, job boards are typically found online. They are an easy and convenient way to find job postings that match your skills and interests. You can tailor your job search on the board to find the perfect opportunity, and you can also set job alerts there to receive a new list of job postings every day.

Many opportunities are available on the Internet. Use online job searches to find a job that inspires you anywhere in the world if you are open to relocating. You can also use job boards to find a great job that you can do remotely.

Besides using search engines like Google, try websites like Monster.com, CareerBuilder.com, or Jobs2Careers.com. Many types of job boards cater to specific types of job seekers. For example, some job boards focus exclusively on executive-level jobs, jobs for minority candidates, jobs for neurodiverse candidates, jobs for single mothers, jobs for refugees, jobs in a particular industry, or jobs for returning citizens.

8. Use a job aggregator

Job aggregators are websites that collect job postings from various sources on the Internet, including job boards and career sites, and post them on their own website. Aggregators like Indeed.com, ZipRecruiter.com, and Glassdoor.com work like the Google search engine, but instead of returning web pages in their search results, they show job postings.

The main benefit of using these aggregators is that you can find a large number of job opportunities in one place. This saves you from having to browse many different career websites and job boards. In addition, many of these sites offer the ability to set job alerts, so you can be notified of new opportunities via email or the site's mobile app.

You can also add your resume to a job aggregator's database so that other companies that use it can find your profile and contact you about a new job opportunity.

9.   Attend job fairs and meetups

Networking is key when looking for a new job! Make sure to attend job fairs and meetups with companies you're interested in and participate even online. Many companies request that potential attendees fill out a registration form before joining any events they are hosting. In addition to requiring basic information such as name and contact details, they often ask for a link to your LinkedIn profile so they can check who you are.

Recruitment teams and hiring managers often go through the attendee list and check LinkedIn profiles to make a pre-selection list of interesting attendees that could be contacted by their recruitment team. If you attend those events, you are raising your chance that your LinkedIn profile will be reviewed by a hiring manager rather than just a recruiter.

If you are a recent graduate looking for your first job, you should consider attending job fairs. These fairs are organized specifically to help you stand out and connect with companies looking for future employees. One of the benefits of attending job fairs is that you have the opportunity to meet and speak with employers in person so you can get all the answers you need.

10. Collaborate with an employment or headhunting agency

Executive search and employment agencies cooperate with a large number of organizations. This means that contacting them will help expand your search and provide information about companies that you were not even aware of.

Some agencies work with clients to find candidates before a job is even announced to the public. This is often done when an organization is trying to replace current employees or if they are coming to a new location and want to keep it a secret.

Agencies can also help you understand your value on the market by sharing the salary ranges that are typical for your industry, your position, or the position you are seeking. And even if they don't have any opportunity for you at the moment, your resume will become part of their database so they can reach you when the right opportunity appears, which could be sooner than you think.

Agencies work for a commission. That commission is paid by the hiring companies, so candidates should not have to pay anything to them. Try to stay away from any agency that is requesting payment for their services. With so many agencies out there, it's also worth shopping around to find the one that will work for you before you make a decision.

Ultimately, the best way to find a job is often through good old-fashioned networking. If you want to improve your resume or LinkedIn profile, consider hiring a professional career or interview coach who can help you for a fee. Some recruiters in employment agencies also offer free resume help and LinkedIn feedback on a limited basis.

11. Participate in an internship or temporary employment offer

If you are a recent graduate and searching for your first full-time job, it may be wise to seek an internship or even a temporary employment offer at the beginning, especially if such an opportunity gets you in the door at a desired company. In most cases, these opportunities turn into full-time offers when you prove how good you are in your job.

Most recruiters agree that it is easier to find a job when you already have a job. Taking on internships or temporary opportunities can help you stay up to date with industry developments and network with the right people at a company.

12. Keep an eye on social media

Nowadays, social media is used for a variety of purposes. Companies often use it to advertise their products and services as well as to promote upcoming events. Using social media is a fast, convenient, and effective way to reach a large number of people. Consequently, many businesses also use social media to advertise job openings.

To get notifications of new jobs from companies you're interested in, follow those companies on their social media pages and use hashtags to find out when they're posting new jobs. Effective hashtags include the name of the company and keywords like *job, jobs,* or *career.* If you know what hashtags a company is already using, you can start following those hashtags to see if they have any open roles.

FINAL THOUGHTS

If you're looking for a new job, it's important to have a plan. There are a lot of options out there, and it can be overwhelming to try to figure out where to start. You can include everything from online job boards to networking events to your plan, and you can mix and match to find the best option for your needs.

If you're not sure where to start, I recommend focusing on referrals and LinkedIn. These are two of the most effective tools for finding job openings, so be sure to add them to your search plan.

2. The Job Search Plan

Losing a job is a stressful experience that can prompt people to start applying for positions without a clear plan. Although it is possible to find a job without a strategic approach, it is much more likely that you will be successful if you take the time to develop a job search plan.

A well-crafted plan will save you time and help you focus your efforts on the most promising opportunities. By taking a strategic approach to your job search, you will increase your chances of finding the right position for you.

The majority of people are not knowledgeable about the entire process of looking for a job. As a result, they make common mistakes that decrease their chances of being hired. For example, they send an incomplete resume or apply for jobs they are not qualified for.

If you want to find your dream job, you need to start by creating a job search plan and be strategic about your job hunt. Creating a proper plan will help you increase your chance of landing a great job and shorten the time it takes.

WHY IT IS IMPORTANT TO HAVE A JOB SEARCH PLAN

Starting a job search can be a daunting task, but having a plan in place can make it much easier. Decide what you want, how to achieve it, and which companies to target. Then follow your plan and stay on track so you make the most of your time and don't waste time on companies that don't interest you.

It is common to apply for multiple jobs at once when looking for work. If you apply to multiple companies at the same time, it can be difficult to keep track of all the applications and follow-ups, especially since different companies require different types of resumes and cover letters. Applying for multiple jobs at once can make the process more complicated and increase the chances of making a mistake. If you don't have a plan for job searching, the chances of error increase.

MAKE A STEP-BY-STEP JOB SEARCH PLAN

Creating a list of tasks and activities for a particular goal that you can cross off when you've accomplished them can be very motivating.

1. Figure out what you want next

The first step in every career plan is to set the proper goal. What kind of job role are you looking for and is the job title more important to you than money or is money more important to you than the job title? Are you looking for a local position, a remote one, or a position in a different city or even a different country? Are you looking for a full-time job, part-time job, or a job that will give you flexibility so you can work four days instead of five?

The more honest you are with yourself, the better your new opportunity may be. Once you have reflected and answered these questions, you can set your goals to achieve your final objective, landing a job that meets your expectations. Figuring out what you want will set the course for your job search.

2. Set your job search goals

When looking for a job, it is important to break your goals down into smaller, more manageable tasks. Instead of relying on a broad goal like "Get a job," try to create several specific goals such as "Research job openings," "Submit job applications," and "Attend job interviews." This will help you to be more efficient and reach your final goal more easily.

To reach your goals, be clear about what you need to do and set weekly targets, such as a specific number of applications to send out, specific people to contact on LinkedIn, and specific companies to research.

Making a weekly plan for all of these tasks and then completing them one by one can be rewarding itself, but don't forget to reward yourself every time you finish a task. The reward does not need to be something big. Consider something related to your ability to enjoy this new chapter of your life while you are between jobs, such as a walk in the park, searching for new music, or spending time with friends.

It is important to set realistic goals when looking for a new job. Temporary and controllable goals will help you stay on track and motivated. Bear in mind that even if you set a goal to apply for twenty positions per week, say, sometimes you won't be able to reach that number, not because you haven't put out the effort but because of a lack of new job openings.

Remember: Don't expect to find a new job right away. Having unrealistic expectations can sidetrack you from your goals.

One of the best pieces of advice I give to clients is to start using the *"If this, then that"* method for setting goals. If their goal is to apply to twenty job openings per week but there are only ten new job openings on the market, they could instead send ten more LinkedIn connection requests. This method is effective because it keeps you motivated and busy. As you take action, you will see results, and many of my clients found their jobs this way.

They didn't apply for many job openings, but they connected with more people on LinkedIn and started discussions with new people. As a result, they found new opportunities. They connected with old friends and colleagues as well as new contacts. They also joined groups and started following companies they were interested in.

By being active on LinkedIn, they were able to identify new job openings that weren't widely advertised. They were also able to learn about companies that were a good fit for their skills and interests. In addition, they were able to make a strong impression on potential employers. As a result of their efforts, they landed jobs that were better matches for their skills and interests.

3. Set a schedule for your job search

Job searching can be difficult, especially if you are still employed. Finding time to search for a job or schedule an interview during working hours can be challenging. Even if you are between jobs, you should make a schedule to help you focus on achieving your goals.

In your schedule, set aside specific times to work on your job search. Dedicate certain hours of the day or certain days of the week to job applications, networking, or research. If you are currently unemployed, try allocating the first two hours of each day to job hunting, followed by a break and then two more hours of job hunting later in the day.

If you are currently employed, you can book smaller time blocks in your calendar and apply for a new job opportunity during your breaks. Bear in mind that some companies track the activities of their employees, so you should not be using your work computer for personal matters during working hours—you could be fired for that. Find some time at the end of your workday to apply for new jobs. Do this every day, as companies frequently post new roles. If you wait until the weekend, you could easily miss the right opportunity.

If you want to increase your chances of being invited for an interview, apply for open roles every day. If you are one of the first people to apply, you will also be one of the first candidates that the recruiter screens. If the recruiter receives ten to twenty applications in the first week or two, they will review those and set up several prescreening calls.

Candidates who apply later may not be considered if the recruiter has already found several candidates that are a good fit and have already been presented to the hiring manager. The goal of every recruiter is to fill the open position as soon as possible. Adding more people into the process will only delay that goal.

If you apply during the first two weeks after the role is posted, you will be among the prescreened candidates and not in the second group of backup candidates who are contacted only if the interviews with the first group of candidates don't work out.

Bear in mind that not every recruiter works this way and not every position that is open will get dozens of candidates. Companies that are focusing on the local market and looking for local people might be struggling to find the right talent, so even if you apply after a month, you might still be the only person who applied.

4. Use tools and apps

Progress tracking. You don't need to track everything in paper notes or in a computer notepad. Use an application like Google Spreadsheets or Microsoft Excel to track where you have sent your applications.

Store the links to job applications on your Google Drive so you can connect those applications with the positions and companies where you apply. This will enable you always to find the job description of the role, even if the position is already unposted from the company's career site or job board.

Calendar applications. Setting up calendar reminders to follow up with employers about your applications or for interviews is a great way to stay organized. You can even use a snooze option in your Gmail mailbox, postponing any emails from a company or recruiter and temporarily removing them from your inbox until you need them. Your email will come back to the top of your inbox when you want it to, making it a great reminder to reach out to the company or recruiter to follow up with them.

A word of caution: If you're snoozing an email and email notifications, there's a good chance you'll forget about it entirely and miss the opportunity to respond. Even if you do remember to check your email later, the other person may have already moved on. In short, when it comes to email, it's always best to err on the side of caution and reply as soon as possible.

If you use a calendar app like Calendly[3], you can easily share your availability

---

[3] https://calendly.com/

for prescreening calls and interviews with recruiters and hiring managers. This will not only speed up the interview process as they can check your availability with one click, but it will also minimize confusion about variance in time zones (if the interviewer is from a different country).

Email tracking. If you want to level up your email game, you should start using an email tracking tool to see if recipients open your email. There are many of these tools on the market like Vocus[4], Mailtrack[5], Gmelius[6], and SalesHandy[7]. They often offer free limited versions or trials for a couple of weeks or a month, so you don't need to spend any money on them.

The paid versions usually offer more features, such as templates, real-time desktop notifications, per-recipient email tracking, and automated workflows. Some of them even help you turn your Gmail account into a Kanban board, which is a visual task organizer. This will help you visually track the progress with each company you have contacted.

5. Automate your work

Some registration forms only ask you for a few items, but others want to know almost everything about you. When you are applying to dozens of roles every week, filling all those forms can take hours of your time. Save your time by setting up autofill in Google Chrome or using one of many autofill Chrome plugins.

Checking career sites and job boards every day can also take ages. You can save time by setting job alerts on sites like LinkedIn or Indeed. These sites will email you on a daily basis with any new matches to your search.

Use these tools to help you search more quickly and easily.

6. Simplify whatever you can simplify

Do everything you can to make the process of finding a job quick and easy. Streamline the process as far as you can to ensure that you do not have to end up giving the assignment of searching for a job much more time than it requires.

Create templates for your resume, cover letter, follow-up emails, and other correspondence in order to make it easier to tailor your applications to specific companies and situations. Even create an email templates in text

---

[4]   https://vocus.io/
[5]   https://mailtrack.io/
[6]   https://gmelius.com/
[7]   https://www.saleshandy.com/

expanders[8] like Briskine[9], Magical[10] or TextExpander,[11] as they will speed up the communications with recruiters and even your networking activities on LinkedIn.

Remember that your communication style reflects your values and principles, so make sure your templates reflect them too.

7. Decide how public you are about job search

Are you open about your job search because you are currently between jobs or are you searching for a new job opportunity discreetly while working at your current job? Your strategy for finding a new job opportunity can affect how successful you are. Being discreet may help you avoid any troubles, and being open may help you find a new job opportunity faster.

If you are transparent about your job search, ask people for recommendations and for endorsements on LinkedIn. This will make your LinkedIn profile look more interesting, and it will improve your chance of landing a job. If you want to keep your search to yourself, in the next chapters you will learn about several options how to search for a job without alerting your current employer.

8. Create a list of skills, keywords, and job titles

Start thinking about your skills and the keywords you could use to describe them during your job search. This will help you better understand what your talents are.

Using these keywords to search for jobs will help you find positions that don't use the expected job title. For example, you might be searching for a *developer* role but a company might be advertising for a *software engineer.* That is why you should also spend some time understanding what job titles companies are using.

Keep in mind that job titles can also vary depending on the location where you are applying. That's why you should take note of and list all job titles you find during your search via keywords.

---

[8] Text expander is an app that lets you summon up content with a couple of keystrokes.
[9] https://www.briskine.com/
[10] https://www.getmagical.com/
[11] https://textexpander.com/

9. Update your resume

If you have been out of the job market for a while or haven't searched for a new job for a long time, create a new resume from scratch. Don't simply refresh the one you were using years ago.

Creating a new resume can improve it and make it more aligned with what employers are looking for. You should even consider customizing your resume for the specific position you're seeking. Your resume should reflect your experience and skills, but it should also emphasize the skills that are required for the specific position. Your cover letter should also be tailored to match the specific requirements of each company you apply to.

By taking this care, you'll show the recruiter and hiring manager that you have the skills they're looking for and that you're the perfect candidate for the job.

10. Create a list of job sites

When you're job hunting, it's important to have a list of places where you can reliably check for new opportunities. But it's not enough to just have a list of job sites; you also need to set a schedule for how often to visit them.

That way, you can make sure you're not missing any new postings. In addition, it's also helpful to add the link for creating an account and adding your resume on each site as well as where to activate job alerts. That way, you can save yourself some time when you do eventually find a job posting that interests you. By taking these simple steps, you can make your job search more efficient and, ideally, land the perfect position in no time.

If you are afraid that you will forget all passwords for those job sites, you can also use one of the password managers (LastPass[12], 1Password[13], Dashlane[14], etc.) on the market. They will help you store all the login details in one place.

11. Create a suitable workspace

Creating a dedicated workspace is important for your job search plan even if it's just a corner of your bedroom or the kitchen table. Having a place where

---

[12] https://www.lastpass.com/
[13] https://1password.com/
[14] https://www.dashlane.com/

you can focus on your job search and where you can keep all of your notes and materials will help you to stay organized, productive, and on track.

12. Prepare for your interviews

Interviewing for a job is a process that can be daunting, but it's made easier with the right preparation. When you don't have any interviews lined up, it may be hard to motivate yourself to prepare for one, but it is a good idea to add the step to your job search plan.

To improve your interview skills, practice answering potential interview questions with a friend and even record yourself. This will help you find out where you can improve, learn how your answer sounds, feel confident, and get ready for any interview that comes your way. With the right preparation and over time, you will become a pro.

13. Contact recruitment agencies

You may want to consider contacting multiple recruitment agencies in order to speed up the process of finding your new job. However, it is important to be selective and only work with those agencies that can be helpful to you.

If you know anyone who has used an agency recently, ask them for a recommendation. You should also contact agencies that focus specifically on your industry, as they are more likely to have the right position for you than are agencies that focus on everything. Niche agencies also know your market better, so they can give you feedback on your salary expectations.

14. Build a list of target companies

To create a list of target companies, research the industry and competitors of the businesses you are interested in working for. This will help you learn more about the companies and their culture as well as discover other businesses in the industry that you may not have known existed.

After you have created a list of target companies, check their LinkedIn company pages to see if you have any first connections working there. This will help you create a list of people to contact for referrals. Even if you don't find a role that matches your expectations, it never hurts to ask as companies can always create new roles for an exceptional person.

15. Attend career fairs and events

When you have a list of target companies, you should also check their company social media sites to see if they are hosting any upcoming online events or meetups. If you are a recent graduate, attending these events is a great opportunity for you, and attending them should be a part of your job career plan.

Networking events and career fairs are great ways to get your name out there. They allow you to learn more about the companies that are hiring and let you speak to people who can help you get a job. Additionally, they give you a sense of what companies are looking for in employees.

Networking events are also a great way to meet new people who are in the same situation as you. Finding others who are going through the same process can help motivate you and give you the opportunity to share tips and tricks about what is working and what is not. In a best-case scenario, someone could tell you about a fantastic opportunity they were not suited for but you are. Take every chance you can to network.

16. Create a Kanban board

You can also use a Kanban board to visualize your job search strategy. A Kanban board will track the progress you're making and help you remember where you have applied, who invited you for an interview, who hasn't yet answered, and who has said no.

On the board, create several columns to track the progress of your job applications, such as Applied, Rejected, Prescreened, Prescreened feedback, First round, Second round, Rejected, and Offer.

FINAL THOUGHTS

Creating a job search plan can help you stay motivated and focused during your job search. It can also help you track your progress and determine what is working well and what needs improvement. Remember that your plan is not set in stone and can be adjusted as needed.

You should evaluate your plan regularly to see what you can improve to get better results. Don't be afraid to think outside the box. Some candidates create their own personal websites dedicated to their job searches or even use AdWords, Instagram, and Facebook ad campaigns to target employers.

3. Protecting Your Mental Health While Job Searching

Looking for a new job can be very tiring, both physically and emotionally. Especially when you are between jobs and the bills are coming in, it can be difficult to keep your energy up. Not only do you have to deal with the uncertainty of job hunting, but you may also have to deal with a lot of rejections from companies.

Applying for jobs can take up a great deal of your time, and you may feel anxiety about job interviews. Even if you make it through the prescreening process, there's no guarantee you'll get the job. Rejections from companies and recruiters can be very exhausting and can harm your mental health. That's why it is important to talk about it.

When we step into adulthood, we start taking on different responsibilities. For many people, financial independence is related to self-worth. Losing that value can have an impact on their self-confidence while applying for jobs. People who worked in senior roles, such as a Senior Director, often negatively experience having to accept or apply for a role at a lower level, feeling that they're taking a step back in their careers. Rejection and feelings of uncertainty can breed depression and anxiety.

Many psychiatrists agree that hunting for a job can stir up emotional turmoil, forcing job hunters to face several challenges and side effects, such as a lack of purpose. Following are several strategies for managing mental health while searching for a new job.

MENTAL HEALTH SUPPORTIVE STRATEGIES

1. Have a plan

In the previous chapter you learned about the importance of having a plan. Having a plan for your job search will help your mental health too by making it possible to stay organized and by filling your days with purpose and order. Although the plan won't replace the security of having a job, it will give you the confidence you need.

Keeping busy while formulating a plan will leave you less time to think about problems, rejections, and other hardships that could lead to depression and anxiety. Keeping yourself busy is the key to a healthy and happy mind.

2. Stay social

The process of looking for a job can feel lonely. It can be difficult to find people to talk to about it. You spend hours looking at job postings, writing cover letters and resumes, and talking to no one other than recruiters.

Although your job search might not be going as planned, it's important to stay positive and interact with the people around you. Make sure you take some time away from your job search to spend with your friends and family; you never know if they have heard about a new opportunity that would be a good fit for you.

Bear in mind that you are not alone and that you have people who care about you and are willing to help. If you are feeling stressed or hopeless, consider talking to a career coach or psychologist for help.

3. Learn new skills

If you are currently without a job, you may have a lot of free time on your hands. This could be a great opportunity to start learning new skills that you've been thinking about for a while. Such skills might include learning a new language, mastering a new technique or process related to your industry, or becoming more proficient in a software that will help you in your next job.

The skills you learn will not only help you be more marketable; you can also share with an interviewer that you spent your time in between jobs learning something new, showing that you are the type of person who is always striving to improve and grow and that you are open to learning new things.

The candidate who is busy and learning new things is more likely to stand out from the crowd. As a recruiter, who would you pick: the candidate who sits at home waiting for the next job opportunity or the one who is trying to learn new things?

4. Let yourself feel low

When it comes to mental health, it's important to remember that every coin has two sides. On one side, you have to celebrate every small win and concentrate on the positive vibes. On the other side, you have to face the fall. Sometimes, feeling low is completely okay. Getting frustrated is natural and expected.

Don't limit yourself in this process. Understand how frustration and anxiety feel and how far you can go before reaching your limit. Try to learn from difficult situations. Remember that in order to reach the top, you have to experience some problems and setbacks along the way. These experiences don't mean that you're finished.

There will be other opportunities to reach your goals. When my clients feel down about their job searches, I always recommend they write down their achievements. This will improve their mood and remind them of how capable they are. When they're asked in an interview to share examples of things that make them proud, they can use their lists as inspiration.

5. Be compassionate toward yourself

Although it may seem obvious, it's important to be kind to yourself when you're going through a hard time. This means giving yourself time to think, reflect, and come up with a plan, as well as gathering your forces to move forward.

You have to be sympathetic and supportive of yourself, both in action and verbally. If you find that your concentration is failing and you're focusing more on failure, you have to change the narrative. Stand in front of the mirror and talk to yourself with compassion, rather than blaming yourself.

If you have failed in a job interview, don't beat yourself up. Instead, tell yourself that you did your best to get through another tough day of job applications. Don't take rejections too personally. There are usually reasons unrelated to your application for why you weren't invited for an interview.

6. Appreciate yourself by practicing self-care

Even though this book is about finding a job, it's important to remember to take care of yourself too. These things include getting a good night's sleep, eating a balanced diet, and staying active. They can help you feel your best when you're looking for a job. Don't forget to do the things you enjoy too.

Mental health care or *self-care* doesn't refer to bingeing web series and relishing leisure time in spas. Self-care is all about freeing yourself from negative vibes and loving yourself.

7. Identify your triggers

Some people enjoy feeling a degree of stress when applying for a new job because it helps them get things done. This type of stress is called *eustress*[15] or healthy stress, and it develops when you are challenged but not overwhelmed and motivated but not panicked.

If, however, you start to feel overwhelmed, depressed, or anxious, pay attention as they are signs that your stress level is getting out of control.

8. Take a break

If you are making job-hunting a full-time job, balance your life in a way that is similar to the balance you achieve when you have a job. Following a routine is a very important part of balancing life and work.

Limit your job search to a certain number of hours per day. Start your day with your normal routine, such as meditation or exercise. Then set a time limit for how long you will spend job searching each day and be sure to take breaks.

Try to stick to your working hours, as they'll be when you have the most energy. The golden rule is not to work the whole day—you need time to rest too. Even at work, you take coffee and lunch breaks, so you deserve the same when you're looking for a job.

9. Reach out for help

It is very important to ask for help when you need it. Reaching out for support is not a sign of weakness. Instead it is a sign of proactivity and strength. It can be helpful to speak with someone about your problems and how they are impacting your life and career. Ask people you trust to look at your resume and LinkedIn profile and discuss your plans with you.

If you need help, you can reach out to a recruiter you know or hire a career coach. These professionals have years of experience helping candidates find new jobs, and they know what works.

As a career coach and recruiter, I helped people improve their job search skills and get job offers faster. We work together on search plans, resumes, answers, and presentation. After learning all the tricks about how to get their resumes and LinkedIn profiles in front of recruiters, my clients are able to attract the right people and are contacted with new job offers more frequently.

---

[15] https://en.wikipedia.org/wiki/Eustress

10. Don't forget your family

Having a job brings security so, when you are between jobs, you can lose that feeling of security, and the resulting stress can come between you and your family. To reduce the chances of that happening, always keep your family in the loop. They are more likely to support you if they know what is going on.

FINAL THOUGHTS

Although losing a job can be really tough, remember that you have achieved a lot in the past and those accomplishments won't go away overnight. You should be proud of what you have accomplished during your career so far.

Mental health is important not just for your well-being, but for your career as well. If two candidates are equally qualified, but one is acting and feeling confident while the other is feeling down and depressed, who would you choose? The way you act and feel during an interview can make a big difference.

Even if you haven't received replies from the employers to whom you have applied, don't assume that means you're not eligible or qualified. Don't be too hard on yourself and remember that there are many things you can't control. Focus on the things you can.

There are many things you can change to make yourself happier. For example, focus on your cover letter or resume, learn a new skill, or work on your networking skills. When you see the progress you've made, you will feel a lot happier.

Every hardship will eventually go away, and your stress will not continue forever. Your unemployment is only temporary.

4. How to Get Your First Job Without Experience

Employers often want candidates who are already familiar with the ins and outs of the job, but how is anyone supposed to get that experience if no one is willing to give them a chance?

Experience is something you can only get by working for it. And, without work, you will not be able to get the experience you need to get a job.

JOB-SEEKING STRATEGIES FOR THE INEXPERIENCED

The way to get around this conundrum is to incorporate the following twelve strategies.

1. Work your way up

One way to get your foot in the door is to look for internships or entry-level positions. Many businesses are willing to take on interns with little to no previous experience and provide on-the-job training.

Even if you don't land an internship, there are still ways to make yourself more attractive to potential employers, such as volunteering at a business in your area or taking on a project-based job. Project-based jobs can help you gain experience and make some money until you find a permanent job.

In the end, after interning or volunteering, you might end up with a promotion and a great job.

2. Expand your knowledge

You may have a degree, but if you don't have relevant work experience, your resume can look like a blank piece of paper. But there are things you can do to fill in the blanks. Add activities you did during your studies, especially if they are related to the job you are trying to get. Also share certifications that demonstrate you are serious about your education. Volunteering experiences are valid too.

Remember that your resume is also a chance to show your personality and soft skills. Even if you don't have any concrete work experience, you can find ways to show that you're trying to learn. For example, ask to shadow an employee for a day or take online courses. Most online trainings and courses offer certification for a small price or for free. Adding these certifications to your resume and LinkedIn profile can help you to stand out from other candidates and expand your knowledge.

3. Get to know who you really are

It's important to know your strengths and weaknesses before an interview so that you can be prepared to answer questions about them. Talking to family members and friends can help you get an objective opinion and an outsider's perspective on the qualities you possess. You can also use the service of a career coach to help you prepare for interviews.

Once you know your strengths, it's important to showcase them in a positive light. Highlight examples of times when you've used your strengths to achieve success. If you're asked about a weakness, be honest, but focus on the steps you're taking to improve. By being prepared and knowing who you are, you'll be more likely to impress the interviewer.

4. Embrace your inexperience

Remember that everyone, including your interviewers, had to start at the beginning in their careers. Lacking experience is common, so don't let it discourage you. It's up to you to work your way up the professional ladder.

Meanwhile, try to learn as much as you can and improve your skills, even if you don't get paid to do so. If you can't find a side project or volunteer opportunity, attending events in your field of interest is a great way to become familiar with what's going on.

There is a little "hack" that I recommend that could help you to land a job faster. Find the companies where you would like to work and then find a manager who is working in the role you want to have after several years. Contact them via LinkedIn and ask them for ten to fifteen minutes of their time.

Instead of asking them for a job opportunity, ask them for advice on how to start your career in the industry. If they say yes, you'll have a chance to introduce yourself to a potential hiring manager.

5. Get in touch with industry experts

LinkedIn is a great place to make connections with professionals in your industry and to ask them questions. Most people who are active on LinkedIn are happy to help others in their fields, but you don't want to bother them with too many questions. Try to be helpful to them if you can and show that you're interested in learning more.

Having a vetted industry expert as a mentor can help you land a job, and then only the sky is the limit.

Use the approach I described earlier. Reach out and ask if they would be willing to share their advice on how they got into the industry and any tips they would give someone starting out in their career. Compliments never hurt, so feel free to flatter them a bit to get their attention.

6. Enhance your network

Networking is a recommended strategy for experienced and inexperienced candidates alike. It never hurts to search for contacts when you are looking to get hired, find a new job, or advance your career. Look for professionals who have the same vision and determination as you do.

Start networking as soon as you know when you're graduating. The first step should be establishing an online presence by creating a LinkedIn profile. You can also connect with friends or classmates; they might know of some job openings too or already be working full-time or part-time in companies that are hiring. The more you expand your network and the more people you meet, the better. Having a wide network of professionals will help you immensely.

If you are invited for an interview, send a connection request to the interviewer the day after your meeting so your LinkedIn network will organically grow. Then, even if the company or the interviewer don't hire you, you'll still have gained a new connection. LinkedIn could also help you reach out to people who are working in the company you're eyeing. Such a contact could open the door for you by delivering your resume to the hiring manager.

7. Ask for help on LinkedIn

Looking for a new opportunity? One of the easiest things you can do is post about it on LinkedIn. Your post will attract the attention of people in your network, and their reactions (likes and comments) will make your post visible to a broader audience.

You never know who might see your post and reach out to you with an exciting new opportunity. So if you're looking for a change, don't be afraid to put it out there on LinkedIn.

8. Show that you want to continue learning

If you are lacking knowledge in a certain area, the best thing you can do is be curious and willing to listen to others. Be open to learning new things and admit when you don't know something. As long as you are willing to learn, you will be able to compensate for your lack of knowledge.

An employer is turned off by a candidate who comes across as someone who knows everything. You want to show that you are fully committed to growth and willing to learn from others.

Once you have some experience, your resume will grow and you will steadily progress up the ranks to reach your goals. Just make sure that you keep your skills up and stay motivated.

9. Work on your speaking skills

Finding a job without any experience can be difficult because you have to showcase yourself even though you don't have any practical experience. For many newcomers, the first interviews can be very nerve-wracking and challenging; it is difficult to talk about your skills in a professional setting when you're not used to it.

If you want to improve your speaking skills and reduce any fear or worries, it will certainly help if you have a good story to tell. Practice sharing your career-starting story that shows your appreciation for the industry and the reasons you were attracted to it.

You should always be professional when representing yourself to a potential employer, but don't be afraid to show enthusiasm for the work and excitement for the opportunity. Once you do that, you can expect good results.

10. Underline your strong desire and motivation

Even if you don't have experience, you have something valuable: a desire to land a job. Your application shows that you are motivated enough to apply even if you don't fit the description that well. If you have this kind of desire when it comes to a job, do your best to make it obvious to the potential employer.

When sending your resume, be sure to attach a cover letter that describes your motivation to work for the company and industry. Show your passion and interest in the industry.

For this, you will have to do research to find out as much as possible about the employer. Then, when you're asked why you want to work for them, you'll be capable of providing a very good answer.

11. Apply even to "reach" job posts

Although it is acceptable to apply for any role for which you feel you are a good fit, especially when you are at the beginning of your career, it is also important to be realistic about your experience level. Applying for a senior, manager, or director role right after you finish school will likely result in a rejection.

Most roles require specific skills, but some employers also look at people without experience who might have the right potential and who can grow into the role. So it can pay to apply even to jobs that require more experience than you have.

12. Follow up after an interview

After an interview, it's a good idea to follow up by email. In your email, express your enthusiasm for the job and your appreciation for the opportunity. Being nice can help you stand out and may give you an advantage when competing for the job.

Remember that everyone likes to feel appreciated, and if you treat a recruiter or hiring manager well, they will get a chance to see how you will treat your future colleagues if they hire you.

FINAL THOUGHTS

Landing your first job can be difficult, especially if you don't have any experience. However, don't get discouraged if you don't get the job after your first interview. Many other graduates out there are also struggling to get their dream jobs. If the company you want to work for has high standards, consider finding a less ideal job first that nonetheless offers you the opportunity to refine your skills and gain experience.

Always try to expand your network and meet new people, especially in your own field. Use every opportunity as a networking opportunity and add to your LinkedIn network every person you meet during your interviews. Not only you will expand your network faster this way, but you will also stay in touch, and you never know when someone will contact you with an amazing opportunity.

Remember that you bring with you a fresh perspective that can help companies adapt to the customers of today. Your vision and energy can be exactly what a company needs.

You can find a new job via social media, but you can also easily lose an opportunity or even your job because of social media posts. Before you start searching for your first job opportunity, assess your digital footprint and increase your privacy for your Facebook, Twitter, Instagram, and TikTok accounts.

You do not want to lose a job opportunity because of photos or posts you shared many years ago. Try to hide or remove anything that could have a negative impact on your job search and career. In addition, be careful about what you post on social media from now on because it can affect your future career.

5. How to Get a Good Job After Age Fifty

Finding a job after you finish school can be a challenge because you don't have the skills that many companies are searching for. But searching for a job after fifty can be just as challenging, although for different reasons. One is that you are now *overqualified* for many positions. Another is age discrimination, which involves treating an applicant or employee less favorably because of their age.

If you're over fifty and looking for a job, it's important to be realistic about the challenges you may face. But don't give up—there are plenty of employers who value experience and maturity. With a little effort, you should be able to find a job that's a good fit for you.

Age discrimination is illegal in many countries, but that doesn't stop employers from doing it. They may be more likely to hire someone who is younger and cheaper to train. Or they may think that older workers are less productive or capable of learning new things.

Many labor laws fight age discrimination. For example in the United States, the Age Discrimination in Employment Act (ADEA) forbids age discrimination against people who are age forty or older. It does not protect workers under the age of forty, [16] although some *states* do have laws that protect younger workers from age discrimination.

It can be hard to prove why your job application was rejected. Instead, consider altering your resume so that your exact age is not shown. Don't let your age keep you from looking for a new job and advancing your career.

Although it may be difficult to land a great job when you are part of the fifty+ age group, it is not impossible. If you can prove to the employer that your experience and knowledge are valuable to the company and you know your way around technology, you have an equal chance of getting hired.

---

[16] https://www.eeoc.gov/age-discrimination

ADVICE FOR THE OLDER SET

Following are a few pieces of advice that are meant to help you get back in the game, regardless of your age.

1. Make your age an advantage

Don't see your age as an obstacle. You've gained a lot of skills and experience from your time spent in the workforce. You have qualities and abilities that are rare among younger employees. Your work ethic, promptness, and ability to manage difficult customers are just a few examples. Many companies are looking for people like you, people who have a lot to offer!

2. Make your resume ageless

When you're looking for a job, don't use the same resume you used a few years ago. To increase your chances of getting hired, give your resume a fresh new look. The first thing you need to remember when writing a resume is that employers take less than a minute to scan a resume by eye. You'll need to be clear, short, and concise.

I recommend focusing more on the achievements of the past fifteen years, as your experience may be vast. There is no need to list all jobs that you did twenty-five to thirty years ago, as you are not doing the same job or in the same role.

Rather than discussing your irrelevant work experience from twenty years ago with the employer, try to focus on mentioning your abilities, skills, and knowledge that are relevant to the job you're applying for. Emphasize your people skills.

It's also important to make sure your resume is up to date and looks professional. One way to do this is to search for resume templates online. You can find templates for all sorts of different professions and industries, so you're sure to find one that's a good fit for your qualifications. Once you've found a template you like, simply fill in your information and customize it to your liking.

Be sure to use short sentences, paragraphs, and bullet points to list important details. This will make them easy to read and notice. With a little time and effort, you can create a resume that will help you get the job interview.

When you are applying for a role that requires ten or more years of experience, and you have thirty or more, you don't need to start your overview in your resume or your cover letter with "I have thirty+ years of experience." Instead say, "I have fifteen+ years of experience." This will look better and still be the truth.

Some recruiters and hiring managers reject candidates with long careers because they think they are not ready to learn new things or would be too expensive. Reducing the number of years of experience on your resume will help you avoid this.

There are also a few other things you should consider doing:

- Remove any key age indicator dates like when you graduated from college.
- If it is not required, don't add a photo to your resume.
- Don't add your date of birth to the resume. This information should not be part of it anyway, and it is not relevant information for the employers.
- Show the employer that you are tech-savvy. For example, use a modern email address like @gmail.com instead of @msn.com, @aol.com or other old-fashioned email platforms that have been around for decades.
- Embrace social media by adding to your resume the link to your LinkedIn profile. Make sure your LinkedIn profile matches your resume.

3. Make your LinkedIn profile ageless too

LinkedIn is a great way to make connections with other professionals and experts as well as to display your experience and expertise. If you don't have a LinkedIn profile, you should create one. Having a LinkedIn profile gives you an advantage—employers may reach out to you with offers via the platform. Having a LinkedIn profile shows that you are interested in technology and building an expanding network.

You can also leverage your LinkedIn profile for finding a job faster by turning on the "Open to work"[17] feature on your profile. This will privately signal to recruiters that you're open to new opportunities and are actively looking. Or you can turn this option on for everyone on LinkedIn if you are ready to market your availability to the whole world.

If you do that, don't forget to use the *add your location* and *desired industry* features to help recruiters contact you with relevant offers.

Although you don't need to have a profile picture on your LinkedIn profile, having one can increase the chances that you will be discovered. If you are going to use a profile picture, make sure that it is professional and representative of you. Also, make sure it doesn't give away too much about your age.

Use LinkedIn to show that you are tech-savvy and recruiter-friendly. Many

---

[17] https://www.linkedin.com/help/linkedin/answer/a507508/let-recruiters-know-you-re-open-to-work

recruiters search for candidates on LinkedIn, so if you're not there you're missing out.

4.   Maintain a digital presence

To ensure that your job search is not hindered in any way, hide or lock your other social media profiles while you are looking for a new job. Employers will know that you are on social media, but they will not be able to access your posts and photos so they will not be able to determine your age.

5.   Don't wait for a job to come along

Most certainly you know what kind of job you want, but if you can't find that job, would you rather stay unemployed? If there is a way to work and make a decent income, then you should do it. Meanwhile, you can continue looking for jobs that are closer to your expectations.

With this being said, don't rule out temporary jobs or project-based jobs. If you can handle it, you should go for it. Besides making it possible for you to pay your bills, these jobs will add to your resume and, above all, boost your confidence.

Many of my friends who are over fifty got their new permanent jobs due to project-based jobs they were willing to take on. Some of them even started as freelance consultants. You never know—maybe the temporary or part-time job will evolve into a full-time one.

6.   Constantly work on expanding your knowledge

You can always learn new things, no matter how old you are. This is why it's important to show a prospective employer that you're always working on yourself and staying up to date with the latest developments in your field.

There are a few ways to update and improve your skills: Enroll in courses and workshops specific to your industry, participate in events meant to introduce industry news, and become an association member if the association is relevant to your industry. This kind of activity will not only prove that you are still interested in your career and professional life but also that you have no problem learning new things all the time, an ability that is very much appreciated by employers.

Adding a Coursera certification to your resume or LinkedIn profile can help you stand out from the crowd while you are searching for a new job. When recruiters check your LinkedIn profile, they will see that you are constantly working on yourself and may be more likely to consider you for a position. Your network may also react to your post, which could attract the attention of other hiring managers and recruiters.

Don't forget to add your new certificates to your LinkedIn profile. When you add a date to the recent certifications, the visitors will notice it and see you as a person constantly working on your education.

7. Get help finding a job, if you need it

If you're having difficulty finding the right job or don't know where to start, it's always a good idea to ask for help. Asking a recruiter or career coach for help can expedite the process and improve your chances of finding a job.

You have a large network of contacts that you've built up over your career. You might be able to utilize them by reconnecting with them. The more people you contact, the more job opportunities might appear. You never know—the person you contact may not be able to help you now but may consider you for an opportunity in the future.

8. Become a boomerang employee

A boomerang employee is an employee who leaves an organization they work for but then later returns. If you have a good relationship with the company where you worked in the past, reach out to them to see if they have a position for you. People who worked with you in the past may still be employed there and able to vouch for you.

9. Prove that you can work on a team

If you're over fifty and looking for a job, there's a good chance you'll come across managers who are much younger than you. In this case, the managers may be reluctant to hire someone your age because they may see you as difficult to manage.

If you want to have good chances of being hired, show the employer that you are a team player. This means showing them that you are willing to learn from people younger than you. It is possible to do this in your resume, in your cover letter, and during an interview. Show your enthusiasm and that you are open-minded when it comes to working with younger people.

WHAT ELSE YOU SHOULD KNOW

When you are over a certain age, it's not uncommon for interviewers to make comments about seasoned candidates being "overqualified" or "too expensive."

If the question of compensation comes up, you have several options for how to handle the situation. You can ask for the same amount that you were earning or even more, or you can be flexible about your salary expectations. If you believe your age is standing in the way of your getting hired, be open to salary negotiation.

1. Be flexible when it comes to your paycheck.

Many career coaches recommend being flexible when it comes to your salary expectations.

When asked about salary, you can tell the hiring manager that you're more interested in finding a role that you're passionate about and that pays well than in finding a role that pays a lot but makes you miserable.

When asked by a recruiter during the first prescreening what your salary expectation is, you can share that you are flexible about your salary and do not have a specific range in mind. Then wait on the proposal from them. If they are pushing to get your answer, buy time by telling them you want to speak with more people from the company to better understand the role and what the salary range and bonus structure look like.

If the recruiter shares the salary range with you and it is below your original expectation, do not react negatively or comment on it. Some seasoned candidates could feel insulted by a lower salary and react to it with sarcasm. Even if you feel the urge to react, don't say anything. If you say something like "That is low" to a recruiter, your resume might not be even presented to a hiring manager and be eliminated at the beginning right after the prescreening call to save time.

Your goal is to get an interview with the hiring manager. If they see your experience, they can consider you for a different role in a very different salary range.

Try to understand how a company structures its salaries. Consider lower than expected salaries —you can make up the difference by negotiating more vacation days, a flexible working schedule, and other perks. Many companies also offer company shares or stock options that could be part of your compensation.

2. Approaches for the overqualified

If an interviewer says that you are overqualified for a position and questions whether you would be satisfied with a role, have an answer ready. My recommendation is to answer something like this: "I consider myself as someone who will bring years of experience and expertise to the company and not somebody who is overqualified for the role."

Many people over fifty who are looking for a job will hear that they are overqualified; employers often feel overwhelmed by the experience of taking on such a person or meeting their salary expectations. If you are applying for a job that is below your current qualifications, you have the onus of explaining your choice. If you applied for the job, explain why. If you have skills and experience that would benefit the company, explain how.

Hiring managers often perceive candidates with lots of experience as people who are looking for a high-level role. Some hiring managers feel threatened by more experienced employees, and others are afraid that overqualified candidates will be resistant to change and clash with teammates.

You can easily allay their fears during the interview by demonstrating your enthusiasm and willingness to learn. You should also express that you are not the type to think you know everything and that you prefer to work as part of a team and not alone.

3. Consider a second career

There's no rule saying you have to do the same job for the rest of your life. Maybe you can pursue a different passion or use other skills you have and build a second career. Many people become happier after they consider a career change, and this could be true for you too.

Make a list of things that you are good at, things that you find most meaningful, and things that bring you joy. Maybe you will realize that you want to pursue a completely different opportunity than your current career.

A number of people from my LinkedIn network have completely changed their careers, and they're now happier in their current jobs than they were in their previous jobs, regardless of their ages. They chose happiness over chasing money, and money has followed them as a result. Most of them are now earning more than they did before.

4. Stay positive

Although it can be difficult, try to stay positive throughout your job search. This means avoiding negative self-talk, keeping your energy up, and staying hopeful.

There are many people out there who feel the same way every day. We have all experienced that feeling several times in our lives, so it is not unfamiliar. You need to keep pushing forward until you succeed. Having a negative mindset or being angry at recruiters or hiring managers will not help, so try to be positive. If a company rejects you, it is their loss; something better will be coming your way soon.

FINAL THOUGHTS

It can be difficult to remain patient and optimistic when job hunting, especially if you've been at it for a while with no bites. It's important to remember that any rejection from a company during your search will not change what you already achieved or stop you from setting another goal.

You know your own strengths and weaknesses better than anyone, so focus on how you can present yourself in the best light possible to potential employers. With the right attitude and proper planning, you will find your new role soon. Whatever you do, don't give up. Rome wasn't built in a day, and your perfect job won't be found that quickly either.

As Les Brown[18] once said, "You are never too old to set another goal or dream a new dream."

---

[18] https://en.wikipedia.org/wiki/Les_Brown_(speaker)

6. Digital Footprint

Do you ever think about how your personal life, including what you post on social media and what you say, can impact your professional life? I'm talking about things outside of work.

Although you may think that your personal life is private, the things you do and say in your spare time can still have an effect on your job prospects. In reality, these often disregarded details could have a serious effect on your chances of landing a job you want.

How can this be possible? The answer lies in your digital footprint.

WHAT IS A DIGITAL FOOTPRINT?

Your digital footprint is a record of your online activity. This includes everything you do on the Internet, every email you send, every photo you share, every website you visit, and any information you share publicly or via online services. The majority of your digital footprint, like the websites you visit and the emails you send, will remain hidden from public eyes even though it continues to exist.

But if you share publicly your thoughts and pictures via social media, anyone can access them, forever. Even if you forget about the embarrassing photo from the company party or the Tweet that you sent when you were angry five years ago, the Internet doesn't forget. So be careful about what you post.

We only hear about the negative consequences of social media postings when they happen to a celebrity, but they happen also to regular people. Every year people lose their jobs because of inappropriate Tweets or old posts that resurface.

Nowadays, it is easy for potential employers to find out about you by searching your name on the Internet. Many applicant tracking systems scour social media, giving recruiters and hiring managers access to your Facebook, Twitter, and other social media profiles with one click.

That's why it is so important to check your digital footprint before you start your job search, so you can see the results that will be visible to others who Google your name and look for you on social media. By removing photos, posts, and Tweets that could be considered inappropriate, you can improve your first impression.

WHY YOU NEED TO HAVE A STRONG ONLINE FOOTPRINT

You've found an open position at your dream company and you match all their requirements. You spend hours fine-tuning your resume and your cover letter. Then you never hear back, or you get a template message that they chose somebody else.

What happened? You will likely never know. But you should assume that any potential employer is not going to rely entirely on the resume you provide. There's a high chance they will also check your social media profile.

What may seem like harmless behavior to you, such as publicly badmouthing a colleague or manager, writing negative reviews about hotels, or commenting angrily on social media posts, can come back to haunt you when you're looking for a new job.

Even comments during an election year directed toward people who may have an opinion different from yours can work against you. You have the right to express yourself and defend your beliefs, but employers may prefer someone diplomatic and discreet, capable of respecting the opinions of others.

Many companies have a policy that a person can only be hired if feedback from the interview panel is unanimous. If just one hiring manager doesn't like your online rant, you might not get the job.

Based on a CareerBuilder[19] survey, approximately 70 percent of recruiting companies use social media to find and screen candidates and determine which of them are most suitable. Of those that do social research, 57 percent have found content that caused them not to hire candidates.

That data is from a survey done in 2018, so you can imagine that today the percentage of companies using the power of social media is only higher. In other words, if you applied for a job recently, there is a very good chance that your social media profile, regardless of the network you're using, has been examined.

Recruiters and hiring managers could be looking for any content that could be seen as sexist, racist, or bigoted. They know that hiring someone with these views could have a negative impact on the team and company brand.

---

[19] https://www.prnewswire.com/news-releases/more-than-half-of-employers-have-found-content-on-social-media-that-caused-them-not-to-hire-a-candidate-according-to-recent-careerbuilder-survey-300694437.html

WHAT EMPLOYERS ARE LOOKING FOR

You might be wondering what employers are actually looking for when they go through your online profile. They want to see that you are opinionated but that you respect other people's views and opinions. They want to see that you are informed and know what is happening in your industry. They want to see creativity and to see you express yourself with clarity and without vulgarity. They want to see that you are passionate. Finally, they are looking for signs that you are the right person for their team *or* not the wrong person for their team.

If you're one of the few people without a social media profile—no Facebook, LinkedIn, Twitter, Instagram, Pinterest, TikTok, or YouTube—don't forget to consider legacy sites that you used when you were a teenager or message boards and forums where your conversations live on in perpetuity. Don't forget about comments you've made on blog articles, Yelp reviews, and so forth.

We often forget about the accounts that we create, but the information we publish and share on those accounts will stay online forever. Even if a site ceases to exist, much of its information can still be found through the "Wayback Machine,"[20] which is a website that allows you to view archived versions of the entire web from the past. The majority of people will not spend their time using the Wayback Machine to find out about you. However, many websites scrape[21] Instagram and Twitter profiles for posts that they keep even if you deleted the originals.

If you are already active on social media, spend a little more time to think about what you are posting and how those posts support your personal brand. Publish meaningful status updates, such as your thoughts on your area of expertise and general matters. Look at what distinguishes you from other people and consider how best to convey your value to your potential employers. Try to build and maintain a positive presence online.

HOW TO TIDY UP YOUR DIGITAL FOOTPRINT BEFORE YOUR JOB SEARCH

Do you want to make sure your online presence won't create any problems during a job search? Then it's time to clean up your digital footprint before you even plan to look for a job.

Following are some tips on how to check your digital footprint and what to do about it.

---

[20] https://archive.org/web/
[21] https://en.wikipedia.org/wiki/Web_scraping

1. Google your name

There is nothing easier than Googling your name. If you have a unique surname like me, you will find results from a simple search on your name. If you have a more common name, you can Google it with the addition of your city or job title.

Examples:

- "John Smith" Austin
- "John Smith" "New York"
- "John Smith" "New York" "Finance Manager"

You can also add your current and previous companies to see if you are still associated with them.

Examples:

- "John Smith" Google
- "John Smith" "American Express"

 Quotation marks are Boolean search modifiers[22] When you use them, the terms must appear exactly as they appear between the quotes for the result to show. By using them you are searching for an exact phrase—in this case, your full name.

Don't forget to check under the tab *Images*[23] and *News*[24] on Google or Bing[25]. Play around with the custom range timeline for your search results so you can discover the latest posts about you.

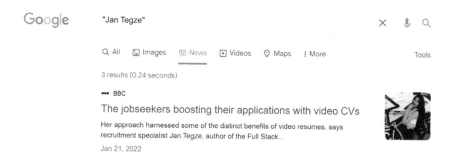

---

[22] You can learn more about these operators on https://jobsearch.guide/.
[23] https://www.google.com/imghp
[24] https://news.google.com/
[25] https://www.bing.com/

Some tools will help you track any new search results about your name. One of the free options is Google Alerts.[26] This service sends emails to the user when it finds new results such as web pages, newspaper articles, blogs, or scientific research that match the user's search term.

Tools like Awario[27] and Peakmetrics[28] also track press, online news, social media, and broadcast news.

Simply add your name and specific keywords to the tool, and when somebody mentions your name online you will receive an email notification about it.

2. Keep your social media profile private

How do you make sure your digital footprint is clean? The first step is to turn the status of your social media profile from public to private to limit the visibility of your posts for people whom you do not know or the general public.

If you want to make sure that nothing from your personal life will create any inconveniences, then all your social media accounts should be private. If you want to keep your accounts public, don't use your full name or your real name. This will limit the chance that somebody will find you via Google.

Making your social profiles private also ensures that you are not sharing with potential burglars the fact that you are not at home.

3. Maintain an effective public profile

A public social media profile could bring more benefits than inconveniences when you are looking for a job. This is especially true for those looking for jobs in the media sector. For those people, a good-looking profile on social media could be a great addition to their resumes.

If this is the case for you, take a close look at your timeline. Review and inspect it to weed out any details that should not be there or that could affect your reputation and credibility. Make sure you don't leave behind any posts, images, or comments that could be detrimental. Clean the timeline well and remove any details that could work against you.

I recommend that clients remove their old post and Tweets from their social profiles. What could be considered dark humor one year could be offensive in the next five or ten years. Removing old posts and Tweets from your social media accounts will ensure that the profiles reflect who you are now and not who you were ten years ago.

---

[26] https://www.google.com/alerts
[27] https://awario.com/
[28] https://www.peakmetrics.com/

4. Control who can tag you

One of the downsides of using social media is that you can end up in places without intending to. This can happen if someone else tags you when making a post on their own social media profiles. Everyone else from your list of friends and followers, including employers, will be able to see that post if the person sharing it has a public profile. Once you are tagged, employers can find you via social media sites or even just by Googling you.

Luckily, you can control this and avoid being tagged in ways you don't like. Facebook, Instagram, Twitter, and other social sites give users the chance to disable the tagging feature when it comes to other users. Once the feature is disabled, no one can tag you without you knowing about it.

5. Get rid of old social media accounts

Most people have old social media accounts they've forgotten about. Recruiters do not use only the most popular social media networks to find info about you. Even profiles created on old networks like Myspace[29] can pop up in a search.

To track down old accounts, just search for your name on Google and see what information comes up. Once you track down all your profiles, close them or make them private.

6. Use social media to your favor

If you do not have any online presence, you should consider building one, especially on LinkedIn. You can also join Twitter and share a few interesting articles there so you present yourself as a tech-savvy person to a potential employer.

It is very easy to create a great reputation and professional image with the help of social media. But what is private should remain private. Instead of posting a photo of you drinking at a party, post an image of you volunteering for an organization or working on a project you enjoy in your spare time. Don't stage such photos—show the admirable things you actually do.

---

[29] https://en.wikipedia.org/wiki/Myspace

FINAL THOUGHTS

Nowadays, with so much information available online, employers won't hesitate to research job candidates over the Internet, including using special engines to scan social media profiles for undesirable information. In this context, it's important to have a good digital footprint.

Make sure that every aspect of your digital footprint is professional. This includes having a professional-looking email address in your resume. An inappropriate email address—e.g., "sweety.pie.69@" or "big-lover@"—will decrease your chances of being hired.

You can improve your chances of having a successful career by being mindful of the content you post online. It's important to be aware of your digital footprint before starting your job search.

In a majority of countries in the world, it's completely legal for employers to check public social media platforms, but checking anything beyond public accounts falls into a gray area.

Since it's legal for employers to check public social media accounts, you should consider making your personal accounts private if you are not using social media to make a living.

7. The Resume

When starting your job search, one of the most important steps is to create a resume or CV (curriculum vitae). What's the difference? A resume is used for a job search, and a CV is a much longer document that details the whole course of your career and is used mostly for academic purposes.

Your resume is typically between one and three pages long. An introduction to employers, it outlines your qualifications and showcases your experience, education, and skills.

The resume you give to employers is their initial introduction to you. Everything contained on that one to three pieces of paper will dictate if they progress with your application or not.

Recruiters and hiring managers usually spend something between ten and thirty seconds on the initial screen or page of your resume to determine if they need to pay more attention to it. If your resume lacks value to them during the initial screening, your chances of making it through the process are slim.

The reason it is important to have a well-written resume is that it is one of the ways you can get an interview. Your personality and character will get you the *job,* but your resume needs to get you the interview first. A poorly written and generic one will get you rejected from the start.

A well-written resume, on the other hand, can help you create a positive first impression, outline your experience and skills, and highlight your education. It is more than just a piece of paper—it can help potential employers quickly and efficiently assess your qualifications.

Keep in mind that your resume is only as good as the information you provide; it won't automatically get you a job. You'll still need to convince the recruiter and the hiring manager that you are the right person.

Beware of those false resume-related promises on the Internet such as "This ATS friendly resume will get you a job," or "This resume template landed me a job at Google, and it will help you too." It is not the format, font, or design that gets you the job; it's the information contained in it.

SHOULD YOU WRITE YOUR RESUME IN FIRST OR THIRD PERSON?

Some career coaches say that using first-person pronouns on a resume sounds too informal and maybe even unprofessional. The third person is accepted as a standard resume convention. Looking a bit formal, it keeps your resume impersonal and reduces the chance of sounding too egocentric. Even people in more senior roles write their resumes in the third person.

However, first person *can* work well for resumes as it helps you describe your professional attributes and additional details to enhance your employability. When you write your CV in the first person, it can feel more natural and personal. This is because you are writing about yourself in a way that you would naturally talk to someone.

Although, some career coaches will disagree with me, my recommendation is to use first person but leave out the pronoun "I." Pronouns are unnecessary in a resume, and using the "I" over and over again will sound repetitive.

Here are examples of the three options:

- **First person:** I am a successful Key Account Manager specializing in B2B Software.
- **Third person:** He is a successful Key Account Manager specializing in B2B Software.
- **First person without pronoun:** A successful Key Account Manager specializing in B2B Software.

By avoiding using the same pronoun over and over again throughout your resume, your resume will read more naturally. And you can use this approach to create short, concise bullet points highlighting your past achievements:

- Copyedited manuscripts.
- Led project teams.
- Coordinated design of manuscript.
- Bid on projects.

HOW TO WRITE A GREAT RESUME

Many websites allow you to create a resume for free, but you should always check if there is a hidden price for the service. Also check how reliable the service is before you start working on your resume on their platform. Many of those services let you create your resume for free, but they will ask you for payment at the end of the process, usually right before you want to export your resume to a PDF file.

The service you choose, whether free or with a charge, should offer you the ability to export your resume into a Word document (.DOC, .DOCx, .RTF) and a PDF (Portable Document Format) file, as these are the types of files employers and recruiters usually want to see. Also make sure that your resume is ATS (Applicant Tracking System) friendly. Many paid services offer templates with crazy graphic elements, which you should avoid.

You can create your resume yourself using a text editor such as Microsoft Word or Google Docs. This is a better option than using a paid service because you can easily customize the text in your resume and also make custom-tailored versions of it to send to different employers or different types of positions - without having to pay any extra fees. If you don't know how to create a resume in Word, you can use a free Word design or template optimized for content.

The most common type of resume is the chronological resume. This resume lists information within each subcategory (education, work experience, skills, etc.) from most recent to oldest.

You can find free resume templates via the Internet by searching for the right keywords. Keywords like **"Free Resume Templates"** or search phrase **filetype:docx "Resume Template"** will help you find them.

When you are selecting a template for your resume, try to keep it simple. Using too many colors, fonts, or graphic elements can divert the attention of people reviewing your resume away from the important information.

Colors can make your resume pop on screens, but keep in mind that the average recruiter and hiring manager need only dozens of seconds to review your resume. Most likely, they're skimming for specific keywords and phrases. That is why you need to make it clear right off the bat how you can add value and what skills you can bring to their company.

In the next section of this book, you will learn about best practices for creating a professional resume that will grab the attention of a potential employer. You will also learn several tricks that will help you get your resume directly in front of the hiring manager.

RESUME HEADER

Every resume starts with a header that should include your name and contact information including your telephone number, email address, and links to your websites or social media profiles, such as LinkedIn. The main goal of this section is to make sure that the resume is associated with you and that recruiters know how to find you.

What to Include

- **Name.** First name, last name. If you have a middle name, you can add it.

- **Phone number.** Always include your country code. You never know if one of the recruiters or the hiring manager doing a prescreening of your resume is in a different country from you. Use space between numbers: +1 555 555 5555. This format is easy to read for most people.

- **Email address.** Email is probably the most widely used form of contact between recruiters and candidates. Use a professional email address and never one like funnygirl78@ or ladybug25@. The best email address has some of your name in it: carmen.doe@, carmendoe@, or carmendoe2@.

- When job searching use an email address that includes your full name, first name / last name, initials, or a minor variation. For both safety and ageism reasons – don't use your birth year in an email address!

  You can also invest some money to buy your own domain name and create your own personal email address: firstname@surname.com. Your email address should be simple, easy to remember, and quick to type out, so avoid including too many numbers and words.

  Be aware that where your email is hosted may give off a certain impression too. If you are using a very old email provider like msn.com or aol.com, consider upgrading to gmail.com or outlook.com. Although you may disagree, some hiring managers may judge technical relevancy based on your email host, and you might come off as a little outdated and possibly unskilled with technology.

  Employers could even guess your age range based on the type of email address you are using; if you're older, changing your address into something new might help you.

 Try to avoid using an email address from the company where you are currently working. When you leave that company, you will lose access to that email and any future job offers will be inaccessible.

- **LinkedIn URL.** If you have a LinkedIn profile, always include a link from it to your resume. But don't forget to update it. Your LinkedIn profile can provide recruiters and hiring managers extra information about you not available on your resume. If you have recommendations from executives on your LinkedIn profile, for example, they could boost your credibility.

- **Personal website or blog.** As you can't add everything about your career to your resume, use your personal website to share additional information with an employer. Your personal website could also highlight your attitude toward your professional life. Use the website to clarify your career path and aspirations.

- **Social media.** If you are a marketer, designer, or developer or you have something to show as part of what you offer to an employer, you can add a link to your portfolio. For example, designers can add their profiles from Behance.net, and developers can share their profiles from GitHub.

- **Address.** The city and state/country where you live should be enough. Bear in mind that recruiters often search for local candidates first, so if you aren't local but are planning on moving to the company's location, mention that fact or say that you are willing to relocate.

What Not to Include

- **Date of birth:** Refrain from listing your birth date. Nobody needs to know how old you are. It could even be an obstacle to landing an interview. Nobody should be asking for your age as part of their job application process or during the interview. These actions can form the basis of a discrimination lawsuit.

- **Personal information.** Don't include your marriage status, your height, or your weight. None of that information is important to employers and it shouldn't be in your resume.

- **Second email or phone number.** Additional emails or phone numbers will only confuse recruiters and hiring managers. Choose the primary way you want to be contacted and leave it at that. Do not use the phone number of the company where you are currently working. When you leave your current company, you will lose access to your old phone number so recruiters will not be able to reach you.

- **Profile photo:** Resumes in the United States and the majority of other countries should not include a headshot or any profile picture. The recruiter or interviewer does not need to know what you look like in order to evaluate your application, and using a profile photo in your resume could lead to hiring prejudices and be a reason why your resume is rejected.

  You already have a professional photo on your LinkedIn profile, so there is no need to add a profile photo to your resume. Of course, there are some exceptions to this general rule; for example, if you work as a TV anchor, actor, or model, you may be expected to include a head shot in your resume.

- **Full address.** Avoid including your full home address on your resume. Although it used to be part of your contact details, no one needs to know that anymore. It can even harm your chance of getting a job out of state or in a different city. Your potential employer could remove you from the process just because they calculate it will take you more time to get to work.

- If you are from different state or country, including your address information, even just a city of state, might also be a reason not to hire you because the employer doesn't want to deal with relocation. Some employers could also check if your address is in a problematic neighborhood and exclude you for this reason. Last but not least, disclosing your full address could open you up to identity theft.

- **Official ID numbers.** When you are applying for a job and you are a visa and work permit holder, avoid sharing the numbers of your permits in your resume. Don't share such information before the company asks you for it. The same goes for any government ID, Social Security number, or personal identification number. This information is your private data and should not be part of your resume as you never know who will have access to it.

- **Social media profiles:** Social media is critical in today's hiring market. Your personal web page is a fantastic way for employers to get to know you before an interview. But your Facebook, Instagram, Twitter, and TikTok profiles should not be part of your resume. Your potential employer could find something there that they take as offensive even if you posted it as a joke.

- **Date of the resume creation.** Showing the date when your resume was created will not help you in any way, and it might even hurt you. It might, for example, give the impression that the information in the resume is outdated.

When you add your LinkedIn profile to your resume, the majority of recruiters will check it. But you should know that they could also check your profile via their LinkedIn Recruiter account, which will show them what type of roles you are looking for if you have turned on "Open to Work" functionality.

You don't want this if you are specifically applying to an Associate HR Consultant position, for example, but your LinkedIn profile shows that you'll consider anything in management.

This is what recruiters see in their LinkedIn Recruiter accounts:

Open to work ⌄

Job title
Territory Sales Manager • Sales Manager • Sales Executive

Job type
Full-time

Locations
On-site: Greater Dublin • Greater Barcelona Metropolitan Area • Greater Madrid Metropolitan Area

Workplace types
On-site • Hybrid • Remote

RESUME HEADLINE

A resume headline is a brief description located just below your name and above your summary.

As the name suggests, a resume headline is the shortest way to summarize your accomplishments. Your resume headline is like your tagline: It should be catchy, short (one sentence), and to the point.

You can use your headline to advertise your skill set and professional goals or you can use it to summarize your accomplishments. It might even consist of a short explanation for why you are a great fit for the role even though you have no experience in it:

- Passionate communicator for sales jobs
- Fashion enthusiast for a social media position in retail.

Make sure your headline catches the reader's attention.

If you are unable to think of a headline for your resume, don't worry. Use a simple headline for your current job title, such as "Senior Data Analyst," under your name.

When creating your headline, think about your career achievements, your role in the workplace, and the description of the job you're applying to.

For example, if a company is looking for an employee with a specific certification, then create a headline that revolves around that certification. Let's say you are a network specialist and you obtained several certifications from your field. Your headline can be *Security professional (CISM, CompTIA Security+ CISSP) with 8+ years' experience in the software industry.* An experienced digital marketer could write, *Certified digital marketer with 10+ years in the marketing sector.*

These are perfect examples of how you can formulate a resume headline that is descriptive, interesting, and engaging. If you wish, pair the headline with a resume summary.

RESUME SUMMARY AND OBJECTIVE

The summary is the heading statement at the top of your resume, after your header and headline. It gives recruiters and managers a quick overview of who you are and tells them whether they should read your entire resume. This section is just like what you say in speed dating, when you only have a couple of minutes to market yourself and impress a potential date.

Write a few short lines to catch an employer's attention and convince them that you are capable of the job in question. The summary needs to be interesting and catchy because most hiring teams spend only a few seconds looking over a resume before making up their minds. You only have a few moments to attract attention and give employers a reason to consider you for a role. Highlight your career achievements and skills. It's important to make this summary clear, concise, and readable, as well as unique.

Avoid using any template summary text that you find online, as many other applicants will likely use the same information. Instead, focus on listing specific examples of your skills and achievements and use numbers to quantify your successes. Consider adding to the last sentence a personal attribute, something that will make the recruiter see beyond your professional skills. A resume summary, often used in conjunction with the resume headline, contains no more than three sentences. The best summaries are not in the first person, they use action verbs, and they avoid pronouns.

Here are some examples:

- Profound experience in developing android applications using Android Studio and various other SDK tools. Looking forward to pursuing my career in application development.
- Senior Account Executive with 10+ years of experience in the software and security industries. History of establishing new territories and building relationships to form bonds and establish business commitments. Increased

sales revenue by 57% in 2021. Rated the best Account Executive in 2020 and 2021.

If you have less experience and you want to demonstrate your motivation for getting into a new field, skip the summary and use an objective instead. An objective is, in a nutshell, the goal of your resume. You can use it to emphasize the overall skills that you have. Do not say that you have no work experience and don't say that you are motivated to learn. Recruiters and hiring managers receive many of those messages every week and it just bores them, and they will automatically dismiss you because you have not told them anything that shows them your value.

Instead, tell them what you are capable of. Mention anything that you have accomplished—at any job—and if you earned certifications or underwent training, ranked highly, or maintained individual satisfaction ratings. Include any statistics that you have.

Like a resume summary, the resume objective should not be written in first person and should include how you want to grow at the company and what you hope to achieve.

Here's an example:

Results-driven student with a passion for data analytics, looking for a full-time position in a company that will maximize my potential.

WORK EXPERIENCE & KEY ACHIEVEMENTS

Work experience is yet another important section of your resume. This section of your resume is essential for hiring managers and recruiters. They need to know you have skills, but they also need to know that you have experience applying those skills. Because this section is so important, you need to include the right keywords and write it in an engaging, compelling, and consistent format.

This section demands you to list the company names where you have worked in the past along with the locations, dates of employment, titles, and job roles. Use bullet points and action verbs.

Do not forget that at some companies like Google and Facebook the hiring managers are flooded with hundreds of resume submissions. It is your duty to make yourself and your resume stand out from the crowd, and the best way to do this is to make sure that the work experience section of your resume gets attention.

The work experience section should only include aspects of your life that are crucial to this position. Do not add every single thing you are currently doing or did at work. Your goal should be a resume that will go back no more than ten to fifteen years in history. In many industries, sharing experience that dates back more than fifteen years just isn't very helpful for recruiters and hiring managers. In addition, listing more than twenty years of experience can clutter up your resume and make it too long. Of course, if you spent twenty years at two organizations and didn't work anywhere else, add both companies to your resume.

When you are writing your resume, add your work experience in the most common format. Every employment record that you will have in your resume should include Job Title, Company Name, Location, Dates Employed, Description, and Key Achievements.

Example 1

ACME Company, **Talent Acquisition Director,** January 2020–Present

- Leading and supporting Global Talent Acquisition teams.
- Designing effective cost-saving talent acquisition strategies to support high growth across the entire organization.

Example 2

Talent Acquisition Director, ACME Company
January 2020–Present

- Leading and supporting Global Talent Acquisition teams.
- Designing effective cost-saving talent acquisition strategies to support high growth across the entire organization.

Bear in mind that a resume without dates or with only a few jobs can be a red flag for recruiters and hiring managers. You can leave off your oldest jobs when editing your resume, but your resume should provide a clear synopsis of your work history to potential employers. Be careful not to show unexplained working gaps.

The following example shows how your role changed at the organization even though *manager* is the only position directly relevant to the job you're seeking:

ACME Corp.

- **Manager,** 2003–2006
- **Shift Leader,** 1999–2003

Job Title/Position

The job title should go at the very top of each entry of work history so it's visible. Make it bold too so the job title will stand out from your text. That way, when potential employers scan the resume, they will immediately see it. You can even use a bigger font for the job title, company name, location, and dates employed.

 Not every company uses the same job titles across an industry so, for example, "Technical Support Level 3" at one company could be called "Senior Tech Support" at another company. That is why you should check what job titles are used in the company where you are applying, so you can customize the job title.

Company Name/Location

Under your job title, add the name of the company as well as the location where you worked. If you worked abroad, you can add the country there too. You can also add the industry of the company right after the name. The format you choose is up to you, but you need to use the same format for every job you add.

Example of different formats

- ACME, New York
- ACME, London (United Kingdom)
- ACME, Information Technology, New York

Do not add any company logos, as those could negatively impact how the ATS system will recognize your resume and parse the text into keywords. Any graphic element has an impact on how the robots will read your resume.

Dates Employed

Always add the timeframe of your employment under each work record. The standard format that employers are expecting is M/YYYY (example: 1/2018–7/2020). Use only the month and year when you start and the month and year when you end your employment. If you are still working in the company, use the word *Present* for the end date (8/2020–Present).

If you worked somewhere only for several months and you don't want to share how long your tenure was, just list the range of years (2021–2021).

Key Responsibilities

Use bullet points to discuss your roles and responsibilities at your various jobs, sticking ideally to no more than five and using only a single line for each bullet. Those bullet points demonstrate your value and what you managed to achieve at your places of work. Be specific about what you accomplished, referencing specific results and data. Include anything that you did to help better the workplace.

Example

Senior Recruiting Manager, ACME
2015–Present

- Leading and supporting Global Talent Acquisition teams.
- Designing and executing the selection and recruiting processes for all level searches across the organization.
- Taking ownership of global TA reporting.
- Implementing innovative recruitment strategies.
- Advising hiring managers on strategic staffing issues, including industry talent trends.

If you prefer to describe your responsibilities in paragraphs, consider making bold the important parts or the keywords in that text that are mentioned in job requirements. They will stand out from the other text and get the right attention from the reader.

If you have a limited work history (you are a graduate without previous work experience), do not be afraid of listing your temporary jobs. Include completed training courses, the number of times you were employee of the month, and details about what you accomplished, like modernizing the inventory system.

Showcase that you brought something important to every job you worked at and that you learned valuable skills while there. Do not just list the things that you did, like stocking shelves or answering the phone. Use strong action verbs to demonstrate responsibilities that will transfer over to the new job.

Key Achievements

Beneath the bullet points, add any key achievements that are relevant and set you apart. These can also be bolded to highlight your skills. Most people fail to include key achievements, but they can assist you during the hiring process.

Use statistics about high ratings or quality results, being the leading salesperson every year, or creating specialized software for the company. These details show what you are capable of.

When you add key responsibilities and achievements, try to be specific and use quantifiable metrics to show recruiters and hiring managers what you accomplished.

Examples

> *Not so great:* I was responsible for leading a team of six employees.

> *Much better:* I was team leader for a sales team that exceeded sales KPIs by 120%+ in 2021.

Follow these tips for listing your achievements in your resume:

- Try not to use paragraphs of text when writing about your work experience. It's better to use bullet points and fewer words because it makes it easier for your employers to go through the list quickly. Increased readability can double your chances of getting hired.
- Always begin with your most recent jobs. Add fewer details about your older job roles. Keep in mind that most employers and recruiters are only interested in your most recent or current job roles and accomplishments.
- If you have any gaps in your work experience, show how you filled that time. Add your freelance work experience, certifications, or education. If you are a freelancer, you can simply write "Self-employed" or list the clients you worked for. Some recruiters and hiring managers consider any gaps in a resume as red flags.

If you've been out of the job for a long time, consider adding a sabbatical to your resume. The sabbatical looks better than unexplained gaps, and people understand the need to take some time off between jobs.

Education

Your academic credentials are important to future employers. However, other sections are *more* important, so don't let your education take up too much space. Only mention details about the educational institution, when you attended it (unless you're over fifty), and the type of degree you earned. (There is no need to include your graduation date in this section if you're not applying for your first job.) Put your education section after your work experience. (But, when writing an academic CV, put your education above work experience.)

When listing your education, place your highest degree first. If you achieved a bachelor, master, or doctoral degree, there is no need to add that you also have a high school degree. For hiring managers, the highest achieved degree is more important than other education.

In this section of your resume, you also need to list all relevant certifications and trainings that make you stand out. Be sure to include your field of study as well.

Also include any honors, awards, extracurriculars, or research labs. Only list your GPA[30] if it was high (above 3.5); otherwise, it can leave a bad impression.

What to include in your education section:

- Your most recent degree (or education in progress)
- The full name of your institution (school or university)
- The location of that institution
- The graduation year (or expected graduation date) and the years attended (only necessary if you're applying for your first job; don't include if you're over fifty)
- Your field of study and degree major
- Your GPA (only if it's above 3.5)
- Any academic honors

Examples

- California State University, Fresno
  Bachelor of Science in Software Engineering
  Graduated in 2020 with a 4.1 GPA
  Honors: Dean's list

- 2020 BA in English Literature
  Harvard University, Cambridge, MA
  3.9 GPA

- Harvard University, Cambridge, MA
  May 2020
  Bachelor of Science in Software Engineering
  3.8 GPA

- Florida State University College of Business

---

[30] In some countries, grades are averaged to create a grade point average (GPA). GPA is calculated by using the number of grade points a student earns in a given period of time. https://en.wikipedia.org/wiki/Grading_in_education

BS • Finance
2005–2008

If you have more than one degree, use the same format for all of your degrees.

If you did not earn a degree, don't include this section. Hiring managers will find your work experience much more relevant at this point in your career. Highlight your work achievements in your resume and in your cover letter.

SKILLS

Your skills mentioned in your resume should primarily relate to the job you're seeking. Include a variety of both hard and soft skills.

Soft skills are the life skills that you learned and developed over time. You worked on yourself to achieve these things, like public speaking, verbal and written communication, empathy, or time management. These soft skills have to do with organization, management, and communication. They cannot easily be measured, but they are vital to being a successful individual.

Hard skills are mostly linked to technical knowledge and experience such as of specific tools or software. Hard skills are quantitative abilities that you can measure easily. They include things like speaking a foreign language, being proficient in a graphic program like Adobe Photoshop, and knowing computer programming. These skills vary by the type of job and industry unlike soft skills, which are universal.

Both hard and soft skills are important and can demonstrate your range as an employee. Hiring managers want to know what you are capable of and what you think your best assets are to help the team. Choose hard skills that apply to the job description and use keywords to emphasize soft skills like analyzing, listening, computer use, and organization abilities.

- **Soft skills:** organization, strong decision making, logical reasoning, self-motivation, responsibility, integrity, discipline, teamwork, time management, focus, patience, kindness, stress management, diplomacy.

- **Hard skills:** Java development, software development, data presentation, foreign languages, data mining, technical reporting, bookkeeping, SEO, SEM, HTML/CSS.

Don't use bullet points in this section as they will take up too much space. Rather, list your skills in a single paragraph separated by commas. Start with the skills in which you are most proficient.

Example

> Expert in Adobe Photoshop; proficient in Excel, Word, spreadsheets; familiar with PHP

Try to be specific with your skills. Instead of just saying, "Relational Database Management," say, "Experience with Oracle, MySQL, SQL Server, MySQL, phpMyAdmin." When you are specific with your skills, readers will easily recognize that you know what you're talking about. In addition, employers' database searches will find relevant keywords in your skills section.

Don't make false claims. Don't claim you are proficient in Photoshop when you are barely a beginner. These things can come back to haunt you.

Stick with no more than ten skills and use a basic proficiency rating level: familiar, proficient, expert. Technical skills require a bit more specific explanation. For example, if you put *proficient* next to *computer programming,* it doesn't mean much. Instead, you should name the different coding languages you know like HTML, CSS, or JavaScript.

Avoid using graphic elements for your rating system. Four stars out of five or percentages will confuse most recruiters and hiring managers because they don't represent any meaningful way of measuring experience. Also avoid using word clouds of keywords. Applicant tracking systems and AI can't read graphic elements.

ADDITIONAL EXPERIENCE

In the "Additional Experience" section of the resume, include anything like your hobbies, community work, volunteer work, certifications, or skills that are not precisely related to the position but are relevant to work in general and may give an indication of how passionate you are about a particular topic.

Try to use the last part of this section to make yourself memorable.

ACTIVE VERBS

Your resume is one of the most important tools you have when it comes to finding a new job. It gives employers a snapshot of your experience, skills, and accomplishments. So when it comes to writing your resume, it's important to choose your words carefully. Avoid weak and passive verbs, stay away from business jargon or clichés, and watch out for tired words and phrases.

Passive verbs can undermine the strength and effectiveness of your resume. Instead, use strong, active verbs to describe your accomplishments and focus on concrete results. Use language that is clear and concise and be sure to proofread your resume carefully before submitting it. With a little care and attention, you can ensure that your resume makes the best possible impression on potential employers.

What Are Active Verbs?

An active verb[31] is a verb that shows what you did as opposed to a passive verb that shows what you were or what you experienced.

Examples:

> *Active*—Led a team of five designers.
>
> *Passive*—Was the leader of a team of five designers.
>
> *Active*—Studied HTML, earning a programming certificate.
>
> *Passive*—Attended an HTML class and was awarded a programming certificate.

Even active verbs themselves can vary in terms of their dynamic effect. For example, the active verb *negotiated* conveys more energy and involvement on your part than does the active verb *discussed*.

Examples:

> *Okay*—Negotiated a new contract with company drivers.
>
> *Better*—Discussed contract terms with company drivers.

Passive verbs have the effect of making you seem passive too, and active verbs make you seem like a person who is a doer. In a resume, you would use active verbs to highlight your skills, experience, and accomplishments.

Keep in mind that you should try to avoid using the same verb more than

---

[31] https://jobsearch.guide/action-verbs-for-your-resume/

once on your resume, so be sure to mix it up! For example, if you increased sales, you can use these different verbs to highlight your achievements: accelerated, achieved, advanced, amplified, and boosted.

You can find a list of all these verbs by Googling "Active verbs to use on your resume."

RESUME TIPS

Recruiters are mostly interested in your skills and work experience, but that doesn't mean you should ignore the design and formatting of your resume. A cluttered resume is visually confusing, doesn't give a good impression, and is difficult to read. Bad design and unclear organization are enough of a reason for a recruiter or hiring manager to outright reject you. How will you be able to do a good job for their company if you can't even put together a decent presentation of what you have to offer?

A well-formatted, sleek, polished, and organized resume will increase your chances of getting hired. The most important criterion is clarity. Anyone should be able to read and understand your resume. Clarity is achieved largely through consistency. If you boldface one job title, boldface all job titles. If you list dates *after* titles, always list dates *after* titles.

More Resume Tips

- Don't lie! Avoid listing degrees, skills, and knowledge that you do not have. Work with what you have and upsell yourself that way.
- Utilize keywords and action verbs[32].
- Check again how the companies want to receive your resume. Failing to follow directions will quickly get your application tossed out. See if they want a specific subject line and addressee in your email. If they do not have any information listed, just put the position title you are applying for, your name, and the word resume in the email subject line.
- If you want to include references, add a separate page to your resume.
- Use an easy-to-read font that is not smaller than 11 pt. A good practice is also to use standard fonts that most people have on their computers. Avoid lots of underlining, many colors, and personality-laden and unprofessional fonts like Comic Sans.
- Stick to the same use of formatting, colors, and dates throughout your resume.

---

[32] https://jobsearch.guide/action-verbs-for-your-resume/

- Do not forget to leave sufficient space between different sections of your resume. There is a good chance that the reader will overlook a section if it isn't differentiated by space.
- Proofread, proofread, proofread! Use software to double-check your grammar and then have someone look it over too.
- Save your resume as a PDF. A PDF maintains the formatting regardless of what computer it's on.
- Title the file with your name in a simple way, like Michael_Ramirez_resume.pdf or michaelramirez-resume.pdf. Don't add years or versions into the name of the file.
- Ignore the complicated recommendations you can find online about getting your resume noticed. People will tell you to include the job description in your resume to get attention from robots. Don't do this. People will tell you to use larger or smaller font sizes—ignore them. People will even tell you to create your entire resume in a white font. No! Forget that. These are terrible ideas. Be clear, be consistent, be focused on the job. That's it.

HOW TO EXPLAIN CAREER GAPS IN YOUR RESUME

If you have been out of the workforce for a period of time, there is no need to feel ashamed or embarrassed. People take extended breaks from their careers for a variety of reasons, including raising children, caring for elderly relatives, or going back to school.

Career gaps aren't always a bad thing. There are numerous easy-to-explain reasons you might have a career gap, and most employers are understanding of these types of situations and will value the skills and experience you've gained during your time away from work.

There are also some more challenging reasons, such as health problems, being unable to find work, redundancy, being fired, or burnout. These can be more difficult to explain on your CV; try to focus on the positive aspects of your break from work.

For example, if you took time off to raise your children, you can highlight the skills you acquired during that period, such as multitasking, organization, and patience. Similarly, if you took time off to care for an elderly relative, you can highlight your experience in managing medication schedules, coordinating with doctors, and providing emotional support. By framing your career break in a positive light, you can show employers that you are a well-rounded and experienced individual.

Whatever the reason for your career gap, be honest about it in your job applications and interviews and focus on how you've grown as a result of the experience.

FINAL THOUGHTS

It can be difficult to compose a perfect resume that will help you stand out. However, by following the guidelines provided in this chapter, you can write a great resume that can help you get your dream job.

Bear in mind that creating a good resume takes time. You don't want to rush through the process and deliver a sub-par application. Spending just a little bit of extra time polishing up your resume can make the difference between getting a job and ending up at the bottom of the resume pile.

The best way how to beat those ATS systems is to be qualified for the job you are applying for! Make sure that your resume doesn't work against your qualifications.

Some people add "Harvard," "Oxford," or "Cambridge" into their resumes in invisible white text as a way to pass automated screenings.

Don't keyword stuff into your CV or add the entire job description in white, invisible text. Although these tricks may seem smart, employers will be able to tell that you are trying to deceive them.

RESUME LENGTH

There are many misconceptions about resumes, many of which have to do with length. Resumes need to be clear and concise while covering the most important areas and achievements of your professional life. How long should your resume be to make sure it aligns with what recruiters and hiring managers want to see and helps you stand out from the competition?

Some career coaches say that a resume should only be one page long and that anything above the limit could hurt your chance of getting selected. However, providing limited information about your professional experience can actually hurt your chance of being selected even more. If you are a candidate with more than ten years of experience, trying to condense that to fit one page is extremely difficult and will cut down on your ability to show how experienced and capable you are.

The goal here is to find out what structure allows you to place your best foot forward so that your resume gets you an invitation for an interview. There is no specific guideline to follow when it comes to a resume's length. Your resume length can vary based on various factors like your years of experience, the industry in which you work, and the job you are applying for. Your primary goal should not be to focus on the length of your resume but on the content.

In the next paragraphs, you will find general guidelines on resume length and ways to determine the best length.

One-Page Resumes

You've probably heard that the best resumes are one page long, but this isn't the case anymore. Experienced professionals shouldn't try to make their resumes fit on one page, because it will require them to skip important information that's crucial to their success.

A one-page resume is considered suitable only for recent graduates and entry-level candidates looking for their first professional job or for people who do not have a lot of professional experience. A one-page resume is also acceptable if you haven't moved around much and your experience is limited to one or two companies where you didn't change roles.

These days, candidates at the beginning of their careers enter the labor market with far more experience than did candidates at the same level many years ago. This is because today's candidates usually also have experience volunteering, in part-time jobs, or in internships. In addition, today's world presents candidates with many more online learning opportunities.

If there's sufficient information worthy of mentioning in a resume, don't be afraid to exceed the one-page limit. Of course you should avoid filling your resume with "fluff" just to make it longer.

Two-Page Resumes

The two-page resume is the ideal choice for most people because it gives enough space to share information about experience, career, and work achievements. Two pages allow you to dig into your accomplishments in more detail and also provide more context.

Why is this option more suitable than the one-page resume? Just think about the fact that recruiters are looking for candidates with the best set of skills, qualities, and abilities to fill in available positions. This can be determined only by reading well-made resumes that provide information regarding education, training, experience, and acquired skills, all of which usually take more than one page to share.

Use the first page to show your relevant skills and your relevant experience. On the second page add things that are less relevant to a job, like your education and hobbies. Don't forget that recruiters may spend only several seconds scanning a resume, and you want them to read the most important parts first.

A two-page resume works best for those with at least ten years of experience on the job market. With this level of experience, you'll have sufficient space for all the information worthy of mentioning on a resume.

Length only matters so much. If you submit a two-page resume and the person reading it decides you're not a match for the job, they will stop reading. On the other hand, if you do seem to fit the job requirements, they will want to know more about you.

If you have in your resume something that is relevant to the job (based on the requirement in the job ad), make that part more visible by **boldfacing** it. If you do, you will help the recruiter find the right keywords, and they will spend more time with your resume.

Resumes of Three Pages or More

Do you feel that a longer resume of three pages or more would be best because you have so many things to say? If your answer is yes, take into consideration that recruiters don't want to spend too much time reading resumes.

It's important to remember that a resume is not the same as a PowerPoint presentation. When you're creating a resume, you only have a limited amount of space to work with. This means that you need to be selective about the information that you include. Start by reading the job requirements carefully. Then, tailor your resume to fit those requirements. Don't try to include everything—just focus on the information that will be most useful to the employer. If you can keep your resume clear and concise, you'll make a much better impression.

If you are considering a multiple-page resume, do an in-depth analysis of why you need the space and just how much space you need. The goal here is to figure out what you must say and how you can show the recruiter you have concrete experience in the field—no more and no less. Give recruiters the information they wish to find and leave other details for the interview.

The longer resume option is most suitable for those in executive positions with impressive track records. It is also a good choice for those with a wide array of publications relevant to their job or with academic activities.

If you need to include case studies, technical background, skills, or highlights of different projects or if you're applying for a federal job, which may require a higher degree of detail, then you might need a longer resume.

The Rule of Thumb

If you are starting out in your career or you have a limited work history, one page should be fine. If you have more experience, it is best to keep your resume to two pages. This way, you can highlight your most relevant experience and skills without overwhelming the reader.

However, if you have a lot of experience or you are applying for a senior-level position, a longer resume may be appropriate. In these cases, you should focus on including only the information that is most relevant to the job you are applying for. Remember that the goal of your resume is to get an interview, so don't include anything that wouldn't help you achieve that goal. If you're not sure whether something should be included, err on the side of caution and leave it out.

The recommendation is to limit your resume to no longer than three pages. Everything that is longer will do no good for you.

The exceptions to the rule are government resumes or resumes that need to include all your patents, licenses, or other specific and technical information in addition to your work history. In most cases, the right length is between two and three pages. If you need to share more information with a reader, you can always leverage your LinkedIn profile and redirect the reader there.

HOW TO SHORTEN YOUR RESUME

Shortening your resume can increase readability and make it easier for recruiters and hiring managers to understand your qualifications. The more information you put on your resume, the more difficult it will be for the reader to see the highlights of your career. Some of the things you have included will not be relevant to recruiters. That is why it is a good practice to remove unnecessary content from your resume before you start sending it to employers.

Start with your personal data. Your date of birth or marital status are not relevant to any job, and you should remove them from your resume. Your home address and references are also not required and therefore should be removed.

After removing personal data, you can play with formatting, size of text, and bullet points to save space. But don't go crazy—your goal is not to use the smallest font possible to squeeze your resume into fewer pages. Always focus on the accuracy and quality of the information you are sharing as well as the presentation. Make it readable.

Consider these suggestions when you are trying to make your resume shorter:

1. Use or remove bullet points

If you have more than five bullet points in any section, consider combining them into a paragraph.

Example

- Train, mentor, and coach recruiters on recruiting methodology, cutting-edge sourcing techniques (and tools), relationship building, negotiation, and closing techniques.
- Take ownership of recruiting KPIs and global reporting.
- Implement innovative recruitment strategies.
- Manage internal communications regarding hiring.
- Organize job fair presentations.
- Create annual hiring practices handbook.

Turn the list into a paragraph:

> *I help to train, mentor, and coach recruiters on recruiting methodology, cutting-edge sourcing techniques (and tools), relationship building, negotiation, and closing techniques. I also set recruiting KPIs, create global reports and internal hiring practice guidebooks, implement innovative recruitment strategies, manage internal communications regarding hiring, and organize job fair presentations.*

Bullet points are easier to read so before you start replacing them with a paragraph, try first to remove unnecessary info.

2. Change text size and font

If you're having trouble making your resume fit within a specific number of pages, try changing the font size of your job titles or use a different font for your entire resume.

There are several font sizes and font types that are recommended. The best font size for resumes is 11 to 12 points for paragraph text and 14 to 16 points for section titles and headers. Easy-to-read font types are Calibri, Arial, Garamond, Verdana, Helvetica, and Tahoma. The most common font to use is Times New Roman. These fonts are also common to most computers and they are easy to read by ATS systems.

3. Adjust spacing

Experiment with the spacing between paragraphs, the overall spacing of your resume, and the formatting. Just make sure that, by reducing spacing, you're not also reducing readability.

4. Remove photos and graphics

If you have a photo or graphic elements in your resume, remove them to save space. Any graphic element you have in your resume could cause problems for ATS systems anyway. You already have your profile photo on LinkedIn so there is no reason to have it in your resume.

Don't add logos of certifications you received or companies you worked for. It is better to list them as text because not all recruiters are familiar with the logos and the ATS system will not be able to read them.

The same goes for emojis: Do not use them in your resume at all. Not only is it unprofessional to do so, but an ATS system could turn an emoji into nonsense code.

Photos also have an impact on the overall size of your Word or PDF file. Large Word files or PDFs may not be uploaded. Save yourself that potential headache.

5. Remove unimportant sections

Not every section in your resume is important. Your goal is to keep it simple. Following are some sections you can remove.

6. Hobbies

There is no reason to have this section in a resume in the first place. Interviewers are usually not interested in your hobbies. If they are, they will ask you during the interview.

7. Reference section

There is absolutely no reason to add a reference section. Instead write "References available upon request" or some similar statement. Recruiters do not have the

time to contact your references at the beginning of the prescreening; in any case, they should inform you before they start contacting them.

If the company asks you for a reference, you should be able to give your contact a quick heads up and loop them into the job you are applying for. You can always provide your references after the interview via email or phone.

8. Temp jobs and early career jobs

If you have a LinkedIn profile, you can add all the information about your previous employers there. The internship role that you did twenty years ago is not relevant for the role that you are trying to get now.

9. Home address

Many candidates add their home addresses to their resumes. My recommendation is not to do this. Keep only the city (and country) where you live. There is no need for anyone during the prescreening process to know exactly where you live.

FINAL THOUGHTS

The first page of your resume is the page with the potential to attract the attention of the recruiter and hiring manager. Make sure that the first page has the most relevant information. To do that, you need to read the job description carefully and then tailor that first page to highlight what the employer is looking for.

Always focus on content, keywords, and accuracy of information instead of length. As I recommend to my clients, the best length is two pages, but you should primarily focus on relevant content, clearly articulating your accomplishments, and making sure that the information you have in your resume is current and accurate. You can always edit your resume after you create the final version.

The final length depends entirely on you and how much information you want to include. However, do your best to limit your resume to the information that is useful and valuable for the job you are looking to obtain.

8. How to Get Your Resume Noticed

As discussed, there are a few things you can do to make sure your resume stands out from the rest. First, tailor your resume specifically for the job you are applying for. Make sure your skills and experience match the requirements of the position. Second, use strong active verbs to describe your experience and skills. Third, make sure your formatting is clean and easy to read. And fourth, proofread your resume for errors.

The good news is that, once you've got your resume in tip-top shape, there are many things you can do to get it noticed. Since your resume is all about grabbing the attention of your employers, it is important to know what can make a recruiter spend a bit more time considering you for the role. Your resume can get you the best and worst attention of employers, recruiters, and hiring managers. Your goal is to get the right kind of attention by showing your skills, qualifications, and motivation.

The most challenging part of applying for a job is obtaining an interview and getting the chance to talk to your employer in person. This will be the moment that you will show your soft skills and personality and talk about why you are a great fit for the role. To get to that stage, you need to submit a resume and a cover letter. Unfortunately many candidates don't make it through the first round of screening or, as many call it, the six-second scan.

THE SIX-SECOND RESUME SCAN

This initial six-second scan is how the employer finds details that are worth considering. If you get an employer to spend more than six seconds looking at your resume, then your chances of getting an interview are considerably higher.

Is the initial scan really only six seconds long? I asked the same question when I read my first article about this phenomenon, an article that promised to customize my resume so I could pass the six-second screening test.

Employers, especially at big organizations, receive a high number of resumes for most of the roles they open. As you may suspect, the recruiters or hiring

managers do not have the time to read all the resumes, so they will quickly scan them to see if a candidate is worth a more in-depth analysis.

I'm a recruiter, and I know that recruiters take way more time than six seconds with each resume. This six-second resume scan myth is just one of the many misconceptions in our field. That's why I want to share with you how this scan really works.

This misconception started when a company offering resume rewriting released the results of a "study" it had conducted. Subsequently, many career coaches embraced the myth, offering to help people rewrite their resumes to help them pass the six-second test. A study from Careerbuilder[33] shows that one in six (17 percent) hiring managers spend thirty seconds or less, on average, reviewing resumes. According to a more recent CareerBuilder survey, a majority (68 percent) spend less than two minutes.

If you want to get your resume noticed, follow these guidelines to help your resume pass screening robots and make recruiters and hiring managers spend more time considering you.

1. Write a "screener-friendly" qualifications summary

Recruiters look for candidates who have the highest chances of turning into reliable and productive employees. A well-written qualifications summary at the top of your resume—a few brief sentences outlining why you are the best person for the job—can help you be selected for the next stage within a few seconds. Showing the recruiter that you have the needed qualifications won't just help your resume pass the initial assessment but will also considerably increase your chances of landing an interview.

To create the summary, write down a list of qualifications taken from the job's description. Many job descriptions will provide a set of skills, abilities, and qualifications desired by the employing company for the job, which will facilitate this task. Then make sure you mention several of those in your summary or even in your resume. Tailor your summary to the job description, mentioning the same phrases, and describing your achievements that are connected with the responsibility part of the job description.

During my career, I learned that the first three requirements in a job description are, in the majority of cases, the most important requirements for the hiring manager. When you are applying for a role, match those requirements. Provide concrete examples of related tasks you have worked on and the results.

---

[33] http://press.careerbuilder.com/2014-03-13-Hiring-Managers-Rank-Best-and-Worst-Words-to-Use-in-a-Resume-in-New-CareerBuilder-Survey

2. Make your resume skimmable

Given that your resume often serves as your first impression, it's worth taking a few minutes to fix any issues with formatting. Your resume, when paired with neat formatting, will help differentiate you from other applicants.

To make it skimmable, focus on margins, spacing, and fonts, making sure that all three contribute to easy reading and don't, in fact, make it more difficult. You can also improve the skimmability of your resume by adding divider lines between sections or using boldface and italics to highlight important information such as company names and job titles.

Keep your formatting the same throughout the entire document. Consistency helps with skimming.

3. Use the right keywords

Many recruiting companies have turned to screening systems for the initial evaluation of resumes. Using keywords is helpful even if the resume will be screened by real humans. Screeners, whether inanimate or human, will look for specific words and expressions to determine if your resume is worthy of an in-depth analysis. Keywords help you speak the hiring manager's language.

Avoid mentioning the same skills multiple times in your descriptions of your older jobs. If you want to mention a skill, emphasize it at the last job you had where you used it.

4. Focus on results

How do you emphasize results in a resume? Use numbers and metrics to give concrete evidence of what you achieved and accomplished.

For example, don't just say you do advertising campaigns. Instead, provide numbers connected to your advertising campaigns. For instance, how much does the ROI increase after your input? How many new customers does the company win over? How much do sales go up? Basically, prove to the recruiter and hiring manager that you fit the role and can deliver the results the business needs.

Example

- Increased billable hours in the first quarter by 25%.
- Added 21 clients in the first half of 2021 for $8.6 million in additional revenue.

5. Pair Your resume with a good cover letter

Some recruiters do not require a cover letter. If they do, take the time to write a good one. The best part about cover letters is that you can personalize them to fit a job application, underlining experiences that are most relevant for the job.

BEFORE YOU SEND YOUR RESUME

There are a few things you should keep in mind before you send your resume to a recruiter or upload it via the registration form. You want to get your resume noticed, but you don't want to attract negative attention.

1. Make sure you're a fit for the job

It is always a good idea to only apply for positions you are qualified for. You would be surprised how many candidates apply to positions that they're utterly wrong for.

Aiming for a higher position than you currently have is okay, but you need to be realistic and know what an appropriate goal is. Applying for Senior Manager roles with one year of experience is unrealistic and will likely lead to your resume being rejected.

In time, as you gather more experience and participate in training sessions and courses, you will be able to aim high. Until then, make sure you are a good fit by reading a job's requirements carefully. If you fall short in 70 percent of those requirements, don't bother to apply.

Even if you don't meet *all* the requirements, make sure you can at least tick off the minimum set of requirements, the ones that are considered crucial. You can learn the rest on the job if you demonstrate you have the willingness and ability to learn fast. You can and should mention that in your cover letter.

2. Limit the fluff

A complex resume does not equal a higher chance of getting hired. On the contrary, a resume that is too long or difficult to read, especially one that is full of fluff, will be left on the side. There is no point in adding information that is irrelevant to the available job just for the sake of having a resume stuffed with many sentences. That type of resume wastes recruiters' time.

A resume is not your life history but instead a way to emphasize the characteristics, skills, experiences, and qualities that recommend you for a

specific job. If you choose to mention experiences that are not that relevant, keep it brief.

3.   Check and double check

Are you happy you finished your resume? You probably want to click the "send" button as soon as possible so you can be done with this part of the job search. Restrain yourself! Don't send your resume until you have checked it and checked it again. ATS does not recognize misspelled words at all, but humans do, so mistakes will hurt you no matter what. Check for typos, misplaced punctuation, repeated words, inconsistency, and misspellings. Check your work again with digital tools meant for proofing documents such as Word's spelling and grammar check and Grammarly.

Is your email address right? Do you write dates the same way throughout your entire resume? Are you consistent in font size? Are there any extra unwanted spaces in sentences?

When you're done with the proofreading, save your resume by giving it the right name. The receiver will see the name of the file you've sent. Don't name it *resume*, which will make it indistinguishable from every other resume. Personalize the name of the file: AntoniaFrenchResume.pdf.

FINAL THOUGHTS

When writing your resume, remember that it is not a comprehensive list of all your skills or your entire job history, which would include every summer job you've ever had. Think of your resume as an advertisement—you don't want to bore your audience with too much detail. Instead, focus on the relevant information.

If you want to increase your chances of getting an invitation for an interview, create a cover letter that is tailored to the position you are applying for. A cover letter gives you an extra space to market your skills and demonstrate to the recruiter and hiring manager that you are the right fit for their open position.

9. The Cover Letter

A cover letter is an opportunity to show your potential employer who you are before even meeting them face to face. By following these tips, you will be sure to make a great first impression and improve your chances of getting the job you want.

WHAT A COVER LETTER IS

Your resume is a more factual document that outlines your experience, training, and education. The cover letter is a great opportunity to introduce yourself and showcase your personality. However, you don't want to go overboard. The cover letter should be used to impress the employer and make a good impression.

The first thing to remember when writing a cover letter is that it should be original. Do not use any templates or pre-written forms. A cover letter should represent who you are, so it's not worth writing it if you're just going to copy it from the Internet.

You will find out, later on, what to include in a cover letter, so composing it will seem less daunting. Although there is not an official format you can use when writing a cover letter, try to make it fit the industry and company you're sending the application to. This means that if you are looking for a job in the finance industry, you should try to be factual and specific in your application. If you are looking for a job in marketing, you may want to think outside the box and show the employer how you can make ideas come to life.

Another piece of advice is to organize the letter well. In other words, present the information in a way that is easy to read and understand.

A great cover letter starts with a well-written introduction that briefly states why you are interested in the job and how your skills and experience make you the perfect candidate. Then it provides examples of projects, work, and accomplishments that are relevant to the job you're looking to get. Last, but not least, a cover letter should contain a call to action. During the recruitment process, you should "sell" yourself to the employer in a subtle yet effective manner. Make them think you are their best choice. Then give them something to do about that.

WHAT TO INCLUDE IN YOUR COVER LETTER

Although it is tempting to write a long and detailed cover letter, remember that a cover letter is a supplement to your resume, not a replacement. You don't need to include a comprehensive overview of your professional experience if it is already in your resume.

Employers do not have time to read long cover letters and resumes, so they will scan them for the information that is interesting to them. Focus on the aspects of your experience that can help you get the job. This means mentioning those parts of your career that fit the situation and emphasizing your skills and qualifications. If you can demonstrate how you can be a valuable asset to the company, you are more likely to be hired.

Your cover letter should also show that you are interested in the position. Just as you want the employer to want you, the employer wants you to want to work for them.

A proper cover letter should do the following:

- Emphasize the parts of your experience that recommend you for the job you're looking to obtain. Read the job's requirements well and precisely pick those professional experiences that are a match.
- Underline the skills that make you suitable for the job. Every job description will also include a list of desired skills. If you have some or all of the skills, make sure you mention them in the cover letter.
- Reveal your reason for wanting to work there. This part is very important for every employer. If you have a good reason and you combine it with passion and determination, you will make a good impression.

When applying for a job, take company culture into account. Your cover letter is a way for you to show recruiters that you would easily connect with your future team. If you want to improve your chances of landing your dream opportunity, research the company values and the team you will work with and use this information to your advantage. The more the recruiter feels you will fit in, the higher the chances you will get called in for an interview.

When providing such information, you prove to the employer that you are a great choice. You make it clear that you have what it takes to meet the company's requirements and do a good job at work.

What should you do if you do not meet all the requirements of the job description? In case you are a graduate without experience, for example, think of your skills and qualities that could recommend you. And show the employer your desire to learn and improve.

Candidates commonly mention skills in general terms in their cover letters, like "effective in finding solutions to problems." Don't just stop there. Also give a real-life example of your actions being essential to solving a problem. If your example is pertinent to the available job, that's even better.

COVER LETTER LENGTH

Ideally, the cover letter should be one page long and divided into three paragraphs, and you should target a word count of around 300 to 400 words. There is no need to create a longer cover letter as many recruiters will not even read it if it's too long.

To make it even easier to get started, following is an outline of the cover letter structure.

HEADER

The header should include your name, phone number, and email address. Add the country code to your phone number, as the recruiter or hiring manager could be located in a different country.

Next, add a date and the name of the hiring manager with their job title. If you don't know their name, you can just leave this information and keep only the company name.

The date line should be separated from your address and the recipient's address.

Add the name of the company right below the name of the hiring manager.

Use a professional email address and not an unprofessional email address like sugarbaby47@example.com.

Example

Janelle Mendoza • +1 000-000-0000 • janellem@example.com • LinkedIn: linkedin.com/janll-24/

January 21, 2022

Marcus Jones, HR Manager
Ready Storage Inc.

You can also add your social media profiles or personal website if these links will add some value to your application. If not, simply add a LinkedIn link so they can check your LinkedIn profile.

Note: When you are applying to several open positions at different companies, always check the company name. Nothing will kill the first impression as using the wrong company name.

SALUTATION

In the next step, you are ready to start writing the content of your cover letter. Start by addressing the specific hiring manager rather than using generic phrases like "Dear Sir/Madam." This approach will help you stand out among other applicants by showing the hiring manager that you have done proper research about the company before sending in your application.

If you do not know the name of the hiring manager, use the generic salutation. It's important to use a formal and professional greeting when you don't know your letter or email recipient well.

Always do your research about the company culture before you reach out to the hiring manager. For some companies, using the first name in the salutation is the right way to start your cover letter; for other, using the first name could lower your chances of being invited.

If the company has an open culture and you know the name of the hiring manager, use it in the salutation. If you do not know the gender of the recipient and can't tell from their name, just use the person's first and last names.

Examples

- Dear John, (if you know the recipient)
- Dear Mr. Doe, Dear Ms. Doe, Dear John Doe,
- Dear (Company) Team,
- Dear Hiring Manager,

Don't use these salutations:

- Dear Sir or Madam,
- To Whom It May Concern,
- Hello there,
- Hey, Hi, Hello, etc.

Example

Janelle Mendoza • +1 000-000-0000 • janellem@example.com • LinkedIn: linkedin.com/janll-24/

January 21, 2022

Marcus Jones, HR Manager
Ready Storage Inc.

Dear Mr. Jones,

COVER LETTER PARAGRAPHS

As discussed earlier, your cover letter will have three paragraphs. We'll go over the content of each one.

First Paragraph

The first paragraph is used for an opening. The goal of this paragraph is to grab the reader's attention with several of your top achievements. Keep it short and point out two to three top achievements. Keep the rest for the interview and for your resume.

The generic openings in most cover letters will not grab attention.

Bad Example

Dear Mr. Doe,

My name is Julie Smith, and I would like to work as branch manager at ACME LLC. I have previous experience as a branch manager at ACME 2 and at Different ACME, and because I worked as branch manager for the last four years, I am the right fit for the open position your company is trying to fill.

Good Example

Dear Mr. Doe,

My name is Julie Smith, and I would like to help your company ACME with expansion and increasing profit. For the last four years, I worked for ACME 2 and Different ACME where I was able to help them be more effective and increase earnings: During my work for ACME 2, we generated **67% more profit** than in previous years and at Different ACME, we generated **89% more profit** than in previous years. I believe that my previous experience as a branch manager makes me the right candidate for the job.

It doesn't matter so much that you worked in a similar role before; many other candidates who are applying also worked in similar positions. Maybe they even have more experience than you. What can make you stand out are your achievements. And those achievements that you mention in your cover letter could be the reason you get invited for an interview. Those achievements demonstrate not only that you have the right skills, but also that you have results behind you.

There are many ways to get the attention of the reader. One of the easiest ones is to put in bold your achievements.

Second Paragraph

In the second paragraph, you need to explain why you are perfect for the job. Detail your experience, skills, and qualifications that match the role.

Only discuss the skills that are relevant to the job. That's why it is important to check the job description and see what requirements are listed first; they are usually the most important ones.

Using the right keywords or similar phrases will help you to get attention. In addition, you need to convince the hiring manager that you are a perfect fit for the *organization*.

This paragraph is also the place where you can share proof that you were successful before and that your skills will likely help the company to reach better results.

For example, if they are looking for a "Good key account manager," saying, "I worked as a key account manager and hit the sales KPI every month" will not demonstrate anything. If you say, "As a key account manager I was able to exceed company KPI by more than 200% and bring in $500,000 U.S. every month," you will better demonstrate your worth for the company.

Third Paragraph

Explain why you are a good match for the company and why the company is the perfect fit for you. All you have to do is use any search engine to research the following information:

- Company culture
- Long term goals, plans, or overall mission
- The business model of the company you are applying for
- Their products and services
- Their other activities like supporting local communities

Once you are done with your research, figure out the things that you love about the company. Those may be the products or services they are offering. Or it may be work culture or something else that you find yourself passionate about as well. Then in the third paragraph explain why you want to work for that company.

CLOSING

In the closing of your cover letter, you should add a call to action. This shouldn't be something as meaningless as "Call me." Instead, say something more professional that also reinforces a point you have made earlier: "I would welcome the opportunity to discuss your sales objectives and find out how my previous success at ACME 2 can be used to foster sales growth at ACME."

If you can't think of anything, you can always say, "Thank you very much for your time and consideration. I look forward to hearing from you." This is clichéd but still professional and meaningful. You can even show your proactivity here by saying, "I would love the opportunity to have a short meeting this week so that I can fully understand your expectations and vision for the role. I can stop by the office or have it via Zoom if you are available."

By mentioning "this week" and not a specific date like "this Tuesday," you are giving the reader room to pick a time in their busy schedule that works for them.

Formal Closing

At the end, close the letter in a formal manner. You can conclude with one of the following phrases: "Sincerely," "Best Regards," "Kind Regards," or "Best Wishes."

Example

Janelle Mendoza • +1 000-000-0000 • janellem@example.com • LinkedIn: linkedin.com/janll-24/

January 21, 2022

Marcus Jones, HR Manager
Ready Storage Inc.

Dear Mr. Jones,

I am hoping to get the chance to apply my experience as a marketing manager to help Ready Storage attract more customers. As marketing manager at ACME Storage, I tripled the size of our mailing list and increased our Facebook followers by 300 percent. My marketing strategies were followed within six months by a 25 percent increase in customers.

I used my knowledge of WordPress to build a new more friendly and interactive website for ACME Storage, and through that site we were able to launch the campaign to increase our email list. I also used my experience with MailChimp to design a monthly electronic newsletter that I wrote and sent out to our mailing list with coupons and other enticements. After just four such newsletters, we were able to cover the discounts in our offers and exceed them through new sales by 15 percent. For my previous employer, Banana Shakes Inc., I designed and created a promotional event used by all our franchisees to triple sales on the event day.

Ready Storage values its community, and I admire its commitment to giving back. I envision celebrating this company culture through fundraising events that increase brand-name recognition while supporting housing efforts in Ready Storage's urban settings. People who have trouble finding affordable housing are often the ones most in need of storage options, so linking the two efforts makes good marketing sense.

Thank you so much for your consideration. I hope to get the chance to speak with you directly about my ideas for expanding Ready Storage's consumer base, increasing its name recognition, and further associating the company with causes popular in the company's locations.

Best Wishes,
Janelle Mendoza

The cover letter is not yet ready to be sent to the employer. Make use of proofreading tools to check the letter before sending it. Once the proofreading is done and you are happy with your writing, you are good to go.

Note: *Some candidates add postscripts (P.S.) at the end of their cover letters to promote their success one last time. As people cannot resist reading a postscript, this works especially well to focus on your most marketable attribute.*

LAST FEW TIPS

While writing your cover letter, always keep a few key things in mind. Your cover letter should be attention-grabbing for the reader or the hiring manager. Make sure to write only factual information. Use the cover letter to convince the hiring manager that you are the most suitable candidate for the job and the company. Following are some more tips.

Tell a Good Story

The cover letter is a great opportunity to tell your story as a professional. If you have a great story connected to your career that is worth mentioning because it demonstrates why you are the right candidate, don't hesitate to include it. The employer will appreciate it.

Make Sure the Tone Is Appropriate

Doing some research and getting to know the company will show you what tone is appropriate and whether you should be extremely formal or more friendly and laid back. As with the other details, personalize tone too for each job application.

Be Honest

It is never a good idea to lie when looking to get hired. Making false assertions about your skills, experience, or background can become a serious issue when you are not able to deliver on your promises.

Never Include Negative Points

In your cover letter, don't mention any issues you had at your last organization. Don't mention a difficult boss or problem colleagues. Don't talk about a working situation you didn't like or how you were unhappy with your salary or benefits. You would be surprised how many people have a tendency to share negative things in their cover letters.

Add a Personal Touch

The whole idea of the cover letter is to set yourself apart from all the other candidates. So try not to sound like the others and avoid using clichés. A unique personality is easier to remember, so play your cards carefully on this one if you want to succeed.

End with a Call to Action

Formulate your call to action with care, without being too incisive, and without crossing boundaries. The goal is to give the employer a reason to contact you. So be polite and diplomatic, letting the employer know that you are available and willing to provide any further information and that you're enthusiastic to meet them and have a good conversation.

Always Proofread

Never send a cover letter and resume without proofing them first. Typos and grammar mistakes can lead to the rejection of your application. Ask friends and family members to read what you have written. An eye from someone else could spot mistakes you didn't notice and give you useful feedback about the readability and flow of the content.

Don't Use Templates

Most people write their cover letter by looking at examples of cover letters on the Internet. Try to create your cover letter without using templates as a reference. Templates will stifle your ability to create a unique cover letter that will help you to stand out from the crowd of other job seekers.

Use the Right File Format

Always try to send your cover letter as a PDF because PDFs maintain formatting. During my career, I saw many cover letters save as Excel files or even as plain text files. I do not recommend that at all because they are extremely hard to read and do not look professional.

Almost everyone is able to open a PDF. If, for whatever reason, you can't save your resume as a PDF, send it as a Word doc. Do not send a URL where they can download your resume!

FINAL THOUGHTS

Is a cover letter still important? My opinion is that cover letters are no longer as relevant as they once were, as they duplicate your digital footprint and LinkedIn profile. However, many companies still request them from job applicants.

Create a cover letter to differentiate yourself from others even if it's not required. It will make a positive impression and could improve your chance to get an invitation to interview.

Another option, if you want to stand out from the other job applicants, is to create a short video introduction (two minutes maximum). Record your video, upload it to YouTube, and mark it as "Unlisted"[34] so that only people who have the link can view it. Then include the link in your resume or cover letter or share it via LinkedIn. You can use applications like Loom[35] or StoryXpress[36] to record short videos.

Based on the data I collected over the years, some video cover letters were viewed between five and ten times. Not only will that type of approach get you attention, but it will also show your creativity and make a good first impression. Employers will appreciate the effort.

---

[34] https://support.google.com/youtube/answer/157177
[35] https://www.loom.com/
[36] http://storyxpress.co/

10. LinkedIn and Your Personal Brand

Social networking websites have disrupted the process of hiring, and your Facebook, Instagram, and Twitter profiles can now determine whether you are a great fit for the job. Today, employers include a background check of the online profiles of candidates.

Many companies now recruit candidates primarily through the Internet, using all the data they have. The traditional resume is not dead, of course, and will be with us for some time. But one day it could be replaced by a LinkedIn profile or something similar. For now, it is the combination and alignment of all your efforts that will make you look like a strongly qualified candidate.

Many recruiters and hiring managers use Google to research candidates before extending an offer, especially if the position is crucial for the company. In this modern age of smart search engines, candidates who are active on social media have the advantage to get better visibility, have a stronger personal brand, and create a better positive impression by including recommendations on their LinkedIn profiles and being connected with positive news on the Internet.

Unlike the human brain, the Internet never forgets. Those inappropriate statements you made in your sophomore year of college or that photo of you drunk that was taken at your graduation party can now come back to bite you in your job application process. By conducting a simple search for your name, hiring managers can see all the blog posts you have made since 2006: blogs about your vacation to Mexico, photos of you smoking weed, your outburst on gay marriage, and your comment on immigration laws.

When that happens, your experience starts to matter less and less. Now the recruiter is trying to determine whether you might wreck the company or ruin the team. They need to know you are just the type of professional they want. I already covered this in the "Digital Footprint" section, but it is important to mention it again as a LinkedIn profile could help you direct the attention of the employer in the right direction and away from a Google search of your name.

WHAT LINKEDIN IS

LinkedIn[37] is a social and networking site that has around 830 million members in more than 200 countries and territories. LinkedIn is also one of the first places that recruiters visit when their hiring managers ask them to start searching for a candidate for open vacancies. For many recruiters, LinkedIn is the only place where they search for candidates because that is where the candidates are.

This site is an important tool in your job search because it allows you to improve your chance to get better job opportunities. Having an online presence on LinkedIn is essential for white-collar workers because they can use it to connect with other professionals and potential employers.

If you're not on LinkedIn or haven't been using it much, now is the time to change your approach. A few weeks before you start your job search, start posting and commenting on LinkedIn. This will increase your chances of being discovered by recruiters.

You can also tailor your LinkedIn profile specifically to the hiring managers for the company you want to work for. By doing this, you'll make it more likely that they'll notice you and consider you for the position. So if you're looking for a new job, don't forget to use LinkedIn to your advantage.

HOW TO CREATE A BETTER LINKEDIN PROFILE

LinkedIn is a powerful tool for job seekers because it provides opportunities to connect with potential employers and learn about unadvertised job openings. In addition, LinkedIn allows users to showcase their skills and experience through an online profile.

If you're looking for a new job, not having a LinkedIn profile could put you at a disadvantage compared to other candidates. You won't be aware of all the great job opportunities that are not advertised.

If you don't have a LinkedIn profile, create one!

The Power of a LinkedIn Profile

The most important thing to understand is that a good LinkedIn profile can do much more for you than just share your work experience. Your profile is a great way to show off your career, and it can help create a professional image for potential employers. It will also provide more information for recruiters than you can contain in your resume or, at the very least, it will confirm what you say

---

[37] https://www.linkedin.com/

in your resume. Besides, a public profile can carry more clout—it is less likely for a person to fake a public profile than a private resume.

Why Do You Need to Optimize and Update Your LinkedIn Profile?

Your LinkedIn profile is often the first impression that you make on potential employers and other professionals. You can think of your profile as a landing page for your visitors, a page where they can quickly find out who you are and what you do.

That is why optimization and update of your LinkedIn profile is essential for your job search. Overall, an updated and optimized profile has three benefits:

1. It is more attractive. A well-optimized LinkedIn profile makes any visitor want to know more about you and what you do.
2. Optimizing your profile allows you to be more visible on LinkedIn search. This is very useful when you are looking for a new opportunity: Your profile will appear in recruiter searches more often if you use the right keywords.
• LinkedIn provides you with the ability to embed keywords and customize the URL of your profile. Both will help get your profile noticed outside of the social network via Google searches—as long as your profile's public visibility is turned on.

Keep in mind that LinkedIn is always changing its design and adding new features, so some things could be different by the time you are reading this book.

Visit **jobsearch.guide**[38] for news and updates.

HOW TO STRUCTURE A PERFECT LINKEDIN PROFILE

Your LinkedIn profile page is the foundation of your personal brand. It is important to keep this page professional. Your LinkedIn profile becomes your online resume, a resume that has a structure that you need to follow if you want to get maximum benefit from it.

Follow these tips for the most important LinkedIn sections.

1. Name

The first field you need to fill is the name field. Use your real name, first name first and then your second name. Always use the names that you are using in life when you are communicating with authorities.

---

[38] https://jobsearch.guide/

If your name is difficult to pronounce, LinkedIn has a feature that records you saying your name.

Reijo Ruotsalainen 🔊 · 1st
UX Designer
Talks about #culture, #society, #community
London, England, United Kingdom · Contact info

You can also add your certifications or school degree into the name field. However, my recommendation is to keep it simple with just a name and surname. The reason is that degrees before your name or at the end of your name can be the reason a recruiter won't select you, as they might make you seem overqualified.

Jan Tegze · You 🔗
Director of Talent Acquisition, Author of Full Stack Recruiter
Brno

Try not to add your name in all lowercase or all uppercase letters. And try to avoid using a different font in your name than in your profile because a LinkedIn search engine will not be able to recognize it.

John Doe · 1st 🔗
User Experience Designer
Prague, Czechia

LinkedIn users can also add emojis and symbols before or after their names. There are two reasons people do this: The first reason is that they want to get attention and make their profile stand out in the search results. The second is that they want to know if the InMail messages they receive were sent via automatization tools.

🔍 Jan Tegze · You 🔗
Director of Talent Acquisition
Brno

Those tools take the first symbol as text, so instead of starting with "Dear Jan," the message will have either a blank space where your name would go in the salutation, or an emoji.

The name you use on your LinkedIn profile will be also used in your LinkedIn profile URL (linkedin.com/in/**yourname**/). For this reason, try to avoid adding any symbols when creating your LinkedIn profile.

If you do add symbols or titles, customize your LinkedIn profile URL via LinkedIn settings. This is one of the first steps to take to help ensure you get the URL you want assigned to your LinkedIn profile.

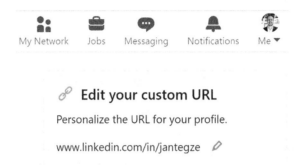

One last thing to remember: There are character limits on LinkedIn. Your first name is limited to 20 characters and your last name to 40 characters. The limit for the URL is 5 to 30 characters.

2. Location and industry

The Location and Industry fields on your LinkedIn profile tell people what industry you are in and where you are located in the world.

Location

You will be asked to fill in the Country/Region and City/District. Both of these will offer you a dropdown menu where you can see a list of all the options. Country/Region is a required field, but you do not need to fill in your City.

Industry

When you are selecting an industry for your industry field, you will be able to see a long list of options. You can only choose one.

If you can't find a heading that perfectly suits your industry, use the next best thing or the industry that is most important to you. You can use the About section to share more info about yourself and your skills.

Recruiters use Industry in filters when searching for candidates. If you are not getting enough offers, consider replacing your current Industry field choice with another.

If you are planning to relocate to a different city or country, consider changing the location on your profile to the new one. This will ensure that you start receiving offers from recruiters looking for candidates in your new location. If you are moving to a different country, there is no need to select a city.

3. Profile/background photo

Profile picture

Your LinkedIn profile is a powerful tool allowing you to introduce yourself to employers. Adding a photo to your profile enables recruiters to put a face to the name. A photo might help you stand out from the crowd and will get your profile more views. LinkedIn members with profile photos can get up to twenty-one times more[39] profile views than members without.

Your profile picture is an efficient way to generate credibility if it's up-to-date, clear, and professional. Preferably it will show you smiling—don't underestimate the power of a smile in a profile photo. Many studies show that photos of people smiling make them look more trustworthy, and multiple research studies by the University of Aberdeen Face Research Laboratory[40] showed that people are more attracted to images of people who make eye contact and smile than to those who do not. If you aren't thrilled about the way your teeth look, try a pleasant closed-mouth grin.

First impressions are important, and your LinkedIn profile photo is often the first thing that people will see when they visit your profile. As a result, it's important to make sure that you're dressed appropriately in your photo. Depending on your industry, this could mean anything from a suit and tie to business casual attire.

The important thing is to look professional and presentable. Always consider how you would present yourself to a potential employer. Would you show up for an interview holding a beer? Then don't take a photo of yourself with one. Don't use a logo of your company, a photo of a famous person, or a picture that you found on the Internet. That last one could get your LinkedIn account blocked.

---

[39] https://www.linkedin.com/help/linkedin/topics/6042/6059/profile-photo?lang=en
[40] https://www.abdn.ac.uk/

If you do not like the way you look in the pictures you have, hire a professional photographer. Not only you will get better pictures for your LinkedIn profile photo, but you will also have professional photos that you can use in articles, with blog posts, or as part of your bio at conferences.

> The default photo setting on LinkedIn is *Public*. If you edit your profile photo visibility settings from your profile page, the system automatically updates the settings on your public profile page too. For example, if you change your profile photo visibility setting from *Public* to *Connections Only*, that change will be applied to your public profile as well.[41]

Showing profile photos[42]
Choose to show or hide profile photos of other members.

← Back

Show profile photos
Which LinkedIn members' profile photos would you like to see?

○ No one

○ Your connections

○ Your network

◉ All LinkedIn members

Members with profile photos can receive up to 21 times more profile views than those without profile photos.[43]

Background photo

The background photo—also called a banner or background image—gives you another opportunity to communicate visually. Visual communication is one of the most persuasive ways to impact the visitors to your LinkedIn profile. The right background photo will help your page stand out, engage attention, and be memorable.

Combined with your profile photo, your background picture is the first visual hook on your page. The profile photo and background picture should work in

---

[41] https://www.linkedin.com/help/linkedin/answer/31/settings-for-profile-photo-visibility

[42] https://www.linkedin.com/mypreferences/d/categories/account

[43] https://www.linkedin.com/help/linkedin/answer/a545557/settings-for-profile-photo-visibility

tandem as a joint visual asset. The recruiter, hiring manager, or potential client will measure your professional credibility based on your visual identity. You can use the background picture to add a logo of your company, values of the company, or products you are selling. A visually appealing background photo will go a long way in making a positive first impression.

You can either use a photo created by your company, one you took yourself, or any royalty-free stock photos you can find on the Internet. All uploaded photos must comply with the LinkedIn user agreement so don't use any photo that is under copyright.

You can also create a picture with software, like Photoshop, or even via sites like Canva[44] or Easil.[45] The dimensions of the LinkedIn banner are currently 1584 x 369 pixels, for a maximum size of 8 MB, in a PNG or JPG format. Make sure your photos look good on mobile phones too.

 Social media image sizes seem to change constantly. To find the current sizes of profile and background images, Google "Social Media Image Sizes Year," replacing Year with the actual year.

4. Headline

Your headline is positioned right below your name on your LinkedIn profile. It is the first thing profile visitors read in search results. You can make your headline more than just a job title by adding text that describes what you are doing and your passion.

Although there's no rule that says the description at the top of your profile page has to be just a job title, I would not recommend including quotes, mottoes, or humorous epithets like "Master of the Universe" or "Sales Ninja."

The headline is the first thing that recruiters scan during their search, and the wrong headline could be the reason they don't open your LinkedIn profile to find out more about you. For active job seekers, the title should be relevant to the position they want or currently have. You can extend the title with text like "Open to Work."

Example

Finance Manager (Open to Work)

---

[44] https://www.canva.com/
[45] https://easil.com/

It is okay to say you are looking for work, but keep your job title in the headline and job title fields.

Your headline has a 220 character limit for desktop and 240 for mobile. Since you've been given two choices, make sure you optimize for a maximum of 220 characters.

 Recruiters search for candidates who have a job title similar to their open roles. Since they scan for the job titles on LinkedIn profiles first, if you don't have the title mentioned in your headline, they will skip your profile.

5. About section (formerly summary)

The About section is one of the most important sections of your profile. As soon as a visitor is attracted by your header and title, they will go to the About section to know more about you. The key to this step is to inspire confidence.

You have a 2,000-character limit for the About section. Be sure to add a description of your career, your skills, and your professional brand in your own words. Use this space primarily to give your audience an overview of your professional life. It is a great place to share your achievements and do your own promo.

This About section is also a place to share your story. Try to present your journey, how you started, what helped you get where you are, and what you plan to do to go further. In your little story, be sure to include your main achievements, your rewards, and even your failures, as this gives a more human vibe to your profile.

The LinkedIn About section is neither your resume nor your cover letter. You may want to include in it what you have done before but, above all, mention your added value, the solutions you can bring to the visitor of your profile, and how you will do that. The objective is to highlight your know-how, personality, and expertise, as well as the solutions you can implement and the benefits a company or partner will be able to derive from your collaboration.

One key thing to remember is that only the first two and a half lines are visible by default on the computer and only a few characters on mobile, depending on the size of the screen. To read the full LinkedIn summary, people have to click on "See more." To provoke people to click through to the rest, make sure to be clear and impactful from the hook and arouse interest.

A LinkedIn About section consists of

- Your key career achievements.
- Your expertise.

- The services you offer.
- Contact information.
- Keywords that are relevant to your role or industry.

Even if visitors don't view your full About section to start, by adding the right keywords you can make sure they'll have another chance when they search for those keywords.

Keyword optimization

Specialties: Global Recruiting Expertise • Leadership • Web3 Recruiter • Technical recruiting • Diversity hiring and initiatives • Talent Acquisition • Technology Staffing • HR marketing • Employer Branding • Social Media Recruiting • Executive Search • Sourcing • Recruiting Best Practices • Recruitment strategies and consulting • Recruitment strategy • Boolean search techniques • Training & Development • International recruitment • Strategic Talent Sourcing • Recruitment Reporting

Anyone searching for keywords like "Diversity hiring" or "Executive Search" could stumble upon my LinkedIn profile because I've optimized it.

To optimize, visit the profiles of your industry counterparts, colleagues, or competitors to see how they present themselves. Don't copy what you see but look for the relevant keywords. I recommend you go on LinkedIn and search for your current job title and location to see who else appears at the top. These people are the first people viewed by hiring teams when searching for somebody like you. Use the information on those LinkedIn profiles as an inspiration when you are building or optimizing your LinkedIn About section.

With an optimized About section you will not only maximize your impact but also prioritize your profile in the LinkedIn search engine. Remember that the algorithm works with keywords—certain keywords that relate to both skills and job titles should be included in your summary.

If you want to limit the number of LinkedIn invites that you are getting, turn on the feature that allows only people who know your email address to communicate with you. You'll still get inMails (a paid service by LinkedIn) from other recruiters but not connection requests. To do this, go to your Settings, select the "Communications" tab, and then select "Who can reach you" and the option "Only people who know your email address or appear in your 'Imported Contacts' list."

Contact information

When you are between jobs, you can improve your chance of being contacted by adding your email address or even phone number to your About section. If you do not want to share your private email, create a new one that you can share.

If you have your own domain name, create an email address with it to share in your LinkedIn summary. This will also give you an idea of where recruiters and hiring managers are finding your email address.

In addition to filling in your usual contact details, take advantage of the fields offered by LinkedIn to specify the geographical location by adding location into the Country/Region field. Fill in the fields to increase the relevance of your profile. And do not forget to add links that direct the reader to your blog, website, and other social media platforms that you want to highlight.

6. Featured section

This section allows you to highlight selected posts, articles, links to external websites, images, documents, videos, or presentations.

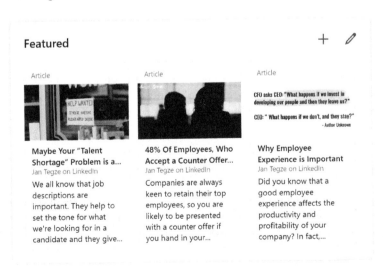

- **Posts.** You can give a second life to your posts by highlighting them in your profile. Try to select posts that are viral, important to you, or that will likely boost engagement.

- **Articles.** You can only showcase articles that you post on LinkedIn. Showcasing these articles will help you to demonstrate your expertise and could help you create a better impression of yourself. To showcase articles not posted on LinkedIn, use the Links section.

- **Links.** You can share websites, external photos, documents, videos, or presentations by selecting the Links option in the Featured section. It will accept PDFs, Word docs, PowerPoint presentations, and jpegs and pngs. You can also add the link to your website, blog, YouTube video, or podcast.

- **Media.** Upload photos, documents, and presentations. This is especially useful for people who want to share parts of their portfolios on LinkedIn.

Enhance your LinkedIn experience with media samples but be aware of the limitations[46]:

- The file size cannot exceed 100 MB.
- The page limit is 300 pages.
- The word count limit is one million words.
- The maximum resolution for images is 36 megapixels.
- The title limit is 100 characters. Each description is limited to 500 characters.

Only the three things most recently added will be visible on your LinkedIn page. LinkedIn constantly changes its system so try to keep up with the latest requirements.

When you add your content to the Featured section you can always change the order in settings. Most people will look only at the items immediately visible on your profile, so I don't recommend adding more than three.

7. Experience

This part of your LinkedIn profile is one of the most important. To create a complete and credible profile, provide a short summary of each of your work experiences. Describe the most impactful job experiences you have had, how they impacted you

---

[46] https://www.linkedin.com/help/linkedin/answer/34327/supported-providers-and-content-types-for-work-samples-on-your-profile

and allowed you to grow, the difference you made and how it helped your employer, the challenges you encountered, and the solutions you proposed. Mention your missions and the highlights of each position, including internships or volunteer experiences.

Your LinkedIn Experience section should both complement and support your resume. This section does not need to be short, so feel free to add as much information as you'd like. However, there are limits to each subsection: 255 characters per title and 2,000 per description.

When you are adding your experience, include title, employment type (full-time, part-time, freelance, contract), company name, location, start date, and end date. Title, company name, and start and end dates are required. When you are adding the company name, try to select the one from the dropdown menu as this will also add the company logo to your profile. When you are adding a new position, turn on notifications so your network will learn about your job and education changes. Updates can take up to two hours.[47]

As a candidate, you can also add a career break to your profile, to account for times when you weren't working, whether it was taken for full-time parenting, bereavement, caregiving, a gap year, layoff, or other life needs or experiences.[48]

Career Breaks allow you to add context and share details about career breaks you've taken outside of regular employment in your work experience. You can select a specific type of career break or leave the career type blank and add details in the description section. Adding a Career Break is optional and will be visible to logged-in LinkedIn members.[49]

Type

| Please select | ▼ |

Location

| Ex: London, United Kingdom | |

☑ I am currently on this career break

I recommend you focus mostly on your most recent work, spending more time and adding more information to the three most recent jobs. Your previous experiences matter too, but recruiters and hiring managers will pay special attention to the last three jobs.

Include relevant keywords and phrases that will attract the attention of your readers and describe your experience.

---

[47] https://www.linkedin.com/help/linkedin/answer/a529062
[48] https://www.linkedin.com/business/talent/blog/product-tips/linkedin-members-spotlight-career-breaks-on-profiles
[49] https://www.linkedin.com/help/linkedin/answer/a597655

Keywords are really important especially in this section, because you want to be found by recruiters and hiring managers. Analyze the job descriptions from companies searching for somebody like you and add the keywords and phrases they use. Companies often use AI sourcing tools to find candidates; they do this by copying and pasting their job descriptions into AI tools. These tools will search LinkedIn and find the candidates whose profiles include relevant keywords.

8. Education, licenses, and certifications

In your Education section, focus on your strengths and specializations. For example, you could highlight your major areas of study and thesis topic. This will help visitors to your profile better understand your journey and will increase your credibility.

Diplomas and certifications are usually among the last things that LinkedIn users add when setting up their profiles. Don't just list your training or diplomas and certifications; instead, add the full name, issuing organization, issue date, and the credential ID and URL if you have them.

When adding the name of your certification, also add the name of the certifying authority and the reference number as a guarantee of reliability.

Example

> **Okay:** The Science of Well-Being

> **Better:** The Science of Well-Being by Yale University

Adding recent certifications to your LinkedIn profile can demonstrate that you are always working on improving your skills.

9. Volunteer experience

Adding volunteer work to your LinkedIn profile is a great way to give potential employers insight into who you are, how you support your community, and what matters to you. Volunteer experience will show recruiters and hiring managers that you care about others and not only about you. There is a 100-character limit per organization.

10. Featured skills and endorsements

LinkedIn allows you to add your skills to your profile. Think carefully about the skills that are most relevant to your profile visitors and those that best represent you. If you are not sure which ones to add, look at the profiles of your colleagues and industry peers for some inspiration.

When you are adding your skills, select three main skills, as LinkedIn shows only three in the preview.

The easiest way to get your skills endorsed is to ask your friends and colleagues. Or you can visit their profiles to endorse their skills, because that is often the trigger for people to return the favor. There is an 80-character limit per skill.

11. Recommendations

The Recommendations on your LinkedIn profile are personal testimonials to illustrate the experience of working with you. They are the proof that your experience and skills are worth looking at, and they will help you attract more potential customers and employers.

In a way, Recommendations are similar to "reviews" on a product or of an establishment. You would rather buy a product that has multiple positive reviews than a product that does not. People believe other people more than they do an advertisement.

Anyone in your LinkedIn relationship network who has met you professionally and has had the experience of working with you is a good candidate to write you a recommendation.

Always focus on quality over quantity. A recommendation from a person who has never worked with you will have zero value. On the other hand, having a recommendation from a colleague who is a senior executive, VP, or even a CEO of the company will increase your credibility tenfold.

Consider recommendations from the following:

- Your past and present colleagues are in the best position to judge your skills and strengths and are more likely to be willing to write you stellar recommendations.
- Your former leaders enjoy an important status, which will be taken into account as a priority by the visitors of your profile.
- Your mentors or teachers (past and present) have been or are at the forefront of your journey. They saw you evolve, contributed to your learning, and were the first witnesses of your progress. Do not hesitate to ask them; they will be proud of your success and your determination.
- As part of your work, you are required to communicate regularly with

people at other companies, and these colleagues, suppliers, and partners are all likely to have a sense of how you work and what your skills and abilities are.

- Your customers can also come in handy when it comes to LinkedIn recommendations. They are your first ambassadors. If they are satisfied with your services, your skills, your communication, or your mastery of a subject, they will be happy to respond favorably to your request for a recommendation.

Only three recommendations are visible in the profile preview. That is why it is important to highlight the best recommendations you receive in those three visible spots. You can choose to hide or unhide a recommendation you've given to, or received from another member on your profile.[50]

Recommendations are limited to 3,000 characters.

 Asking people for recommendations is always tricky. People may not have time to write about you or not know what to write. Consider sharing with them three or five examples of things they might say. They can pick one and customize it, making easier their task of recommending you.

12. Accomplishments

The last section of your LinkedIn profile is the Accomplishment section. This section gives you an opportunity not to only optimize your profile with the right keywords and phrases but also to stand out. It is important to add here all the relevant content that has shaped your journey.

LinkedIn offers you the following options:

- **Volunteer experience:** Adding volunteer experience to your LinkedIn profile is an ideal way to add a little bit of you to your professional profile.

- **Publications:** If you are an author, publisher, or editor, you can share titles of and links to your work.

- **Patents:** If you have filed a patent, enter it in this section. You will need three pieces of information: the name, the assignment office, and the filing number.

---

[50] https://www.linkedin.com/help/linkedin/answer/a542730/hide-and-unhide-your-recommendations?lang=en

- **Project:** If you are working on a project, it may be interesting to talk about it. Professionals may contact you about one of your specific initiatives.

- **Honors and awards:** If you have received an award, please reference it here as this can be immensely helpful in increasing the visibility of your profile.

- **Test scores:** Some tests only make sense if you specify the results. If the result is satisfying and allows you to highlight yourself, take advantage of this section. In the case of final university examinations, for instance, it is customary to specify the subject of your thesis and the training.

- **Languages:** Linguistic skills are extremely useful information for the modern professional world. Again, it is important not to overstate your abilities here. Even if you have studied English for a long time, it is difficult to qualify at the native speaker level. Instead, select the option of "Full Professional Proficiency."

- **Organizations:** You may be a member of an organization relevant to your professional field. Specifying it might get your profile to appear in search results.

- **Causes:** You can add causes you care about.

GENERAL TIPS AND TRICKS

When you are creating or improving your LinkedIn profile, always try to keep all information in it relevant to what you do and remove any trendy buzzwords like "expert," "leadership," "creative," "focused," and "innovative." Not only are they not important, but what makes a resume or LinkedIn profile stand out is tangibility. Not trendy buzzwords.

Use the correct tenses on your profile. For your current job use the present tense, and use the past tense for previous jobs.

Before you click "Save" or "Update," proofread everything. In my own searches I have found tons of people who wrote, "Couch" instead of "Coach" in their job titles. A small typo like that could be the reason a recruiter can't find you, unless they are indeed looking for professional couches. Typos also make you look careless.

During your job search, you should consider investing money into the LinkedIn Premium account[51] as it will give you extra inMails, messages that

---

[51] https://premium.linkedin.com/

you can use to reach out to people without being connected with them. And the best thing is that Premium will allow you to see the names of people who have looked at your profile in the last ninety days. If you know their names, you can check their profile pages and see the career pages of their companies. Maybe you will discover the right position for you.

FINAL THOUGHTS

LinkedIn is a great place to build and stay in touch with your professional network as well as to present yourself to a wider audience. LinkedIn is the place recruiters start searching for candidates, but it is also where recruiters and hiring managers go to learn more about candidates who apply for a role. Often, they are looking for additional information that is not part of the resume.

Recruiters also check other social sites, like Facebook, so it is important to be aware of what they are looking for. Facebook is often one of the first places that recruiters and hiring managers look for information about candidates who do not have LinkedIn profiles. Additionally, team members often use Facebook to learn about their new colleagues. All of this information can help recruiters and hiring managers determine if you are a good fit for their company culture.

Research from Ghent University focused on how publicly available information about job applicants affects employers' hiring decisions. They conducted a field experiment in which fictitious job applications were submitted to real job openings in Belgium. The only difference among these candidates was the unique Facebook profiles attached to their names. Candidates with the most beneficial Facebook picture received approximately 38 percent more interview invitations. The entire study[52] is interesting and I recommend you read it.

When you are optimizing your LinkedIn profile, do not forget to take care of your other social websites too. As you know, one picture is worth a thousand words, and your Facebook profile picture could often constitute recruiters' and hiring managers' first impression of you.

Additionally, new applicant tracking systems can connect your application with all your public profiles on social networking sites, including Facebook, Twitter, and Instagram. This feature allows recruiters to find more information about you with just a single click.

Think about your online presence before applying for a new role, as your online profiles are an extension of your resume and LinkedIn profile. The public data available about you can affect your chances in a positive or negative way.

---

[52] https://journals.sagepub.com/doi/full/10.1177/1461444816687294

HOW TO REACH PEOPLE THROUGH LINKEDIN INVITATIONS

LinkedIn is a great place to meet with industry experts and business partners and stay in contact with your ex-colleagues. It is also a great place for students to start conversations with the CEOs of international companies and a great place to find experts from your field, contact them, exchange interesting information, or follow them to see what new methods they are sharing.

If you have been on LinkedIn for some time, you may have noticed that active LinkedIn users send and receive LinkedIn invitations every week. They are always trying to interact with colleagues, friends, business partners, recruiters, and potential candidates. LinkedIn was created as a professional networking website with one goal in mind: to connect people. Although LinkedIn recommends "only inviting people you know and trust," many of the invitations you will receive will be from total strangers, people you have never met.

Not everyone accepts those types of invitations, so always add a note to any invitation you send.

LINKEDIN TEST

I decided to make a LinkedIn test because I believed that the results would help me to better understand how people were reacting to my LinkedIn invitations.

The first part of that test focused on the invites I sent. I tracked how people reacted to the messages that I sent to them. I sent 200 invites during the test.

The second part focused on the invites I received. During the test, I received 800 invitations, which I analyzed.

First Part

I contacted people in roles and locations that I wanted to add to my network. I do not consider building my network to be a popularity contest, so I always try to be selective.

I started by sending 100 invites without notes: 50 to recruiters and 50 to other people. Here are the initial results:

- 43 of the 50 invites sent to other recruiters were accepted.
- 21 of the 50 invites sent to other professionals were accepted.

Then, I sent 100 invites that contained notes. The first 50 received a templated message, and the other 50 invites got a message that I tailored to each person's LinkedIn profile and experience.

Here are the results:

- 38 of 50 templated invites were accepted.
- 44 of 50 invites I sent with a personal note tailored to the specific person were accepted.

Second Part

Of the 800 invitations I received, I focused on these factors:

- whether they included a note (and, if so, what the content of the note was),
- whether I accepted the invitation when they contacted me with a note or templated message, and
- whether they visited my profile before they sent me an invitation.

I accepted 388 invitations from these 800 people during the test. I also tried to reach out to most of them with a small note.

Why did I approach these people? The answer is simple: They had some reason to connect with me, and I wanted to know what the reason was. What was the trigger for them to send me an invitation? Was it something that I did, posted, or wrote? Or did they just want to know who I was?

In order to give them the opportunity to contact me first, I waited for twenty-four to forty-eight hours after I accepted their invitation. Twenty-seven of them did. Of those, twenty-one with business proposals or job offers, and six just sent thank you notes after I accepted their invites.

And what about the other 361? After forty-eight hours, I contacted them and sent a simple message like this:

> Hi Joe,
>
> Thanks for your LinkedIn invite. I am curious about why you sent me this invite. Is there anything I can do for you, or are you just expanding your network on LinkedIn? :)
>
> Best Regards,
> Jan

In the end, 132 people responded and told me the reason they added me. They gave me interesting feedback, and I was able to understand what I had done to bring my profile to their attention.

The most common reason (67 percent) was *"I am just expanding my network of contacts.*"The remainder had other reasons, including that they wanted to follow my updates or that they had questions (such as about the craft of sourcing).

And what about the other 229 people? A few of them surprised me because I considered them to be top-notch recruiters. But when I contacted them, I received no response.

VISIT THE LINKEDIN PROFILE OF YOUR TARGETS

How many people visited my profile before they sent me an invitation on LinkedIn? Of the 800 people who sent me invitations, only 114 had checked my profile beforehand. That means only 14.25 percent visited my profile before they sent me an invitation. That is a pretty small number.

Many of the LinkedIn invitations come directly from the LinkedIn mobile app. That is why so many lacked a personal note. Even though that option is there, not many people know how to access it. From time to time, LinkedIn also allows users to send invites to hundreds of people with just one click. You will find this in your email address book.

I understand how easy it is to hit the blue button to send an invite on the LinkedIn mobile app, especially given that you do not even have to write a note. However, if you would like to increase the chances of your invite being accepted, be sure to add a note!

And if you would like to follow somebody and get updates, it is better to click "Follow" on their profile instead of adding them.

REASONS FOR REJECTING LINKEDIN INVITES

Adding people to your network is easy. The only thing you must do is click "Accept." But think about the quality of your network. Networking on LinkedIn is not the same as Pokémon—you do not need to catch them all. Target only the people who can bring value to you and your network. You don't want to connect with people who have bad reputations; that could affect your chances of landing your dream job.

Of the 800 invites I received, 773 lacked a personal note. And only 3.38 percent of those sending invites replied with a personal note. I also counted the number of invitations that I accepted and rejected.

	Accepted	Rejected	Total
Invitations with a note.	24	3	27
Invitations without a note.	363	352	715
Invitations from fake profiles.	0	12	12
Invitations from people with "Confidential" instead of a company name.	0	4	4
Invitations from people with logos instead of profile pohotos.	1	13	14
Invitations from people with no career history.	0	28	28

These are a few of the reasons I did not accept a LinkedIn invitation:

- The profile photo was a logo instead of a face.
- The profile was fake or had no information at all.
- The first message was, "Please accept. We have consultants available."
- The invite was from a person who listed his/her current employer as confidential. (This lack of transparency ensures that I won't be accepting your invitation.)
- There was no message at all and the invite came from a person working in a completely different field and location from mine. (There is no need to connect with four construction workers from Uruguay if you are living in Australia and hiring IT people.)
- The person claimed to have a business proposal.

ALWAYS MAKE A CONNECTION

I am always trying to reach people who I can add to my network, and I expect the same from my new contacts. When I added one person to my network in 2015, I got this simple message:

Sales, Marketing and...   •••

Hi there - I love when people use the power of the network to make connections that wouldn't otherwise happen. That said, I do like to know something about the people I connect with. Your profile is interesting. Can you share some info about what you do, and what about my background prompted you to reach out?

Looking forward to hearing from you!

That person and I started a discussion that would not have occurred if she'd just hit "Accept." It was also a great way for us to learn more about each other.

Try to reach out to people after you add them. Just message them with a few words, such as, "I liked your post." A simple message could start an interesting discussion, and it will help you stand out from the LinkedIn crowd. No one is an island, so it is always good to share ideas and discuss points of view.

TURN YOUR VISITORS INTO CONNECTION

If you have a LinkedIn Premium account that gives you the ability to see who visited your profile, and you can turn those visitors into connections. People visit your profile for a reason—because something caught their attention. It could be your reply to someone else's post, a post you shared, an image you posted, or an article you wrote. But what really matters is that they visited your profile.

The way I turn these visitors into new contacts is very simple. I contact them and send them an invitation with a simple text. Here is one variant of that text:

> Hi Joe,
>
> I noticed you recently viewed my LinkedIn profile. I'm curious to know why. What drew your interest? :)
>
> Regards,
> Jan

Because there is a question in that text, people are more likely to respond. As a result, you will add interesting people to your network, but you will also get information about why someone visited your LinkedIn profile.

Of course, always customize the LinkedIn message based on the seniority of your recipient. Sending an emoji in the message to a C-level person might not create a good impression.

HOW TO USE INVITATIONS EFFECTIVELY

It is easy to just hit the "Connect" button and send an invitation. Many people will simply accept it, but more senior people will care more about maintaining the quality of their network than accepting an invitation. The reason they'll reject you is that you didn't add a note to your invitation.

It is good to add something personal between you and that person, and it's better not to use any templates. You can mention that you have some connections in common. Always try to use their name and personalize the message.

> Hi Joe,
>
> I'm looking to expand my professional connections, and it seems we have a number of people in common.
>
> Kind regards,
> Jan

Or

> Hi Joe,
>
> I'm looking to expand my professional connections, and it seems we have a number of people in common. I am very interested in connecting with you, and I would really love to have you as part of my network!
>
> Kind regards,
> Jan

Adding a personal note will always raise the chances that your invitation will be accepted. Here is another example:

> Dear Joe,
>
> I would appreciate having you in my network of contacts on LinkedIn and maybe keeping in touch. :) Please accept my invitation.
>
> Many thanks,
> Jan

If you are sending a template message, try to experiment by creating multiple versions and seeing which works best.

My template is very simple. I always add the name of the person and tell them why they are getting the message. So far, the responses to a note like the one below have been very good.

> Hello Joe,

I am looking to expand my professional network, so I would appreciate it if you could accept my invitation.

Kind regards,
Jan

If I really want to be sure that my invitation will be accepted, I add a more personal note with the specific reason I would like to add the person to my network.

Interact

There is nothing more important than interacting! You got an invitation with a note, accepted it, and then received no interaction from the person for weeks, months, or years. The question is why did you add that person to your network?

I try to contact every single person before I add them to my network.

I add an emoji, so people will not take my message too seriously and so I don't sound like an arrogant person to them. When I send a message without it, people respond more defensively. For instance, they will answer, "It's LinkedIn, and it's about networking. That's why I added you."

Every answer I get could be a hint that something I am doing has had an impact on people.

REACH OUT TO PEOPLE WHO SENT YOU AN INVITATION

You can reach out to people who have sent you an invitation without accepting them. Just click "My Network." Then click "Manage all." What you're looking for is under the "Messaging" icon:

You will see the "Message" link connected with every person. You can just hit that URL and send a message to that person without any need to add them to your network.

Based on my tests, between 50 and 60 percent of people who send invitations never reply, so you don't want to have these people in your network. They could be people who are not going to be active, so don't expect any likes or shares of your posts. Or it could be that their profile is fake, and you certainly don't want to have fake people in your network.

Reaching out to people who sent me an invitation allows me to find out why they sent it. In most cases, they are just expanding their network; but sometimes, my inquiry starts a very interesting conversation.

It's important to reach out to influencers in your network from time to time, especially if these influencers are in the same field.

MAKE A POSITIVE LASTING IMPRESSION

In 2019, I decided to change my approach to a more direct one, beyond just sending a message on LinkedIn. I created a page that was hidden from Google on my website jantegze.com,[53] and in the URL I added the name of the person I was planning to approach. I tested various versions of the messages that I sent to people during the whole of 2019.

When I accept a LinkedIn invitation, I use this message:

> Hi Joe,
>
> Thank you for your LinkedIn invitation! :)
>
> https://jantegze.com/hello/?Name=Joe
>
> Have a great day,
> Jan

Why did I send the message right after I accepted the LinkedIn invitation? I have a few reasons for that. The first reason is to start a discussion with the person who just recently sent me an invitation. That person had a reason to contact me, and I was curious about what I had done to attract them.

My second reason is so I can see if that person is active or not. If people are not replying and there is no activity from their side, I am not going to be sorry if I need to remove them in the future when I need space for others, like when I

---

[53] https://jantegze.com/

hit the 30,000 connections limit on LinkedIn. It is as simple as that, and if they removed me after some time, that message will still be there, so I can always see that I was connected with that person before.

The third reason is to help people get to know me a little bit better via the website that I made for them. It is to let them know that they can approach me via my contact form and to inform them about what I am doing and what I am interested in. It also creates a better first impression than just a simple message.

More than 80 percent of all invitations that I receive during a year are invitations that I do not plan to accept for various reasons. However, the inviters all had a reason to contact me. If you received 1,000 invitations and accepted only 200 of them, there could still be an interesting candidate among those 800 people whom you did not accept. For that specific reason, I decided to contact every single person who sent me an invitation, and I was able to turn some of those connections into candidates.

I created different pages with different messages describing the reason I was not accepting all invitations and also giving people a guide to how they could follow me on LinkedIn or pointing them to a career page so they could easily apply there. I also shared information about myself with people, so that I wasn't just a random stranger.

I tested various messages, and here is one of the examples I sent:

Hi Joe,

First of all, thank you for your LinkedIn invitation. Because you didn't add any message, I don't know what your reason to send me this invitation was. :)

That's why I would like to share with you this page: https://jantegze.com/thankyou/?Name=Joe. Please check it out.

I will wait for your feedback and your reason for sending me this invitation. Or maybe you will share with me how I can help you? :)

Have a great day,
Jan

I also tried to make these templates more interesting by using the first name of the person who approached me. This raised the response rate on my messages. And that specific approach turned some of those people into candidates. In the end, I did not need to add them to my LinkedIn network and I remove them later when I needed space for other connections.

FINAL THOUGHTS

There are many ways to make a good first impression that lasts longer than a few seconds. You don't need to use the same method as the one I am using. You can use my methods as inspiration to help you find your own way to start interacting with your network and people who invite you to connect.

There are many ways to approach new connections. Shannon Whittington[54] has a very interesting approach. I personally love the way she does things because it's more personal. The first message she sent me was a voice message thanking me for accepting her invitation, using my name. The second was a video about her so I could learn more about what she does.

This same video is sent to everyone, but I learned a lot from it about Shannon. The last message was a personal message from her. Again, this was something she created in the moment and that was not sent to everybody.

The reason I love this approach is that it creates a personal connection. I've learned over the years that people, who are willing to invest their time in responding or creating a voice message as a response, are more active on LinkedIn and are willing to share more with you than others. I always prefer to have my network full of people who are willing to speak with me or give me feedback on my work/posts/articles, rather than a network full of people hiding behind their keyboards.

---

54 https://www.linkedin.com/in/shannonwhittington/

GROW YOUR NETWORK

To get the most out of LinkedIn, you should focus on building your network and growing your connections. I recommend aiming for more than 500 connections on LinkedIn. But don't just add anyone and everyone you find. Start by adding the people you know, like your college friends, current and past coworkers, networking contacts, and friends.

The first reason to add people to your LinkedIn profile is to increase the size of your network. A bigger network will make you look more experienced and active on LinkedIn. The second reason is that having more than 500 connections will give you a psychological advantage over other candidates. With 500+ people in your network, you will look like an experienced candidate and somebody who is good at networking.

If your number of connections is only eighty seven people for example, you will look like a person who knows only a few people and is not active in building a wider network. In some industries like in sales, having a bigger network could indicate that you are better at what you do than others.

Networking is also about connecting with the right people, people who not only can help you to expand your network, but may also interact with your posts. Their activity means your posts will be visible also in their networks.

There are many ways to build your network and market yourself. Some people share interesting content, while others share inspiring quotes. My personal recommendation is to start writing articles on LinkedIn or on your blog and share them on your LinkedIn profile too. Those articles will be connected with your LinkedIn profile, and you can also feature them on your profile, so they will be visible to people who visit it.

Although LinkedIn articles don't have a major impact, they are still a great way to reach a wider audience. The articles will be indexed by Google, which will constantly attract new visitors who find the articles through their search. These visitors will be trying to find out who wrote the articles and will visit your profile to learn more about you.

By creating articles, you are allowing people to become familiar with your personal brand. I have found that many candidates reply to my messages because they are already familiar with me and have read my articles. This familiarity increases my chances of getting a response from them. As a candidate, you should also try to engage with recruiters on LinkedIn. You can do this by consuming the content they put out and using it as an opportunity to reach out and start a dialogue. This is especially true if the recruiter is looking for candidates in your industry.

If you are writing interesting and valuable content, you appear to be an expert in your field to potential employers. LinkedIn can also help you reach a larger audience than if you only post your articles on your blog or on medium.com.

My article that I shared on LinkedIn was read by more than 150,000 people. This is significantly more than if I had only posted it on my blog. Writing with knowledge and expertise in your field can also help you land a job faster.

You can attract a larger audience to your LinkedIn profile by writing about a wider range of topics and sharing those articles on other sites like your blog or WordPress. This will help you target different groups of people and get greater visibility for your LinkedIn profile.

If writing is not for you, start sharing links to interesting content from sites such as forbes.com and medium.com. Many newsletters are full of interesting articles that you can share via your social sites, together with questions connected with the topic. This will engage your audience, as well as introduce you to new people and attract new connections, possibly leading you to meet your future boss online.

Remember that posting pictures of math problems or cats is not beneficial to your brand or network. Instead, try to share content that your followers will find interesting.

LinkedIn is an important tool for growing your network of business contacts. However, you should not just add any random person to your network. Instead, try adding people who you believe could benefit from your connections.

Consider the following methods for growing your network.

Be active

This is by far the best way to expand your network. When you are active on LinkedIn and sharing interesting content or posting things that are "controversial," you will get attention. As a result, people will start visiting your profile and they will send you LinkedIn invitations. Most of those invitations will be from people who are not in your target group. But if you are looking to expand your network, this is the best and easiest way.

When you are sharing posts on LinkedIn, try to avoid adding twenty hashtags under your post. More is not always better, especially on LinkedIn. What I found out is the first hashtag in the post matters the most. I try not to add more than three hashtags because the more hashtags I add, the less visibility I get. LinkedIn posts will have a greater impact on visibility if you post quality content several times a week, rather than several times a day.

Comment and like

One thing that works quite well on LinkedIn is to start commenting on the posts of other people. People usually check to see who added a comment or gave them a like. You can combine that with the next suggestion, and this will help you expand your network even more.

When you share a post and somebody adds a comment, you should reply to it. This engagement is important, especially within the first hour. It can be tempting to post and then quickly edit your LinkedIn post multiple times, especially if you're new to the platform and want to get everything just right. However, it's important to remember that each time you edit your post, it loses a bit of visibility.

That's because LinkedIn's algorithm views each edit as a signal that the post is not finished and therefore not ready to be shown to a wider audience. So, if you're unsure about something, it's better to delete your original post and start over than to keep editing it. Of course, this doesn't mean you should never edit your posts; just be aware that each edit comes with a cost in terms of reach.

If you see a like under one of your posts and the person who liked it is someone who you want to have in your network, reach out to them with a similar note, such as "Thank you for liking my post, <Name>." Then add a question into the second part of the message that is connected to the topic. This will increase the likelihood that the person will accept your invitation.

Start sending invitations

You can be proactive and send LinkedIn invitations to the people you would like to have in your network. If you would like to raise the chances that your LinkedIn invitation is going to be accepted, add a personal note. There are also many Chrome extensions that can help you send out these invitations automatically, and you can even add a preselected message for your new connections.

LinkedIn has various limits on how many invitations you can send each day. These limits do change from time to time, but you can always find the number on the LinkedIn page or via Google.

Be authentic

Make sure that your communications stand out from the rest by being unique. As a candidate, you are up against many competitors. Being unique is key, not only because it will make you recognizable to others, but also because it will make you more visible to a larger audience. When you reach out to people, they will recognize your name and be more likely to respond, because you are not just some random person to them—you are the person they know.

I've found that, in many cases, when I reach out to candidates, they respond because they know me or have seen my name somewhere before. This is partly because my surname is unique, but it's also because job candidates check

LinkedIn profiles to see what recruiters are sharing. This can help create a good first impression and convince them to react.

Share your LinkedIn profile URL

If you have more social profiles on Facebook, Twitter, and so on, you can add your LinkedIn profile URL to your bios on those sites to draw visitors to your profile on LinkedIn.

FINAL THOUGHTS

Building your network is not a one-time event that can be completed within a week or two. It is an ongoing process that will take months and years, and it should not be about quantity but always about the quality of people you add. Having the right people in your network can open a lot of doors and bring many new opportunities, but you have to make those connections first.

Before you start building your network or expanding the current one, set the right goals and objectives you want to achieve. When you know what you want to do, design the tactics to reach the goals that you set based on the platform's rules and best practices.

When you start contacting people, try to personalize every message and connection request you send out. This will increase your chance that your invitation will be accepted.

If you want to learn more about how to grow your network faster, visit www. jobsearch.guide[55].

 LinkedIn members can have a maximum of 30,000 first-degree connections.[56]

PERSONAL BRAND AS FREELANCER

As a freelancer, standing out from the crowd can be difficult. With so many of us competing for the same clients and projects, it can be tough to differentiate yourself from the pack. But there are some things you can do to make yourself stand out from the rest.

---

[55] https://jobsearch.guide/
[56] https://www.linkedin.com/help/linkedin/answer/69689/network-size-limit?lang=en

Be an Expert in your Field

One way to stand out from your freelance peers is by being an expert in your field. If you can show potential clients that you know what you're talking about, they'll be more likely to hire you. Showcase your knowledge and skills by writing articles, blog posts, or even books about your area of expertise. You can also give talks or workshops on your topic of expertise. Be active on social sites like LinkedIn or Twitter.

Offer Something Unique

Another way to stand out from the crowd is by offering something unique that other freelancers don't. This could be a particular skill set, a niche service, or even just a different way of working. For example, if you're a writer, you could specialize in writing for a specific industry or target market. Whatever it is that makes you unique, be sure to promote it!

Promote Your Unique Selling Points

Make sure your website and marketing materials highlight what sets you apart from other freelancers. And when you're networking or meeting with potential clients, be sure to mention your unique skills and experience. If you can show potential clients that you're not just another freelancer but someone with something special to offer, you'll be more likely to land the job.

Go the Extra Mile

One way to stand out from your freelance peers is by going the extra mile. This could mean offering additional services, such as rush delivery or 24/7 support. It could also mean doing something above and beyond what's expected, such as creating a custom proposal or sending a thank-you note after a meeting. Whatever it is, make sure your clients know that you're willing to go the extra mile to get the job done right.

Be Responsive

Another way to stand out from your freelance peers is by being responsive. This means returning phone calls and emails promptly, meeting deadlines, and generally being easy to work with. If you can show potential clients that you're reliable and easy to communicate with, they'll be more likely to hire you.

You would be surprised how important this is!

Create a Strong Personal Brand

This means having a professional website and social media presence and using consistent messaging across all of your channels. It also means being clear about what you do and who you do it for. When potential clients can easily see what you're all about, they'll be more likely to hire you.

Having a great online presence, like a modern website, could help you attract more customers and convince those that were not sure if they should hire you. Investing in good website design could make a difference.

Network and Build Relationships

Another way to make yourself stand out is by networking and building relationships. This means getting involved in your industry, attending events, and connecting with other professionals. It also means being active on social media and participating in online discussions. By building relationships with potential clients and referral sources, you'll be more likely to land work.

Keep up with Trends

Keeping up with trends is important, no matter what business you are in. This means staying up-to-date on industry news, new technology, and changes in the marketplace. By being aware of what's going on in your field, you'll be able to offer clients the most up-to-date services possible.

Keep Your Word

A final way to stand out from your freelance peers is by keeping your word. This means doing what you say you're going to do, when you say you're going to do it. If you make a promise, make sure you keep it. Your clients will appreciate your reliability, and they'll be more likely to use your services again in the future.

FINAL THOUGHTS

There you have it! These are just a few ways to make yourself stand out from other freelancers. If you want to be successful in this competitive industry, you need to showcase your skills, build relationships, and keep up with trends. By doing these things, you can show potential clients that you're the best person for the job. But don't stop there! Continually look for ways to improve your services and grow your business. The more you can offer clients, the more likely they are to hire you. Get out there and start making yourself stand out from the rest!

11. Let People Know You're Open to Work

There are several ways to let your network and recruiters know that you are exploring new opportunities. The only thing you need to decide is if you want to let everyone know or if you would prefer a more discreet way.

Following are several tips on how to share publicly or discreetly that you are open to work. Bear in mind that every approach mentioned could bring different results for you. You may want to combine various methods to find the one that will work for you.

ANNOUNCING YOUR AVAILABILITY ON LINKEDIN

LinkedIn is continuously evolving and adding new functions and removing old ones every year. They also often move settings around their platform, so some of the things mentioned here might be working differently or be in different places when you read this book.

On your LinkedIn profile, locate the "Open to" button. This will give you three options. The one you are looking for is "Finding a new job."

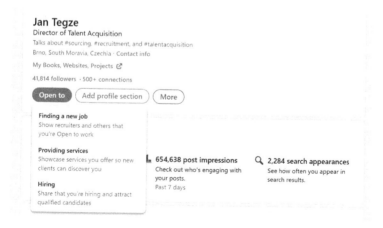

Next you will have to choose how to let people know that you are open to opportunity. Those options are "All LinkedIn members" and "Recruiters only." Both come with several advantages and disadvantages.

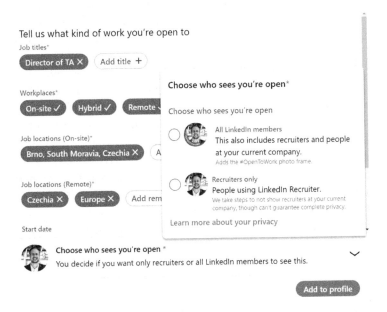

The First Option (All LinkedIn Members)

By selecting this option, you will publicly announce that you are looking for a new opportunity to the whole of LinkedIn. This also includes recruiters and people at your current company and adds the #OpenToWork photo frame to your profile photo.

The benefit of this frame is that it's visible to everyone, so every time you interact with a person, add a comment, give a like to someone's post, or share something on your LinkedIn profile, people can see that you are actively searching for a new opportunity.

According to LinkedIn,[57] the #OpenToWork profile frame increases your chances of receiving inMails from recruiters by 40 percent. One of the results, according to LinkedIn, is that people are 20 percent more likely to receive messages from their community.

I was not able to find more information about the seniority or industry of those people, so we do not know if there are industries or locations in which

---

[57] https://blog.linkedin.com/2020/october/29/the-benefits-of-sharing-with-your-community-you-re-open-to-work

adding this frame to the profile picture will work more or less. But as you can see, this frame raises the chance of being contacted by recruiters.

However, this photo frame could bring some disadvantages too. One of them is the perception that candidates who are open on market are not as good as people who are passive candidates. Passive candidates are hard to get, and this creates the illusion that their value is greater than that of a person who is actively searching.

This bias is an example of a scarcity effect, the cognitive bias that makes people place a higher value on a thing that is scarce and a lower value on one that is available in abundance. This is not necessarily the case for every recruiter and hiring manager out there, but during my career I saw several instances of this effect and heard many stories from my industry colleagues about how the hiring managers preferred candidates who were not actively looking for a job.

My recommendation to job seekers is to add the frame when they are searching for a job as the advantages are way higher than the disadvantages. You can always turn it off at any time. If an employer is less interested in hiring you because you're available, then you probably do not want to work for them.

The Second Option (Recruiters Only)

This option shows users of the LinkedIn Recruiter Account[58] that you are open to a new opportunity. When you want to explore the job market and see what opportunities are available, this is the right option to have active on your LinkedIn profile. When you activate this option, LinkedIn will *not* show recruiters at your current company or related companies that you are open to work. Only recruiters using LinkedIn Recruiter licenses will see. This information is also only accessible via the dashboard and is not publicly available on recruiters' profiles.

Please note: Recruiters outside your company could share with a recruitment team in your company information about who in your company is searching for a job. Recruiters will often exchange this info.

OTHER WAYS TO SIGNAL YOUR INTEREST

There are many other ways to signal that you are open to a new job opportunity. You can create job alerts for new jobs posted by a company through their LinkedIn Page. If you do, you can also signal their recruiters that you are interested.

You can find the option under your profile under Settings and Privacy. Click

---

[58] https://business.linkedin.com/talent-solutions/recruiter

the Data Privacy tab and under "Job Seeking Preference" you will see "Signal your interest to recruiters at companies you've created job alerts for."

← Back

Share job alerts
Use your job alerts to signal interest to recruiters working at those companies?

Signal interest to recruiters   No ⬤

Manage job alerts

Opting into this setting sends a signal to recruiters who may want to contact a member, whenever a member creates a job alert for a company the recruiters work for. Opting into this option doesn't guarantee complete privacy. Learn more

LinkedIn Headline

Another option is to change your headline on LinkedIn and add that you are open to work. I do not recommend this option because when recruiters go through the results of your search, they will only see your name and text you added but not the title of your current or former position. By not using your job title, you are decreasing the chance that recruiters will visit your profile to learn more about you. From my experience, many recruiters first read the current job titles to find people working in the same roles that they are trying to fill.

Jan Tegze · You in
Open to Work
Brno

In your headline, start with Open to Work but add your last job title at the end, that will help you get noticed by recruiters.

Jan Tegze · You in
Open to Work - Director of Talent Acquisition
Brno

LinkedIn Post

If you are transparent that you are searching for a new opportunity, you can try to share it via LinkedIn post. LinkedIn posts are a highly effective way to get in front of a wider audience.

To improve your chance of getting your post noticed, you can share that you are looking for a new opportunity and ask people at the end of the post to like or to comment to expand the reach of your post.

You can even create an image (via Canva[59] and other tools) with your photo, your current role, your location, and the fact that you are actively searching for a job. I did that with several of my clients and the effect was really good as they got noticed quite fast.

The most important thing to remember when creating a social media profile is that people are attracted to faces. A profile photo or even a banner with a face on it is more effective than just a banner. People are also attracted to images that are visually interesting, so don't be afraid to add some color or patterns to your banner. Remember, your goal is to attract people to your profile, so make sure it's something that will catch their eye.

---

[59] https://www.canva.com/

Recruitment and Headhunting Agencies

Recruiters or headhunters are the best sources of information about actual trends in their markets and they are the right people to contact if you want to discuss your job search privately. Many candidates have found their job opportunities this way after an informal discussion with an agency recruiter or headhunter.

Even if an agency has no open role for you at the time of your discussion, they will speak with their clients and they could mention that there is an interesting candidate open to change. Or they could reach out to the recruitment team or hiring managers at the company to explore if they are interested in somebody with your skill set.

One of the things that could also play in your favor is the scarcity effect.[60] If the headhunter mentions that one candidate (you) is exploring the market and available for a discussion, this could create the impression that the availability of someone like you is rare. The hiring manager might perceive you as more valuable and feel the need to act quickly to get you. This perception could also positively influence the offer you get.

Social Media

Another option is to share on other social media platforms like Twitter or Facebook that you are open to work. You can share a simple post stating that you are currently looking for a new opportunity. Add a link from the post to your LinkedIn profile.

Social media is not the right place to announce your availability if you are trying to be discreet about your job search. Even if you share it solely on your private Facebook page, you never know who will re-share it.

FINAL THOUGHTS

The more transparent you are about your job search, the higher your chance of finding your next opportunity. You only need to decide if you want to go the discreet route, mapping out your market, trying to understand what your value is and if there is a suitable position for you or choose the more transparent approach and let everyone around you and in your network know that you are searching for your next role.

When job hunting, always start discreetly if you don't need to find a new

---

[60] https://en.wikipedia.org/wiki/Scarcity_(social_psychology)

job quickly. You can use the scarcity effect during a job interview and your job search to your advantage. If a company believes that you are unavailable on the market and are a passive candidate, they will try harder to get you.

Thanks to that effect, their offer might be higher than the offer they make to those people who are actively looking for a job opportunity. Of course, if you are between jobs searching for the next opportunity, it's best to let your network know about your availability so you can find your new job as soon as possible.

12. How a Personal Brand Can Help Your Job Hunt

Your personal brand is what differentiates you from other candidates and can be summarized by your experiences, strengths, skills, and passions. However, it is also how you are viewed and recognized by others. In other words, your personal brand is your reputation. Having a good reputation is important for any business, and it can also lead to job opportunities that are not advertised.

If you are working as a freelancer or working to find your dream job, building a personal brand has never been more important than it is today. Whether we like it or not, we often judge books by their covers and people by what we see and hear. That is why having a strong personal brand is so important today.

WHAT EXACTLY IS A PERSONAL BRAND?

Your reputation is based on the opinion of others about you and your work. Personal branding is the way you present yourself to others in a way that makes you stand out. It's important to build a recognizable personal brand because it can help you achieve professional success. How you present yourself in the business world is a reflection of your journey so far and your vision for the future. The question is, what should your personal brand stand for?

You may be wondering why it is important to have a personal brand. Many employers do not interview candidates who do not have any information about them online. This means that if you want to increase your chances of getting an interview, you need to work on your personal brand. Just make sure the information is positive and there is nothing provocative or negative about you online.

Even if you don't think you have a personal brand, you do. Everyone has a unique personal brand, whether you like it or not. If you're not actively promoting your personal brand, you're at a disadvantage.

You don't need to be an expert to create a personal brand. You just need a social media profile that accurately represents your professional skills, qualities, experience, and accomplishments. If you want, you can also create a website, but the main idea is to provide high-quality content that employers will appreciate.

Having a strong personal brand can be appealing as it can help you get your name in front of the right people. As you become more recognizable, you will gain advantages in the job search market. A strong brand can attract recruiters and hiring managers, as they will expect that you will not only be doing your job, but also attracting more people to their company.

This is because people tend to trust someone they know or have met more. If you share your personal point of view on subjects, then others' respect for you and their perception that you know what you are talking about increases, as does your personal brand.

To build a successful personal brand, you need to identify your unique qualities, develop them, and learn how to market them effectively. It's just a matter of improving your profile and showcasing your talents to a wider audience. If you're more comfortable creating videos than writing articles, focus on that. Turn your strength into your unique selling proposition.

Your personal brand is the image that employers connect with. It is conveyed through your resume, LinkedIn profile, Twitter account, and public profile. Many people think that personal branding is only for celebrities, such as Kim Kardashian, Katy Perry, Lady Gaga, Cristiano Ronaldo, Jamie Oliver, and Brad Pitt. However, we each have our own personal brands, and we can use the same tactics that famous people use to make ourselves known.

Personal branding has become a requirement for anyone who would like to get noticed by others, get a better job, or take their career to the next level. The fact is that people with a strong personal brand get better offers and more opportunities.

THE REACH OF YOUR PERSONAL BRAND

In today's digital age, it's more important than ever to be aware of the way you present yourself online. Anyone can Google you or find information about you on LinkedIn, Facebook, Instagram, or Twitter. The searchers could be your friends, your colleagues, or a potential date.

Many interviewers do the same. They will Google you, regardless of your position. What they find can have major implications for your professional and your personal well-being, as well as for your potential career opportunities.

If you are a candidate, potential employers may check your social media profiles like Twitter and Facebook to see what things you share. Are they going to find something that sets you apart from the crowd? If so, is it in a good or bad way? To find out, Google yourself. I strongly recommend you do it from time to time. I do it every quarter to see where my name was mentioned.

I Google myself because I want to know when my articles are posted and what comments people are adding to my posts. Feedback is important because it affects how people see you and it helps you develop your ideas further. I also set up a few alerts on my name via applications like Google Alerts.

Your online reputation matters! People form an opinion from it about you before they ever meet you. Your digital identity might literally determine whether you get hired (or even considered) for a new job opportunity.

The more influence and visibility you get through your actions and work, the more people will be Googling your name. Through Google, they will be able to find all your social media accounts, even those that you have not used for a few years or have perhaps even forgotten about. Recruiters, headhunters, and employers often make assumptions about your personality based on what you put on social media. Yes, this may be entirely unfair because the impressions are taken out of context. But people see it, form an opinion, and there you are.

And, of course, turnabout is fair play. You will also get your first impression from the online profiles and activities of your interviewers.

That is why I recommend doing a brand audit and blocking social media accounts during your job search to lower the chance that something negative could be found.

YOUR BRAND ON LINKEDIN

LinkedIn is an essential tool for your career and your brand. It is your personal online resume, but it could also be used as a portfolio of your work (including graphics, presentations, videos, and articles). It can encourage people to find out more about you and your work.

Keep your profile relevant and up-to-date. There is no need to list every volunteer experience you have ever had or post information about how you won a hot-dog-eating contest ten years ago. Customizing your profile picture and headline and choosing a custom URL can help you be more noticeable on LinkedIn. But do not forget to keep your profile updated and active. By active, I mean creating content for your audience or sharing interesting content on a regular basis. You will build your audience this way, and your visibility is going to grow.

Make sure you write and add content that is easy to understand and that contains keywords related to your career ambitions. Look at your LinkedIn profile as an invitation for a conversation and not as a full description of who you are.

Make sure you take into account the time span that others have to learn about your personal brand. Say enough to be interesting but don't take up too much of your readers' time.

What can add value to your readers' work right now? What can you help them solve? What do you bring to the table that is unique? As soon as you see what you want to bring across with your personal brand, give yourself a mental high five! And, remember, having a stellar portfolio is useless if no one ever sees it.

YOUR BRAND ON YOUR PERSONAL BLOG

If you are not actively sharing articles on LinkedIn, Medium.com, or similar websites, then having your own blog is a great way to build brand awareness online. It is not just another source that will appear in a Google search at a higher place when people Google your name. It's also a way to attract new visitors through SEO (Search Engine Optimization)[61]. Also, on your blog, you can share more than just articles with the world.

If you choose to establish a blog, whether video or text based, use it to share insights about your industry as well as interesting tips and content. Your blog will be a great way to increase awareness about you, and your articles, posts, or videos shared by others can help introduce you to a wider audience. Every month, more than sixty thousand people read my old articles on the Internet. So even though I am not publishing anything new, I am still getting the attention of others via the work I already did. That is why it's good to have your own personal blog and share your content on various platforms.

The more content you create, the more online attention you will get. When you share information about your industry, your content is going to be indexed by search engines, allowing others easily to find it. Sharing your thoughts and insights could turn you into an influencer.

Generating content is crucial for success. Being a facilitator and being able to organize and explain information from different sources is also a talent. In fact, it is a very admirable one.

Regardless of how you generate or share your content, your personal brand is directly linked to the way you tell your story and the passion behind it.

YOUR BRAND ON TWITTER

Since it is more informal than LinkedIn, Twitter gives you a little bit more freedom to present your thoughts without damaging your brand. You still need to be aware of what posts you are sharing there, but when you share a photo of your dog, others will not send you messages saying that this content is not good for Twitter, like many people do on LinkedIn.

---

[61] https://en.wikipedia.org/wiki/Search_engine_optimization

Even if your Twitter account is personal, you should try to keep it as professional as possible, because no recruiter or potential employer likes reading hateful Tweets. Keep in mind that every Tweet can still be found, even one you posted five years ago. If you Tweet, "I hate ACME because the company is terrible," do you think ACME is going to hire you? I've seen job candidates say terrible things about companies on Twitter while expressing surprise that those companies were not willing to hire them.

One thing that I recommend is to remove your older Tweets. There are many tools on the Internet that can automatically remove posts that are older than a given number of days, weeks, months, or years. This is a great way to remove posts that could harm you in the future.

If you are new on Twitter and you would like to know how to promote your brand to new people, potential candidates, and employers, try to start following thought leaders and influencers first. You can learn from them how they are using Twitter to promote their personal brand or company brand.

If you are planning to be active on Twitter, try to share something a few times per week. Many people say that you should share a few times per day or use tools like Hootsuite or Buffer for posting curated content automatically. But what I learned, thanks to running various Twitter accounts, is that the frequency depends on your audience. I got more engagement from people when I started posting my own stuff and my own Tweets instead of using tools for posting numerous times a day.

YOUR BRAND ON FACEBOOK

Facebook is a place where we share updates from our lives, photos from holidays, and our thoughts, but it is also the number-one place where people go to check on other people. This is not only because there are more than 2.85 billion active users on Facebook—which is more than any other social website—but also because many people are not on LinkedIn. When somebody wants to find more information about you, they will usually go to Facebook first.

Even though Facebook is a site that we consider a private network, in a few countries it is seen as a LinkedIn replacement, so recruiters often send Facebook invitations to candidates to connect with them. If you are accepting invites from people you do not know or whom you barely know, you are also giving them an invitation to see part of your private life. This could give them access to posts that you shared ten years ago.

If you are planning to add people you don't know or use Facebook as a LinkedIn alternative, I recommend the same thing that I recommend for Twitter: Remove your old posts, photos, or anything that could hurt your brand. Things that you might consider normal could be seen as offensive in other countries.

Also remember that when you add colleagues from work to your Facebook friends, you are sharing your thoughts with them. They can easily share these posts with others in their networks, making posts visible to people you do not even know. These people could develop opinions about you without ever having met you.

Every post you send, every status update you make, and every picture you share contributes to your personal brand. Many tools on the Internet could help people find information about you, even if you're using the maximum privacy settings. You never know if some of your friends or an acquaintance you just added will share your information somewhere else on the Internet.

Ask yourself, "What would someone find on my Facebook page if they went digging through my profile?"

BUILD YOUR BRAND

Building a personal brand is one of the most important things you can do to be more successful in your professional endeavors. You can use your personal brand to create a positive reputation and attract new opportunities. You can also use your personal brand to sell products and services, build relationships, and influence decisions. The key is to create a strong identity that reflects your values and who you are as a person.

What differentiates you? What do you want people to associate with you when they think of your name? What do they see when they Google you or search for you on social sites? How are you unique? What made you successful in the past? What lessons learned have helped you adjust your approach?

Identify What Makes You Different

Identify what makes you unique. What are your special skills and talents? Everybody has some special knowledge.

Pay attention to your everyday life and activities. What do you enjoy doing? Of those activities, what is the part that brings you the most joy? Whatever your mojo is, just make sure that you bring it forward and that you build your brand on top of that. This will allow you to enjoy your work, and this joy will shine through to your brand.

Maybe start with something small, like a simple conversation with yourself about it. Just make sure you are honest with yourself about who you are and where you want to go. Start building your brand in your city and then expand it. Find topics that are close to you and define your most ideal niche.

Be Confident

Do you have confidence in your abilities and knowledge in your field? If so, it will show. The key is not to confuse confidence with arrogance. There is always something to be learned, and there is always something to be gained.

Confidence is knowing who you are and what you have to offer. Arrogance is assuming you have nothing to learn.

Share Your Accomplishments

Share your accomplishments in an accurate way. Don't make blanket statements, such as "I am the best XYZ in the whole city." Instead, share some success stories. Tell what you have done. Share something that makes you stand out, something that is unique. People on LinkedIn love to read about the accomplishments of others if they are personal and don't sound like a PR article.

Don't forget that your personal brand is communicated every time you interact with another individual (online or offline). As you continue to develop your personal brand, stay consistent with your efforts. Keep in mind that your personal brand is your reputation and that people will seek you out for your knowledge and expertise.

YOUR BRAND DURING YOUR JOB HUNT

A good personal brand is a key to the door to any company. If your brand is strong enough it will help you get an interview or be among the first people contacted.

In order to make the most of your resume, be concise and clear. Managers do not have a lot of time to read through lengthy resumes, but they may look for information online if something catches their eye. It can be difficult to tell your entire professional story in a CV that is mostly composed of bullet points and short sentences. Therefore, use the resume to highlight the most important details, while creating a personal brand that can fill in the blanks.

If your resume is interesting and clear enough, the employer will look you up, without a doubt. And this is when a personal brand can be useful and appreciated. Employers will want to find out more about a candidate if his or her resume passes the first evaluation. Use it to tell your story, helping an employer better understand your background, experiences, expertise, and even interests. They will contact you if you are a good fit for the available role and company culture.

The best part about having a personal brand is that it shows what a resume cannot. It shows what makes you unique, setting you apart from the rest. When you use the standard format of a resume to apply for a job, there's no room for particularities. The main purpose of a resume is to reveal your best qualities, abilities, and skills. Thus, a personal brand will provide everything else that is missing from a resume.

If you're seriously considering creating a personal brand, which you should, here is what you need to focus on. Write down the things that make you special and see how you can convey these details in your personal brand. Find those skills that set you apart, those experiences and abilities that make you unique. This is the material that employers will remember.

FINAL THOUGHTS

Quality work requires time and lots of effort; it requires hours and hours of work invisible to others. But achieving fame on the Internet is easier. Anyone with access to the Internet and social media can build an audience, position themselves as an expert or guru, and start attracting clients for their training, workshops, or business.

As my father always said, "Quality will appear over time." I have seen many people who became "overnight stars" perish within a week. I understand that for many people, the dopamine kick caused by likes means the world, but if you're planning to build your brand, don't build it on the basis of "overnight" success, because this shortcut does not exist.

Even if you start building your brand during your job search, it could take months and sometimes even more than a year to see the results. But you should not stop working on your brand even if you find a new job. One day you will be looking for a new one, and a strong personal brand will help you find new opportunities way faster than before.

Bear in mind that having a strong personal brand brings positive benefits throughout your whole career, not just during your job search. If you have a strong personal brand, this will benefit your current work in the form of new deals by attracting new clients and will increase your visibility inside the company, which will lead to promotions. A strong personal brand can help you attract top-tier employers, make more money, and be more successful in your professional endeavors.

13. Job Application Tips

The process of applying for jobs can be both stressful and exciting, but it is always intense. It is important that you take the whole application process seriously and learn right away what things to avoid and what to do to increase your chance of getting a new job. Filling out the application form is often the first step you have to do to get your resume in front of a recruiter and hiring manager.

These days, you'll primarily be applying for jobs online through a company's career site, LinkedIn job postings, or job boards. When you apply for a job through a career site, in most cases you will be redirected to a registration form that is part of the Applicant Tracking System (ATS) that the company is using to track applications and job postings. Even when you are looking for a job on LinkedIn or through a job board, there is a high chance that you will be redirected to a registration form.

The majority of companies use a simple registration form on which they ask you for your full name, email, phone, and resume. They will also ask a few questions connected with your work permit, and, if the company is following OFCCP (Office of Federal Contract Compliance Programs)[62] procedures, you will need to answer several EEO (Equal Employment Opportunity) questions.[63] You will also be asked to agree with their terms and conditions before you share your resume and personal data with them.

It could take you a few seconds to fill out a job application, but it could also take several minutes if there are a lot of questions or if you have to copy and paste your resume. When you are filling out the registration, take your time and make sure you answer all the questions accurately. The registration process is not time-limited, so there's no need to rush. If you try to fill out the registration as quickly as possible, you might make mistakes.

What follows are some tips that you should keep in mind when applying for

---

[62] The Office of Federal Contract Compliance Programs (OFCCP) is part of the U.S. Department of Labor.

[63] https://attorneyatlawmagazine.com/what-are-eeo-questions-why-do-we-have-them

a job, with the goal of increasing your chances of landing an interview for the position.

DECIDE WHETHER TO APPLY

When I started writing this book, I gathered data about job search from various sources including surveys, tests, and interviews with recruiters and candidates. I was trying to understand how candidates apply and how recruiters prescreen and select candidates for an interview.

In one of the surveys, I asked candidates how many requirements they need to meet to apply for a role, and I asked recruiters what percentage of job requirements candidates need to match in order not to be rejected. The majority of recruiters told me that they will reject candidates if they do not match at least 60 to 70 percent of job requirements. The second biggest group of recruiters told me that they reject candidates if they do not match at least 70 to 80 percent of job requirements.

If you don't meet all the requirements in a job description, don't worry—many recruiters will still consider your application. If you meet around 80 percent of the requirements, you should consider applying. If you don't match at least 60 percent, it is not worth your time to apply as there is a high chance that your application will not be considered.

Candidates often hear from recruitment experts that they should apply for any role, regardless if they are a match or not. Keep in mind that when you do this, you will be competing against other applicants who *are* qualified for the job. I believe you shouldn't apply for every open role that you see online, even if you are qualified for it. For example, if you are an accountant, you should not apply to a finance manager or senior finance director role if you don't have the relevant experience.

However, if you believe you are a good fit for the job and the job is something you are interested in, remember that many job postings are just a wish list of things that the company wants in a candidate. Even if you don't have *all* of the requirements, if you can show that you have transferable skills and are a good fit for the company's culture, you may still get the job.

When looking at a job description, always pay attention to the first three bullet points of the requirements. Those are the skills that are most important to the hiring manager, and you should have those skills if you want to be considered for the role. Keep in mind that this tip is based on my personal experience and not research.

FOLLOW THE INSTRUCTIONS

When you are applying for a job, always read the instructions and all questions that are asked. Answer all questions accurately and proofread your answers. Companies use questionnaires to assess and evaluate their candidates during this phase.

Registration is not time-limited, so spend more time reading these questions carefully. If you don't know the answer or you don't understand the question, ask a trusted friend for their feedback on the question; don't contact the recruiter to ask them about it.

Some application processes are not user friendly at all and they require candidates to fill in the application the data from their resumes right after candidates uploaded their resumes. This is time-consuming and frustrating as you already provided all the information in your resume. Nevertheless, despite the annoyance of the task, don't skip the step and simply write, "Refer to resume." This alone could be a reason your application is rejected. It signals a desire to take the easy approach and not follow the rules.

 Some job questionnaires are designed to filter out candidates. When you are applying for a position, if you skip questions or answer no, your application could be moved to the ATS reject folder. For example, if you are asked whether you have a permit to work in the United States, and you don't answer, the recruiter will assume you don't have a work permit and will reject you.

USE A PROFESSIONAL EMAIL ADDRESS

Always use a professional email address when you are filling out the registration. The email should be the same email you have in your resume. If you're using two email addresses, make sure you have access to both. Some candidates use their current company email address when registering, but when they change jobs they lose access to that email address.

If you get an error message that your email is already in the system, assume you already created an account with that email address. If you do not remember your password, you can reset it through the "Forgot your password" link on the ATS.

After submitting the registration, you should receive a confirmation message that your application was received by the company. This confirms that your resume was uploaded to their ATS successfully.

Never ever use your current company email address when you are applying somewhere else. Not only it is unprofessional, but it also guarantees you won't receive further opportunities from the company to which you are applying once you leave your current job.

ATTACH THE CORRECT COVER LETTER

Some companies still require cover letters from candidates when they apply, to see if they are motivated enough to spend their time creating a cover letter in which they express why they want the job. Other companies ask candidates to describe in their cover letters several of their achievements during their careers, and some companies even ask candidates to share major obstacles and how they overcame them.

Cover letters should always be tailored to the specific company. Include the right company name! Nothing will ruin a first impression more than a cover letter that starts with the phrase "I want to work for your company" and then lists the wrong name. This happens often. This is why it is important to double-check all the information in your cover letter before you hit the send button.

Sometimes companies do not give you a way to attach separate cover letters or upload additional files to your application. In these cases, if you want to include a cover letter, attach it to your resume and submit both as one file.

MAKE THE FINISHING TOUCHES BEFORE UPLOADING YOUR RESUME

You're creating a unique cover letter for each employer. You should consider doing the same with your resume, especially if you are applying for positions that are different. When you are applying for a new role, always read over the job application and pay extra attention to two parts: responsibilities and requirements.

These two parts will give you an idea of what kind of person the company is trying to find. Review the description and find words related to traits, skills, or experiences that the company is looking for.

Many employers use applicant tracking systems that compare candidates' resumes against their job descriptions. Relevant candidates are assigned similarity scores based on how well their skills and experience match the job requirements. By using the right keywords and phrases in your resume, you slightly improve your chance that your resume will be reviewed. But be careful: Do *not* copy and paste the whole job description to your resume.

If you want to make sure that your resume catches the attention of the person reviewing it, you can boldface some of those keywords and phrases that are relevant. However, it is important to make sure that your *skills and experience* are highlighted most prominently, as they are most relevant to the job you are applying for.

UPLOAD YOUR RESUME

Before you upload your resume via the registration form or send it via email, always check the name of the file you are sending. Bear in mind that, when your resume is shared with others, the name of the file could help people find it easily and know who it belongs to. You don't want to make it hard for people to find you.

For this reason, include your first and last name and the keyword *resume* in the file name.

Example of good file names:

- resume_jan_tegze.pdf
- resume_jantegze.pdf
- resume_jan-tegze.pdf
- jantegze_resume.pdf

Examples of bad file names:

- MyResume.pdf
- tegze_11-14-2022.pdf
- tegze-resume-v6.pdf

To make your resume look more professional, try to avoid adding dates, using generic names, or mentioning what version of your resume you are sharing with them. Dates could create an impression that your resume is old, and mentioning a version number could create the impression that you've been looking for a job for a while.

DO NOT APPLY VIA SOCIAL MEDIA ACCOUNT

When you are applying for a job, always submit your application through the company's career site or the link provided on their Applicant Tracking System. Sharing your resume on social media sites like Twitter and Facebook is not considered professional, and your application may be lost in the process. Additionally, sharing your resume in this way is not secure.

Do not randomly send your resume to a company email address like sales@ or support@. Doing so will show that you did not expend any effort in checking their career site or finding the right person responsible for recruitment. It will also send the message that you're not responding to a particular job posting but instead just randomly sending in your resume. In all likelihood, your resume sent this way will end up in a spam folder.

When you are applying for the role and you have an option to apply via email, LinkedIn, Facebook, or Twitter, always use the option to create an account via email.

If you decide to close your social media account or if your account is hacked, you will also lose access to the ATS of the company where you have applied for a job. Additionally, by using social media sites to apply, you are giving a recruiter a reason to visit them and they may find reasons there not to hire you.

DON'T MENTION SALARY WHEN APPLYING

Avoid specifying salary requirements in your registration or in your resume. If an employer asks for your salary expectation during registration, there are several things you can do:

- Rather than giving a specific number, mention a range. Never give the minimum you will accept.
- Simply respond, "negotiable" or "I am open to negotiating salary depending on benefits, bonuses, equity, and overall compensation package."

You can share more about your salary expectations during the first prescreening or during the interview when you learn about the role.

Disclosing your salary during the registration could filter you out if it is too low or too high. As you do not know a lot about the job scope and complete compensation package, there is no need to share your salary expectations before you speak with a recruiter or hiring manager.

REVIEW YOUR APPLICATION BEFORE SUBMITTING

Typos and grammar errors can show an employer that you are not paying enough attention. Grammar issues and typos will lessen your chances of being hired. Filling out an application is not time-limited, so take the time you need.

Proofread all your answers to questions that companies ask in their registration forms. Your answers will be reviewed by a recruiter or hiring manager; before *they* review your work, make sure *you* do. In addition, some companies use matching algorithms to analyze your answers, and any typo can lower your score since those systems won't recognize it.

If you forget to upload your resume, you can likely add it through your ATS dashboard after submitting the application. Do not try to apply another time using a different email address. In general, once you have submitted, you cannot make changes. So take care to get it right the first time.

Many Applicant Tracking Systems track your history of changes and uploads, so recruiters may be able to see different versions you have uploaded.

FINAL THOUGHTS

Following these tips can help you complete any job applications more effectively and avoid problems during registration.

When you are asked to create a registration to an ATS, always use a unique password. Ideally, use a password manager (like 1Password, LastPass, or Bitwarden) to help you track all your registrations and passwords.

Looking for job openings that are not advertised on the major job boards? Add the following search string into Google to find the job you are looking for (replace the job title and location with your own):

("Finance Manager") "New York" (inurl:icims OR inurl:greenhouse OR inurl:taleo OR inurl:bullhorn OR inurl:jobvite OR inurl:SmartRecruiters OR inurl:BambooHR OR inurl:Workable) NOT (CV OR Resume)

This search string will help you find all the job postings with the keywords **Finance Manager** and **New York** that are hosted on the websites of the top Applicant Tracking Systems that companies are using.

This tip can increase your chances of finding a job.

14. How to Spot Scam Job Advertisements

The number of job scams exploded as online and remote jobs became more popular. Many job scams are posted anonymously or by fake companies. Be careful when looking for jobs online and learn how to identify the red flags. The worst thing that can happen through such scams is that you lose money or your personal information gets stolen.

The objective of this chapter is to help you spot a fake opportunity right away so that you can spend your time wisely applying for real opportunities. Read the following signs carefully and remember them because they will help you stay away from trouble.

THE AD LACKS DETAILS

If you find a job opening that you do not recognize, try to research it before you consider applying for a role. Always check if information like the company name, the link to a company website, or the name of the recruiter/hiring manager or address are missing. This lack of specificity could be the first sign that the job posting is a scam, especially if you Google the name of the company and you don't get any results.

THE AD USES A SUSPICIOUS EMAIL ADDRESS

If the job posting you found is purportedly for a well-known company like IBM but uses an email address not relating to that company, like @yahoo.com, it is usually a scam posting. Recruiters and hiring managers at reputable companies will always use their company email addresses in job postings!

This is also true for direct contacts from a recruiter. If someone reaches out to you from a free email service rather than from a company email address, beware. Even if they contact you via LinkedIn, for example, if they ask you to send your resume to a Gmail address, be suspicious.

THE AD IS FULL OF GRAMMAR ERRORS

If you receive an email from an employer offering a very tempting job opportunity, and you notice grammatical errors or typos in the message, be wary. Scammers deliberately introduce typos and errors in their emails to make them seem more real. But actual recruiters proof their messages to try to reduce mistakes. So multiple mistakes should raise suspicion. Also, examine the types of errors. Are they the types of mistakes someone who is not a native speaker makes? This could be an indication that a scammer from another country is posing as a recruiter from yours.

THE JOB OFFER IS TOO GOOD TO BE TRUE

When looking for jobs online, be careful of job offers that sound too good to be true. Some of these job offers may be scams, so it's important to read the entire job post carefully and look for clues. If someone is offering you way more money than you think a job is worth and if they are offering it without even putting you through an application process, be suspicious.

APPLICATION FEES ARE CHARGED

You should never send money to get a job. You are looking to get hired so that you will earn a monthly paycheck; you don't need to pay for the privilege. A recruiter or hiring manager will never request money from candidates.

If someone asks you to make a wire transfer of money as part of the application process, run. You don't need to pay for an inventory of supplies to qualify for a job. You don't need to invest in a company in order to be considered for work. You want to get paid and are willing to go through an application process to earn that right. But you don't have to pay to get paid.

THE INTERVIEW PROCESS IS HASTY

Some companies need employees as soon as possible, so they can unroll their processes more effectively. But no manager will rush into hiring people. The interest of a manager or CEO is to find the best candidates for a position, and that takes time.

If you receive a message or email from an employer telling you that you need to go through an interview immediately, it should make you suspicious. Such emails are usually filled with admiration for your work. No one is going to work to convince you that you are the best candidate. You are supposed to convince them.

Interviews don't take just a few minutes. An interview shouldn't first require you to install suspicious communication tools or even familiar tools downloaded from nonofficial websites.

THE EMPLOYER REQUESTS PERSONAL INFORMATION

During the application process or interview, you should never disclose information such as your bank account numbers, your credit card numbers (CCV codes), or details about your PayPal account. A reliable employer will only ask for the means to send you your paycheck *after* you've been hired.

Employers should not ask you to send them a copy of your government ID and other information before making you a job offer. If they do, beware. An employer can ask you for your documentation regarding your visa status or your work permit, but there is never a reason to disclose sensitive information at the beginning of an interview.

THE AD IS ON A SUSPECT JOB SEARCH ENGINE

There are quite a few large websites dedicated to job posts and recruitment, such as LinkedIn, Indeed, or Glassdoor. They are known for gathering the world's most reputable companies and employers and for running detailed background checks on their subscribed members. The reason they do is to detect scammers.

When looking for jobs online, use only reliable search engines and do not follow links to obscure websites. You can look for available jobs directly on an employer's website in the Job or Career sections.

YOU GET SUSPICIOUS SEARCH RESULTS

If you are researching a company that has tried to hire you and the information doesn't add up or has missing links, there could be a serious problem. Websites and social media profiles that are fake look suspicious in most cases. The information they provide is shallow and lacks consistency.

No matter how large or small a company is, one of their main goals is to build a solid presence online. If the online presence is sketchy, the job offer probably is too.

FINAL THOUGHTS

You can find many different types of job scams on the Internet. For example, there are pay for software or training materials scams, pay for a background check or startup kit scams, and even trial employment scams. If you're unsure if a job advertisement is legitimate, doing some research at the beginning of your search can save you time and money in the long run.

Remember that, if you are applying for a job through a recruitment agency, in most cases the company that the job is for will not be listed in the job posting. Recruitment agencies do this so they can introduce you as a candidate and get paid if you are hired. But you can still research the recruitment agency to see if it is legitimate. Some scammers create fake names for recruitment agencies.

If you follow the tips in this chapter, you can avoid most fake job postings.

15. The Hidden Job Market

The hidden job market is often spoken about in hushed tones as if it's some sort of secret society. Despite what some so-called "career coaches" may tell you, the term *hidden job market* refers to open job positions that are not advertised online or formally posted on other channels.

These are the jobs that are either so niche that there's no point in advertising them, open for specific people (friends, referrals, returning employees, etc.), or they are confidential roles for C-level executives' candidates.

Instead of posting a job opening, employers will often use agencies, headhunters, or referrals from their current employees to fill a role, without sharing the role publicly on their career websites. And these jobs will officially open right after the company finds a suitable candidate or when the suitable candidate appears during a search for another role.

Although this job market is "hidden," candidates are more likely to land a job through it than through the common channels because the competition is lower. In the hidden job market, you are not competing against dozens or hundreds of other candidates but just a select few.

Opportunities like these could be your way into a company.

WHY DO SOME EMPLOYERS PREFER THE HIDDEN JOB MARKET?

Many firms would rather minimize their risk by avoiding this costly process of online job applications and other ads. This is a strategy that often pays off since many candidates are referred to the company by other employees, and, as many statistics show, people referred are more loyal, they stay with the company longer, and they turn out to be better applicants.

Another reason companies use the hidden market is to hide the fact that they are planning to expand or open a new branch. They also avoid posting a job if they are replacing someone internally. Public companies might fear leaks of news about significant hiring or replacement of high-level executives, which might affect stock prices.

Even though most companies share their vacancies publicly, the non-hidden job market is not *totally* transparent. Some studies and articles report that 70 to 80 percent of all positions are never shared publicly. From my personal experience and discussion with hundreds of recruiters over the years, the actual percentage is around 5 to 8 percent.

How can you tap into the hidden job market? The answer is simple: It's all about connections and networking.

HOW TO USE YOUR NETWORKING SKILLS

The best way to break into the hidden job market is to expand your connections and advertise your goals to as many people as possible. Utilize networking to learn about job opportunities that haven't been posted yet. Focus on building relationships in order to gain access to insider information about job openings in your network. Somebody from your network might tell you that they are planning to open a role within a week or two.

To gain a head start, determine your key contacts at organizations in your network, people who could introduce you to the right connections within the company. Look for potential hiring managers in your target companies and check their LinkedIn activity for phrases like "For my team, I am looking." If you find these hiring managers, you can try to connect with them on LinkedIn, not only to expand your network but also to ask them if they are looking for somebody with your profile.

Don't start your first message to these people with a direct question about available jobs. First, create a connection with them and add a message to your LinkedIn invitation. Say something generic about expanding your network. Or you can say that you are interested in their company and want to be notified about any opportunity that might arise in the future.

When you send a LinkedIn invitation to someone, they may check your profile to see if you have any skills applicable to a role that they are planning to open. If they see that you have the skills they need, they may approach you directly about the new opportunity.

If they don't approach you right away, they may later on or when they have an opening. When you apply, your name will look familiar to them and this may create a positive psychological association for them because we are more willing to trust people we already know.

HOW TO FIND THE HIDDEN JOB

Following are several strategies to help you find out more about hidden jobs.

Be traditional in your approach

You can test the waters of traditional networking by attending formal networking events, such as conferences or career fairs. You can also reach out to your LinkedIn connections and college alumni. Network with people in your industry to set up informational interviews or discussions.

Reach out to family and friends, keeping them abreast of your job search and professional qualifications. As simple as they sound, these traditional strategies could provide lead advice and information regarding hidden job openings.

Adding people to your LinkedIn network is the quickest way to get visibility and reconnect with your ex-colleagues from previous companies. You can also add to your network recruiters from the local area or recruiters from companies where you want to work. Not everyone will accept your invitation, but many of them will at least check your profile. Maybe they will conduct a confidential search for somebody with your skills.

Remember to improve your LinkedIn profile before you start inviting others to connect with you on LinkedIn.

Expand your networking scope

Networking is a continuous process that should be done on a regular basis, even when you don't need a job. Grow your network by interacting with your industry peers, as they will be able to provide you with valuable information about job opportunities that may not be openly advertised.

Work on casually selling your qualities

One way to sell your qualities is by writing articles shared on your blog, LinkedIn, or other social media platforms. A high-quality article will show the world that you have valuable knowledge and will also attract new connections who find that content through Google and other search engines.

Engage with posts others share on LinkedIn. Watch how others present themselves and notice what is working for them. Don't be scared of putting yourself out there if an opportunity presents itself.

Let your social media reflect your new mission

Be smart about this while you are still employed and hoping to move on, but if you remain cautious and make a small improvement to your LinkedIn profile without broadcasting the change, you will increase your chances of being found by the right person. The best time for making such changes is when you are promoted—this is your opportunity to enrich your profile without jeopardizing your current position.

Give before you get

Helping others on LinkedIn by sharing useful articles and job leads can hep you build a stable foundation for when you need to search for a job. Do not just depend on favors; make a point of building real relationships with people.

You might be surprised how sharing a few articles via LinkedIn with a goal to motivate others or help them on their journey can get you the attention you need. If just one person from your network is connected with a recruiter from a company currently hiring and likes your post, your post could appear on the recruiter's LinkedIn timeline.

Connect with influencers

Look for local industry influencers. In my experience, these people are typically well-informed about new projects and what's happening in their industry. They're also well-connected, and employers often ask them for referrals and tips on potential employees. Connecting with them will also help you stay informed about industry trends.

Use the power of referrals

Leverage your LinkedIn or social network contacts when introducing yourself to the decision-maker. If you are referred to the employer by a mutual acquaintance, you are more likely to get their attention.

Make sure the people you ask for referrals are well-respected. Hiring managers are more excited about referrals from people they like than from a person with a bad reputation or a low performer.

FINAL THOUGHTS

Instead of wasting your time and money on gimmicks and schemes that "career coaches" are offering, focus on building genuine relationships with people in your field. Get out there and start meeting people. Attend industry events, join professional organizations, and reach out to friends and acquaintances. Do not forget to build your network on LinkedIn too!

While there are no guarantees in life, one thing is certain: you won't get anywhere if you don't put yourself out there and start networking. You never know who might have the perfect opportunity for you. And even if they don't, they might know someone who does. You never know where your next lead will come from.

This is how you tap the hidden job market.

16. How to Apply for a Job Even If the Company Isn't Hiring

Whenever I am asked by someone for help with their career search, I always ask them about the companies they are interested in working for and why. Most people don't just name one potential employer. Instead, they give me the names of several companies that they are interested in and their reasons why. The reasons are not just the salary or benefits package; often the reasons have to do with the company culture, brand, mission, and employees.

My next question is whether they have already applied to those companies. Often I'm told that the person hasn't applied because the companies aren't hiring. But this is not a good enough reason not to reach out to your target companies. I ask if the person knows somebody at one of the companies who could introduce them and help connect them with the company recruiter or hiring manager.

HOW TO APPLY WHEN THERE ARE NO OPEN POSITIONS

Even if companies are not currently hiring, it doesn't mean you can't apply for a job. If you can find a way to stand out and get the attention of a recruiter, hiring manager, or company leadership, they might just make room for you in their company.

Keep in mind that all companies want employees who are the best fit for a company's goals and needs. Thus, if the ideal company for you is not hiring at the moment, you can still make a move, using the pieces of information presented next.

Why Apply Even If the Career Page Is Empty

How many times have you given up on companies after seeing that they're not hiring? This is something most people do. They don't see any point in sending over a resume or making their presence felt in any way. But these people are often missing a potentially golden opportunity.

Many companies open some roles only confidentially, because they're looking for someone to replace a person they're going to let go. Companies also choose not to post new roles created for former employees who are returning to work. Still another reason for not posting an opportunity is that the company is preparing a current employee for a promotion into a new role. Alternatively, the company may be creating a new role for someone with a unique and valuable skill set. The point is that, even if a company isn't openly looking for new employees, it doesn't mean that there aren't any opportunities available.

Submitting your resume to a company database will not get the attention of the hiring manager, but applying for a job at a company that is not hiring could increase your chances of being discovered by recruiters when a position matching your skill set becomes available. Showing your interest in a company by applying for a job, despite the fact that the company is not hiring at the moment, could catch the attention of the hiring manager, members of the team they are planning to grow, or a recruiter.

How to Take the First Step

There are a few key things to remember if you want to get hired. First, submit your resume into the company database (ATS) and send it directly to recruiters. This is a strategy that many career coaches recommend, as it increases your chances of being noticed.

However, I do not recommend sending your resume to potential *hiring managers,* as they may not have a role for you and your email will only be forgotten in the pile of emails they get every day. But before you do that, here are several things you need to do.

1. Start by getting to know the company well

You cannot attract a company's attention if you do not get to know the company well. Demonstrating that you know the company will show that you are interested in it and you don't just want any job.

Check out the available products and services. Would you like to buy and use the company's products? Do you know how they are made, what sets them apart, and what their best features are? Also, check to see if the company has an app. If so, download it and use it for a while. Remember that companies appreciate candidates who not only know the products and services but also like and use them, if possible. What are the best features of the company's products and services and do you know how they are made?

Don't stop at finding out more about the company's products and services.

Also look into the company's values. You can find this kind of information on the company's website. Check the news page as well, learning about the latest accomplishments of the business. Get familiar with the company's culture. This is important as it will let you know if you will fit in well.

2. Show the world your value

You need to become more visible in order to appear as an expert in your field or someone with something valuable to offer. Demonstrating your skills and looking like someone who could bring the right expertise will attract not only one company but many others as well.

Show a company that you are more interested than other potential candidates. One way I tackled this problem for myself was by writing an article about Chrome extensions that help recruiters find contact details on candidates. I researched and tested several different tools to come up with a comprehensive list for my article. This gave me a solution to a problem that many people were asking about online. The article attracted many organizations on the market and brought me more than six job offers from companies across the world and also the attention of the people from the company I was trying to attract in the first place.

I found out later that the company was trying to conduct similar tests to the ones I had done, so I saved them time and lots of money by sharing my results. This article helped me show my value to that company and people working there. In addition, I created a good article that was beneficial to the entire recruitment community.

3. Ask for an introduction

If you know someone working at the company you're interested in, ask them to refer you to the hiring manager. This will give you the opportunity to introduce yourself and show your qualifications. If they are willing to refer you, thank them for their help. If the company isn't hiring, their recruiters and hiring managers may remember you if something changes.

FINAL THOUGHTS

Now you know a few simple steps you can take to improve your visibility. I know that submitting your resume to an ATS is recommended by many career coaches, but I recommend being more proactive and not waiting for a day when a recruiter will find your resume in their database.

Try also to resist the temptation to submit your resume to everyone in a particular company. Since the company is not hiring at the moment, your submission via email could be disregarded. That is why networking and creating new connections in that company is the key that will open a door to future opportunities.

17. How to Attract Employers' Attention

There are several ways to get noticed by the employees and hiring managers of the company where you want to work. Use the following strategies to build momentum.

FOLLOW YOUR COMPANIES OF INTEREST

Follow organizations and employers on LinkedIn, Facebook, and Twitter to get information about any major changes they make, like the launch of a new office branch, a merger or big partnership deal, or the expansion of new projects. These events show that growth is occurring within the company and that there might be hiring opportunities.

By following a company's social media, you will gain a better understanding of the company culture, their plans, and their products or services. This will give you a leg up on your competition when you interview with them.

You should also set a Google Alert[64] to get news about your targeted company. It is a perfect way of staying abreast of hidden jobs. Once you sign up, you will be among the first to know when the company might soon be hiring.

To do this, visit the Google Alerts page and enter the fields of interest, such as the company, employers, and names of decision makers.

BECOME A VOLUNTEER AT COMPANIES OF INTEREST

Volunteering with a company is a great way to make connections and learn about the company culture. This is usually a good step for graduates looking for their first job opportunity. When volunteering, as you get to know the employees, let them know that you're interested in working for the company.

The best interview is the one where your work speaks for itself!

---

[64] https://www.google.com/alerts

BECOME A FREQUENT ATTENDEE ON MEETUPS

Tearing a seam in the hidden job market may very well begin with one of the company events. For example, meetups are ideal places where you can make new connections who could have inside information, could land you interviews, or could offer access to decision makers with hiring power. You could even get a one-on-one with prospective employers who are looking to grow their companies and employ more talent.

Another option is to attend bigger conferences that offer the opportunity to meet with more company representatives. Although these conferences can be expensive, especially if you are between jobs, consider attending at least one major meeting each year in your industry or chosen field.

If you are not able to afford to attend an international conference, visit your local industry gatherings and meetups. Or you can reduce or altogether avoid the attendance fee for a conference by volunteering to work there.

BUILDING CONNECTIONS WITH PEERS

Before you are planning to reach out and connect with hiring managers in the companies where you want to work, it is always great to connect on LinkedIn with people working in similar roles in the companies you are targeting. If you know somebody at the company you're applying to, your LinkedIn invitation will have a higher chance of being accepted. Many recruiters and hiring managers are more likely to favor candidates they know, so it's beneficial to appear as though you already have a connection at the company.

If you are connected with your peers, they might reach out to if you are interested in working for their company. This doesn't happen often, but several people I know have been hired this way.

You can either ask these peers directly through LinkedIn if they have a job that matches your skills, or you can try to build a relationship with them before you ask. I don't recommend asking them for help right away because they don't know you and they aren't recruiters. It's better to start building a relationship with them first.

If they ask you why you sent them a connection request, then you can tell them that you are open to an opportunity in their company. You can say something like this: "Hello, Pilar. Thank you for accepting my LinkedIn invitation! I've sent you a connection request because I'm interested in job opportunities at your company and want to get updates on any upcoming events or jobs you're about to share with others via LinkedIn. Best Regards, Carl."

This message will inform them that you are open to a new opportunity, and it is less direct than a first message that says, "Hi, Carl. I saw your company is hiring. Do you have an opportunity for me?"

18. How to Attract the Attention of Recruiters

You already know of several ways to get a new job: by actively applying for new opportunities, by asking your friends to refer you to their company, or through your LinkedIn network. However, sometimes companies try to fill a position solely through recruiting agencies or headhunters.

Since you can't be connected on LinkedIn with every recruiter out there, you can try to get the attention of those who are proactively checking the market for people they do not know and could be a fit for their clients. The best way to get their attention is to be visible to them. To be visible, you don't necessarily have to have a LinkedIn profile, although, as we've discussed, this is an excellent strategy. You don't even have to have a reputation and achievements that make you stand out. The following tips will help you put yourself out in front of the right audience and attract the attention of recruiters, hiring managers, and business owners.

PUT YOURSELF ONLINE AND BE ACTIVE

The majority of recruiters and headhunters start their searches by creating a long list of candidates after checking LinkedIn and other sources. When you are active on LinkedIn, this will help them to discover you and enable you to provide context.

However, you can be active online in other ways too, such as by writing articles or by sharing interesting articles that are related to your field combined with a question that will spark a discussion under your post. This strategy works for LinkedIn, Twitter, and other social sites.

STEP OUT OF THE CROWD

Networking is not about getting to know as many people as possible. It is about getting to know the right people. One of the best ways to get yourself on a headhunter's radar is to be recommended by someone they know. A LinkedIn recommendation from the right person can do wonders.

Endorsements from people in senior positions like Director or VP can help increase your credibility and get you the attention you need in your industry. Their recommendations will help you to step out of the crowd. The greater the number of people who know your name, the greater the chance that a headhunter will hear about you and will contact you with the right offer.

It can be difficult to ask for recommendations, as people you ask may be too busy or they may not know what to write. That's why it's a good idea to provide them with two or three versions of the recommendation you want on your LinkedIn profile. This increases the chance that they will respond, either by editing it or using it as is.

MAKE A LIST OF PEOPLE TO FOLLOW

This is an amazing trick that most people don't know about. I'm going to share with you two ways you can use it to get the most out of it. This trick works because it gets people to pay attention to you and your profile, which is really useful if you're exploring the job market or a new market confidentially.

Option 1: Write an Article

Write a short article entitled "A List of People You Should Follow in [industry name]." The only thing you will need to do is to find the right influencers from your industry and create a top ten or twenty list with them. You do not need to limit your list to people from your city or your country. This simple list should include each person's full name, URL on their LinkedIn profile, link to their Twitter feed or blog, and a short summary of why others should follow them.

If you want to attract even more people, add the current year to the headline of your list. People are attracted to numbers so this will help you get more attention. Add the current year unless you're in the last quarter of the year; in that case, use the upcoming year: "Ten Marketing Leaders to Follow in 2023." Or "Fifteen Tech Leaders to Follow in 2024."

When people share your list, more people will see it, curious about who made the list. By adding some extra info about you at the end of that article with links to your LinkedIn profile, you will piggyback on the traffic that this generates.

If you're sharing your blog post on social media, post it on LinkedIn too and tag any people on your list. If you use Twitter, reshare your article there as well and, again, tag any people on your list. This will get their attention right away and you'll be surprised at how many benefits you'll get from this type of list and how many people will react to it.

This method is effective because people on the list will share it with their own audiences, as we all love to be recognized and be on the list of top people.

Option 2: Put Yourself on the List

There is a second option that some people use. I do not recommend it as it comes with a negative, but during my career I saw several examples.

With this option, you compile a list just like in Option 1, but you include yourself on the list. Obviously, you shouldn't put yourself in the first place, and you should have some experience to justify your inclusion. When you finish this article, find someone from your industry to share the list via their profile.

The drawback of this approach is that by including yourself in the article you write, you are inviting criticism. People tend to react negatively to obvious self-promotion unless (1) you are a celebrity or (2) you're sharing the fact that someone else has honored you. Commenters may tell you that your list is good with the exception of yourself, and, although it gets you attention, it doesn't look good overall.

If you post that article, don't turn on the LinkedIn OpenToWork banner. People will think your article is solely to gain exposure so you can get a job.

SPEAK AT CONFERENCES

Being a speaker is a great way to get your name out there, stay up-to-date on trends in your field, and demonstrate your expertise. Make sure your name, position, and contact info or LinkedIn profile link are visible on event websites and attendance lists—this will help headhunters find you.

Websites and attendance lists are great resources for headhunters to find candidates. By browsing event websites, headhunters can see who is attending the event and what companies are sponsoring it. This information can help them identify potential candidates who may be a good fit for the position. Attendance lists can also help headhunters identify who is likely to be interested in the job and who should be contacted first. By using these resources, headhunters can increase their chances of finding the right candidate for the position.

BE YOUR OWN BEST BRAND

Think about your brand as a product and figure out how to market it and what makes you the best hire. Try to think of what makes you unique and the value you can bring to any organization. Start promoting this value; it will help headhunters find you and let them know why you are going to be a valuable asset for their client.

By taking control of your career, you can make yourself known to potential employers and build relationships that will help you achieve your goals. You are in charge of your career and the only one responsible for it so make it count.

TAKE ACTION AND BE CANDID

If you want recruiters to know you exist, you need to be on their records. However, don't send your resume to them directly. Find a few headhunters from your field and connect with them on LinkedIn. Ask them for a consultation about the market but don't tell them to find you a job. Ask them for a meeting and invite them for coffee. Find out what is new on the market and introduce yourself.

Having trust between you and a headhunter is important. Any dishonest behavior will ruin the relationship and you could lose current and future opportunities. If you can't attend a meeting or are no longer interested, be open and tell the headhunter before the meeting. Always be candid with them!

Remember it's better to have a small number of good headhunters in your network rather than dozens of average ones.

BE OPEN TO MEETINGS

If you are working in a field such as software development, you probably get lots of calls and emails every week with an offer to meet. If you always say yes to every recruiter, you won't have time to do anything else. If you get a call from a headhunter, check their profile on LinkedIn or check references and find out what they're doing and whether they are the right person who knows your field. If you get an invitation for a chat from an experienced headhunter in your field, say yes. Maybe you will lose a few minutes of your time, but you will also get useful information about salaries and other news in your industry.

Good headhunters are not going to push you to take a new job; instead, they will offer you an opportunity to build a relationship with them because they know that even if they can't place you with their client today, they may be able to do so in the future. Plus, you may be able to recommend somebody to them who could be a fit for the role that they are trying to fill.

FINAL THOUGHTS

The more active you are on LinkedIn, the more attention you will attract from recruiters and headhunters. That is why it is important to stay in contact with experienced headhunters once you have their attention.

If you build a good relationship with them, they will call you from time to time to ask you for referrals and tips. These tips and referrals are highly appreciated and always remembered. If you're helpful, people will try to help you.

You might not be looking for a new career opportunity right now, but it's always good to keep in touch with a headhunter because you never know when you may be looking for an opportunity. The key is to become visible. Just as important as getting on their radar is staying on it!

19. How to Find a Recruiter's Professional Details

Not all companies hide who their recruiter or hiring manager is. Some companies list their names on job postings that you can find on a company's career page. But their email address will not be visible in most cases. You may still be able to find their contact information so you can contact them directly.

There are several ways to find a recruiter or hiring manager's email address. LinkedIn is a great resource, but email addresses are not always listed on profiles. Alternatively, you can try finding their email address through a Google search or by using a tool like VoilaNorbert[65] or RocketReach.[66]

VISIT THE LINKEDIN PROFILE

The first and easiest strategy is to visit the LinkedIn profile of the recruiter and check their activity feed or their bio. Many recruiters share new job opportunities on LinkedIn as posts together with an invitation: "Please contact me via email: Martin.Jackson@." Or you might be able to find their email address in their "About" section on LinkedIn right after you click on "See more."

If you can't find their email address on their LinkedIn profile, you can send them a LinkedIn invitation request (of course with a personal message) or ask somebody who is already connected with them for an introduction or for their email address. But all those ways could take time and there is still a chance that your LinkedIn invitation will be rejected or overlooked.

---

[65] https://www.voilanorbert.com/
[66] https://rocketreach.co/

GUESS THE EMAIL ADDRESS

If you know the company where a recruiter is working and how the email addresses of employees are structured, it is easy to guess the person's email address. The most common patterns for company email addresses are firstname. lastname@, lastname.firstname@, and the first letter of the first name and full last name with (s.ramaswan@example.com) or without (sramaswan@ example. com) the dot.

If you know where a recruiter is working, you can also try searching the company website to find their email address. Alternatively, you can use Boolean expressions with operators on Google or any search engine: "Suri Ramaswan" AND "Example Company."

To find the email address format for a company, use quotes to enclose the email address, add a keyword, and combine this with two asterisks and the company's domain name. Google doesn't recognize the @ sign, so replace it with * and spaces on either side of the asterisk.

Example

"email * * ibm.com"

You can also add the keyword "Contact" to your string.

Example

(email OR contact) "* * ibm.com"

At many international companies, a large number of employees use subdomains for their email addresses. For example, IBM uses us.ibm.com for people who are living in the United States. So, in the above examples, you would replace "ibm. com" with "us.ibm.com" if you were targeting email addresses in the United States.

Example

"email * * us.ibm.com"

You can also use one of the email permutations available on the Internet to get a list of email addresses that you can validate with an email validation tool. Try Google "email permutator" to see some of the tools that will help you create more versions of the email address you are trying to validate. Then try to run them via any of the email validators that are on the market, like debounce.io.

You can also use websites like Hunter.io[67] to try to get an email address connected with a specific company (domain name). But in most cases, this method is just a guess based on how emails are structured in that company.

If you need to find Hunter.io alternatives, just Google **"hunter. io alternatives."** Or just type this phrase into Google: **B2B email finder tool**.

VERIFY THE EMAIL

When you find an email address, verify if that email address is valid. You can run the search via Google or use one of the following methods:

1. The easiest way to determine if an email address is valid is to send an email to that address. If you receive an email that bounces back to you, it is invalid; either it doesn't exist, or it is blocked by the recipient's spam filter.
2. There are many online services that can verify email addresses, including debounce.io, thechecker.co, and truemail.io. You can also use free options by searching Google for "Free Email Checker."
3. The third option is to use tool like Discoverly.[68] After you install the plugin on your browser, you can simply enter an email address into your Gmail. If Discoverly knows that person, you will get their LinkedIn profile and other social media links. You can create more versions of the email address (such as suri.ramaswan@, sramaswan@, and suriramaswan@) and paste them all into a Gmail draft to cover all the bases. If you hover over each of these possible email addresses, you will find out which ones are valid.

When you verify the email address and find the correct one, the next step is to ensure that the recruiter or hiring manager reads your message. You need to use one of the email tracking tools that are available on the market.

HOW TO TRACK AN EMAIL

Do you find yourself constantly checking your email inbox for a response from a recruiter? If so, you're not alone—many job seekers do the same. You may be wondering if the recruiter even read your email. Fortunately, there's a way to find out. Recruiters often use email tracking tools to see when their email was

---

[67] https://hunter.io/
[68] https://discover.ly/

opened and how many times it was viewed. So, if you're curious if the recruiter is reading your emails, you can use a similar tool to see the same information.

How does email tracking work? An email tracking tool inserts an invisible image pixel into your emails. That technology can detect the exact time and date an email has been opened by a recipient.

There are several tools on the market you can use, some of them are free with limited tracking options, or you can use the paid version that will help you track even more things and offer you various other options like a Kanban board. Tools like Mailtrack.io[69] and Doubletick[70] offer free plans that you can use for your Gmail account to track your sent emails. Some of those tools will even show you how many times a person opened your email.

If you are interested in getting more advanced tracking and features, you can consider applications like Vocus[71] or Gmelius.

Some tracking tools are blocked by company firewalls, so they may not work all the time.

---

[69] https://mailtrack.io/
[70] https://www.getdoubletick.com/
[71] https://vocus.io/

20. How to Communicate with Recruiters

Many candidates believe that recruiters are only responsible for forwarding resumes to the hiring manager and do not actually help candidates get jobs. However, in reality, recruiters are paid by the company to identify the best talent that is available on the market and bring them onboard, regardless of how the candidate applied—whether through a job board, through a career site, or after being approached by a recruiter on LinkedIn.

Recruiters get dozens of requests from candidates who do not match the job requirements, they are often under a lot of pressure from hiring managers to find new candidates, and they also have a lot of other tasks to attend to. Even if they are working during regular hours (9 am to 5 pm), their candidates often ask them to call them earlier or later than those hours when they may be at work as well.

Being polite and respectful of the recruiter's time during your interaction will help you get on a recruiter's good side, establish a good relationship with them, and stand out among other applicants.

Building relationships with recruiters is key to good communication with them. If you don't get the job, they will remember you and how you treated them, and they will remember your name when any opportunity appears.

CHOOSE THE RIGHT PLATFORM FOR CONNECTING

Although a recruiter may be active on multiple social media platforms, choose one to connect with them on. As a recruiter, I can tell you that there is nothing more annoying than a candidate who will apply for a job, contact you via email, send you a LinkedIn message, and send you direct messages via Twitter and Facebook. All that to express their interest in the open role.

If you want to reach out to recruiters, it is best to use LinkedIn. This is because LinkedIn is a site where recruiters look for candidates and where they spend the majority of their time. Keep in mind that Facebook is also used by recruiters in some countries, but it is considered a private network so bombarding recruiters on Facebook can ruin your chances. I also recommend not sharing your resume or private data via Facebook Messenger or Twitter direct messages.

If you want to start a conversation or get the recruiter's attention, send a LinkedIn invitation with a message to them first. If you don't receive a response, you can contact them via email after a few days. Many recruiters list their email addresses on their LinkedIn profiles, and you can also find them with a Google search or another method detailed in the previous chapter.

BE PATIENT

When contacting recruiters, be sure you have the qualifications they are looking for. Many candidates who do not meet the requirements and do not have the basic qualifications for the job apply anyway, wasting the recruiter's time. Recruiters check dozens of resumes every day, so they may not be able to respond immediately to your message. If you meet the job requirements, the recruiter will get back to you—just be patient and don't expect a response within an hour.

GET TO THE POINT

Recruiters might be handling dozens of people at once, so expecting a response to a two-page email is unrealistic. If you have questions or need to contact them from outside, keep things short and speak clearly. This is more than likely to get you the answer you're looking for.

When sending a message to recruiters, ask yourself if you would want to read it if you were the recruiter. If the answer is no, remove unnecessary parts from the email.

HOW TO CONTACT RECRUITERS VIA EMAIL

If you are thinking about contacting a recruiter via email, there are a few things you should keep in mind. Following these guidelines will help improve your chances of being invited for an interview or receiving a response. This list of dos and don'ts is based on my experience and hundreds of discussions with recruiters from around the whole world.

THINGS YOU SHOULD DO

What follows are general guidelines for communicating with recruiters. Also consider culture and country differences when communicating with recruiters in different parts of the world.

1. Apply first via their career site

If you're interested in the job opportunity that a recruiter shared online, I recommend applying for it before contacting them.

Why not contact the recruiter first before you apply? Due to privacy laws (GDPR) and their internal rules, websites will ask for your consent to share your resume with hiring managers. If you have already applied and they have your resume in their ATS, you can mention in your direct message that you applied for the role; this way, the recruiter will be able to review your application quickly as soon as hearing from you. Otherwise, the recruiter might forget to look, and your message will not have served a purpose.

You can also attach your resume to the email you send. If you are the right fit for the role, having your resume might enable them to reach out to you quickly with an offer for an interview.

2. Be professional

Always maintain a professional tone in your communication; your email could be forwarded to the hiring manager or other higherups in the company. Being sarcastic, demanding, or arrogant will not get you anywhere. No matter how things are going for you, it's important to behave in a way that doesn't upset others. Recruiters are people too, and you wouldn't want to be treated poorly.

If you are rude or unprofessional to the recruiter, your behavior may haunt you for a long time. Recruiters change jobs too and a slighted recruiter might be the person standing between you and your next job.

3. Keep the communication brief

If you receive an email that is two pages long, are you going to read it? And even if you read the whole thing, are you going to be excited to reply to it? I bet you won't!

If you want to get a response from a recruiter or hiring manager, try to keep your email short and to the point. There is no need to send your entire motivating pitch in the email when you can add it as an attachment. Describing all your experience again in the email if you already applied or attached your resume is counterproductive.

4.   Add a phone to your email signature

Adding your phone number to your email signature is a great way to speed up the process of recruiting. That way, the recruiter can easily find your number without having to go to their ATS, and even if they are working from home they can contact you right away.

Format the number in the international standard, including the country code too. Your recruiter may be working in a different country from you.

5.   Reference a job ID number

If you know the job ID number (or requisition ID), always mention it in your email. This number is often part of the job posting or is embedded in the URL of the job posting. Often you can find the number on the career site. It could be several numbers (004787) or a combination of letters and numbers (ID47778).

The job ID number is important to mention because it can help recruiters quickly identify which role you are talking about. A company might be hiring for multiple sales manager roles, in different locations, for example, and the job ID will tell the recruiter which job you're interested in.

THINGS YOU SHOULDN'T DO

Recruiters are not your enemies; their job is simply to identify and present candidates matching the job requirements. They are the gatekeepers to protect their hiring managers' time. It may sometimes seem that recruiters are blocking your access to the hiring manager, but try to turn around that thinking: They are the ones who can get you to the hiring manager.

Also, try to understand what the recruiter has to deal with. If you don't hear back from one right away, instead of assuming they're ghosting you, consider that maybe they have been chasing down the busy hiring manager for feedback for several weeks.

If you want to have a good relationship with recruiters, following are a few things you shouldn't do.

1. Don't try to skip over them

Attempting to circumvent the recruiter by sending your resume directly to the hiring manager will not foster the support of the recruiter. In most cases, when the hiring manager receives your resume, they will simply send it to the recruiter anyway. This is because hiring managers must also follow GDPR and privacy laws, and so they won't be able to work with your resume without your consent.

The recruiter will organize the prescreening call with you, will arrange the interview, and will take care of other recruitment steps. They may not have the final say in whether or not you're hired, but their opinion can definitely sway the decision of the hiring manager.

Also, if you send your resume to the hiring manager, there is a chance that it will be lost among the many other emails they receive every day.

2. Treat them disrespectfully and informally

Remember that recruiters are company representatives; they are not your friends or servants to whom you can assign tasks. This is quite important to understand. If you are the right candidate for the role, the recruiter is the first person to recommend you and share their impression of you with the hiring manager.

Treat recruiters in the same way that you want to be treated. If you treat them badly, don't expect any support from them.

3. Ask what opportunities are available

When a recruiter accepts your LinkedIn invitation, don't immediately ask them about job openings. Most large companies have teams of recruiters, and if you ask one of them about job openings, they will likely refer you to the company's career site. You can save time by checking the career site yourself to see if there are any open positions that interest you.

Asking if a position is still available is also redundant. There is a simple rule: If the position is on their career website, the likelihood that it is still available is 99.9 percent. If you find a role on LinkedIn and you are not sure if it is still available, check the company's career site and you will have your answer.

4. Ask the recruiter to find you a job

Many candidates contact recruiters through email or LinkedIn with a request to find a job for them. But many of these people do not have the qualifications for any of the company's open roles. It is impossible for company recruiters to find a job opportunity for every person who contacts them. In addition, different recruiters within the same company may be trying to fill different roles, so they may not even be aware of all vacancies.

It is better to check the career site first and then send an email with information that you are interested in a specific job opening. Don't forget when you are contacting the recruiter to include the job id (requisition number), the link on that job posting, or any unique code that is connected with this position

5. Ask for the hiring manager's name and contact details

It is not a good idea to ask for the name of the hiring manager and their contact details. Imagine what would happen if a recruiter shared the hiring manager's phone number with every candidate who asked. The hiring manager would have to spend all their time fielding calls, and the recruiters would be superfluous. The job of the recruiter is to filter candidates for the hiring manager, so asking them for the hiring manager's contact information will only suggest that you are clueless about how the hiring process works.

6. Avoid using the recruiter's name

Don't just write "Hello" or "Hi" as your intro. If you already have an email for the recruiter, then you likely know the recruiter's name. "Dear Rebecca" or "Dear Rebecca Jones" are better options than "Hi."

Using the recruiter's name will increase your chance of getting a positive reply to your inquiry. If you are reaching the recruiter over LinkedIn, do the same thing.

And if you don't know the name of the person behind the email address, you can use "Dear Recruiter" or even "Dear Hiring Team."

Try to avoid "To Whom It May Concern" or "Dear Sir or Madam." These salutations not only sound too formal but they also could indicate that you didn't do proper research. Emails with generic salutations look like templates sent to dozens of other companies.

7. Be impatient

Although persistence is a good thing, too much of it can push you over the edge from "eager" to "stalker." All recruiters know that you want to hear back from them as soon as possible, but there are many other things happening behind the scenes that you can't see.

Sometimes there is a delay in getting a response about an interview or feedback due to budget constraints. The hiring manager may be ill or on vacation. The company may be going through internal changes. Someone may even be trying to figure out what position to offer you or what salary to offer you after the interview.

FINAL THOUGHTS

Although you may not always get the job, keep in mind that it was not necessarily the recruiter's decision. Most often, recruiters are just the messengers when it comes to the rejection of your resume or candidacy.

Having a good relationship with a recruiter can help you during the hiring process and benefit your career. Even if you are not selected for a position now, the recruiter may remember you when a new position opens up. Or they may even recommend you to their friends (other recruiters) when they are searching for candidates like you.

Many recruiters also help out the candidates with whom they have good relationships, sharing tips about other companies or helping job seekers improve their resumes. Recruiters can be also great career resources, providing feedback and advice on salary expectations.

Remember that if you act rude toward a recruiter, you may damage your chances of getting a job with the company—and with other companies too.

Sometimes you get the job and sometimes you don't, but not getting a job doesn't mean that you should blame recruiters for it.

21. How to Use a Recruitment Agency to Find a Job

One of the ways to find a new job is to use the services of a job recruitment agency. Many companies now use these agencies to fill vacancies, so by using one yourself you are increasing your chances of being successful. The agency will be able to provide you with information about current vacancies and also give you advice on your CV and interview technique. In addition, they may be able to put you forward for positions that have not yet been advertised.

WHAT A RECRUITMENT AGENCY IS

Recruitment agencies are hired by companies when they need employees to fill in available positions. The recruitment agency takes on all the tasks connected to the hiring process, helping companies find the ideal candidates for open positions. The job description, of course, is provided by the company, as the company staff are the ones that know best what kind of employee they are looking for.

The recruitment agency is responsible for finding suitable candidates for the organization. They use a variety of methods to find the best candidates, such as job postings, networking, and headhunting. They also have a database of candidates they have screened in the past. They will use every possible option to find the best candidates.

TYPES OF RECRUITMENT AGENCIES

Following are some of the most common types of recruitment agencies.

Contingency Search Agency

The most common model for an agency is contingency search. In this model, agencies start searching for the right candidate when they get a request from an employer. An agency only gets paid if they are successful in filling the position, which is why some recruiters may be pushy in order to be faster than their competitors.

Sometimes an employer will give an agency an exclusive time-limited contract. If the agency fails to fill the position within the given time period, the employer can then issue a new contract with a different agency or agencies.

The typical fee for the service of a contingency search agency is around two to three times the monthly salary of the hired candidate.

If you are working with multiple agencies, it's important to make sure that you know the name of the companies where each is planning to present you as it will not look good for your you to be sent to the same company by two or more agencies.

Retained Search Agency

A retained search agency is hired by a company to fill a role or roles. The agency is not competing with any other agency to find a candidate. Such agencies often specialize in hiring for specific industries.

A retained search agency typically asks for an upfront retainer of 30 to 50 percent. The second payment usually happens when the agency presents at least three candidates for an interview, and the final payment usually happens when the candidate is hired. Some agencies break these payments into 30, 30, and 40 percent. Retained search agencies get paid regardless of whether a hire is actually made.

Executive Search Agency

Recruiters working in executive search agencies are experts at finding the best talent, regardless of where it is hidden. They have the skills and knowledge to identify potential candidates anywhere, and they use this expertise to find the very best candidates for their clients.

Such headhunters are often paid a retainer fee. They focus mostly on executive, senior management, and other high-level hard-to-fill roles.

Other Types of Agencies

Niche agencies specialize in a specific industry in which they have a vast network of contacts and that they know well.

Temp agencies and recruitment process outsourcing (RPO) agencies manage the whole recruitment process for their clients.

In most cases, as a job seeker, you will be working with contingency and retained search agencies.

TYPES OF ROLES IN RECRUITMENT AGENCIES

Recruitment agencies feature sourcers, recruiters, and headhunters:

- *Sourcer*: A sourcer creates interest and chases passive candidates. If I could think of one term to sum up this role, it would be *hunter*. Sourcers approach candidates on LinkedIn to find out if they are open to new opportunities.
- *Recruiter*: A recruiter manages relationships with candidates and guides them during the recruitment process. In small agencies or agencies where they don't split the responsibilities between recruiters and sourcers, a recruiter could manage both roles.
- *Headhunter*: A headhunter focuses mostly on executive-level candidates. Often, this person is a recruiter with extensive experience.

WHY COLLABORATE WITH AN AGENCY

There are several advantages to working with a recruitment agency, whether you're just starting your job search or have been looking for a while. If you're not having much luck on your own, it might be time to turn to an agency. And if you want to give yourself the best chance of finding a job, make sure to contact agencies as part of your job search strategy.

1. You don't have to pay anything

The most important benefit of working with a recruitment agency is that its services are free for candidates. If you are asked to pay anything to them, the operation is a scam, and you should stay away. Recruitment agencies don't need candidates to pay them because they get paid by employers when they find the right candidates.

2.   They know the job market well

Recruitment agencies are very familiar with the job market and are usually the first to know about career opportunities. Working with a recruitment agency will help you connect with job opportunities as soon as they become available. The agency will tell you what kind of expectations are realistic and what kind of career opportunities are available.

They also have access to a great deal of information about the job market, including what companies are hiring, the salary ranges being offered, and differences in the job market in different parts of the country. This makes them an excellent resource for anyone looking for a job.

3.   They will help you know your worth

Because agency staff are often privy to the salaries being offered by different organizations, they can give you an idea of whether your expectations are in line with the market.

If you are planning to move to a different country and you are unfamiliar with the job market there, it can be helpful to seek out advice from a local recruitment agency who is familiar with it.

4.   You'll get access to the hidden market

Recruitment agencies are often the first to hear about new job opportunities. This makes them a valuable resource for finding out about roles that are about to open up.

If a new company is entering your city or country, they may use an agency to help hire a few initial employees. Agencies are familiar with the local market, so the new company can use their help in the early stages as they establish their presence. In most cases, these initial roles are not publicly advertised and are only shared with the agency.

5.   They will help you through the process

The recruitment agency wants to match you with the right job, so they will do everything they can to help you. This includes following up on your job application, requesting feedback, and even helping you negotiate your salary.

6. You will establish a permanent connection to opportunities

Once you choose to collaborate with a recruitment agency, you will be entered into their database. As soon as an opportunity that matches your skills becomes available, they will contact you. If that job doesn't work out, they'll reach out again with the next opportunity. This way, you will have constant access to a wide range of opportunities.

7. The agency wants you to succeed

Because agencies work closely with their clients, they are in the unique position to ask for more detailed feedback about why you are rejected. You can thus receive valuable feedback from them that will help you improve for the next opening.

If you don't get the job you wanted, the agency will search for similar opportunities and come up with job offers that best match your skill set and experience. The reason the recruitment agency is so eager to help is that they cannot exist without candidates. It employs its vast knowledge, expertise, network, and partnerships with companies to try to find ideal jobs for every candidate who asks for its assistance. If you are an expert in your industry with a good track record, you will have a good chance of finding a new job via a recruitment agency.

FINAL THOUGHTS

Before working with a particular recruiter, assess what they have to offer. Ask how often people like you get placed. This will give you an idea of how effective they are and if they have experience with candidates like you.

Recruitment agencies can also offer to help you with your resume and LinkedIn profile. If you haven't searched for a new job opportunity for quite some time, they will be able to answer your questions about the current market, give you honest feedback on your salary expectations, and coach you on how to prepare for the phone, remote, or on-site interview.

You can increase your chances of finding a job by working with more than one agency, but always be sure to ask each agency what companies they will be presenting your profile to. If you know the company name and you have already applied there, tell them so you won't be presented there twice.

Remember that, like in any other industry, not every agency is effective. If you have a bad experience with one, don't assume that all the other recruitment agencies are the same.

If you're looking for a new job, working with a recruitment agency can save you time and effort. Recruitment agencies can search for jobs on your behalf while you focus on the things that matter, like your family or other commitments.

Since you don't have to invest anything and you have nothing to lose by collaborating with an agency, it is worth working with some during your job search.

22. Preparing for an Interview

The interview is a very important part of the job search process. If you get to the interview stage, it means that you look good enough on paper to be considered. You've jumped through the application, resume, and cover letter hoops. You are part of a select group that has made it to this stage.

What stands between you and the job now is the interview. After all the work you've put in to get to this stage, you don't want to throw it all away by approaching the interview carelessly. In this chapter we'll go over all the steps you need to take to prepare, and we'll cover the interview process itself.

HOW TO RESEARCH A COMPANY FOR A JOB INTERVIEW

The best way to prepare for an interview is to research the company *before* you are even invited for one. This way, you can make sure that the company is a good fit for you and your professional development. You should also research the company *after* you receive a call from a recruiter inviting you for an interview.

To grow your career effectively, look for a company with a culture that feels right for you. Researching every company before you apply for a position is time-consuming but it's worthwhile; you don't want to find yourself in an interview confronted with the fact that you and the company culture don't fit.

Another reason to research a company is that, when you are asked to come in for an interview, you will be better able to make a good impression, increasing your chances of getting the job. If the interviewer asks, "What do you know about our company?" and you don't have anything to say, you're probably not going to get the job. The interviewer represents the company and likely feels invested in it; they're going to want to see that you are too.

The following steps will take you through the process of researching a potential employer.

1. Visit the company website

The career website should be the first place you visit to learn more about the organization, culture, history, and mission statement. If the company has a dedicated career site separate from the company site, visit the main company website as well. You will learn more about the products and services, the management structure, the names and backgrounds of the organizational leaders, and recent news about the company.

A company's culture, mission, and values are some of the most important topics to learn about. Every business, regardless of its industry, wants to see that candidates are familiar with the mission, values, and culture of the company they are looking to work for.

Apart from helping you prepare for an interview, doing this kind of research will help you figure out if the job is a good fit for you. It will also help you understand how the company wants to be perceived—do they promote themselves as innovators, champions, or challengers? Knowing this will help you see if you can fit into the company's work culture and if their values match your values.

2. Get to know the company's products and services

The employer will expect you to contribute to the business's evolution, which also means knowing the product portfolio and provided services. You should be able to learn a majority of information just from the company website, but check the company's blog section as well.

A blog is a great source of information as it may contain customer comments and impressions. See what people have to say about the company, its products, and its services. Find out what clients' and customers' experiences are. Determine if there are any red flags.

If you uncover any issues, spend some time considering solutions. Employers are looking to hire solution-seekers, the kind of people who know them and their products, consider their opinions important, and look for ways to increase their satisfaction.

3. Learn about the customers

Learning about clients of the company is also important. You need to know who your future stakeholders are. This information may also help you determine if the company is a good fit for you.

4. Browse social media

You can also learn more about a company from their social media sites. Visit their Facebook, Twitter, and Instagram pages to learn more. You will see how the company presents itself online and be able to peruse the comments under their posts.

This research will give you a sneak peek into their culture. Maybe you will find something that will raise some red flags for you, and maybe this will trigger one of the questions that you will ask during your interview.

5. Visit third party websites

Although a company's website and social sites are great sources of information, do not make them the only sources. Think outside the box and see what others have to say about the company or if there are any reviews made by third parties. Online platforms like Glassdoor[72] can reveal useful information about a company, details that can help you during an interview.

Details about a job such as job responsibilities, salary range, the hiring process, and company reviews can be very interesting. Since insider information is difficult to come by, put some effort in this area, as it could give you an edge over the other candidates.

Glassdoor is not the only website that gathers reviews from candidates, employees, and ex-employees. Consider other websites like Trustpilot, LinkedIn, Indeed, and Comparably. Glassdoor reviews should be taken with a grain of salt because they are anonymous and could be fake.

6. Find out what kind of candidates are appreciated by the company

One way to get your hands on information like this is to carefully read the company's job posting and see if you can find any clues. Many companies include their values in their job descriptions, and if they do, they're expecting candidates who apply and are hired to match those values. If the company values include curiosity, for example, they'll be looking for a candidate with a curious mind.

If you can, directly contact an employee, somebody you already know, as they can provide inside information regarding expectations and types of employees. I also recommend visiting LinkedIn profiles of employees working in similar roles to the one you are interested in; this will give you an idea of what kind

---

[72] https://www.glassdoor.com/

of people they hire; it could also trigger their curiosity so they will check your LinkedIn profile.

After they visit your LinkedIn profile, you can send them a connection request. This could lead to a discussion about their company, which might even lead to them referring you. If they mention your name to the hiring manager, it could raise your chances of getting an interview invitation.

7. Find out who the key employees of the company are

Company culture is often set by the CEO executive and senior vice presidents. Knowing the key people in a business can be useful during an interview. You may get to know some of them personally during the recruitment process or interview, so it is worth doing some research in advance on them. Check the About page on the company's website for details about these people. Also check their LinkedIn profiles to see their perspectives on the company and what is going on there at the moment.

8. Look for recent news about the company

Look for recent news about the company to ensure you are familiar with recent accomplishments and updates. This will show the employer that you are interested in their company. Checking out the media page on the website is an easy way to see what the company has been up to recently.

Another reason to check news sites is to learn about the financial stability of the company and the potential for layoffs in the near future or for acquisitions and mergers.

In your search, use phrases like "ACME layoffs," "ACME problems," and "ACME investigations."

9. Find the company on the stock exchange

If the company is listed on a stock exchange, you can learn a lot about them from their earnings calls and from the reports with market analytics. The earnings calls and those reports will give you a unique overview of the company's business model and profitability and may disclose future plans.

When hired, you may be offered a stock option as part of your compensation package. This research will help you be prepared during negotiations.

10. Get to know their competitors

Understanding the company's competitors could help you understand the current trends in the industry and give you some ideas for new job opportunities. You might even find an opportunity that's a better fit for you.

11. Research interviewers

Knowing a little about the person conducting the interview will help you better connect with them and understand their interests. By looking at their LinkedIn profile and the comments and articles they've shared or liked, you can get a sense of what is important to them professionally. You can use the information you found to your advantage in an interview by mentioning that you read an article that the person shared. This will help you connect with the interviewer and direct the conversation in a desirable direction.

FINAL THOUGHTS

Your research at the beginning of your job search and especially before your interview will help you determine if the job is right for you and will also show the interviewer that you are interested in the position. Competition for jobs is fierce, especially when it comes to companies with good reputations and solid brands, and that are known for offering high salaries. This small effort at the beginning could be the deciding factor when the company is choosing between two candidates.

If you're trying to find information about the type of projects a company is involved in, head to Google and type in the company name followed by "projects."

Example: site:companydomain.com projects

If you are trying to find information about IBM and their projects, for example, your search string will look like this:

site:ibm.com projects

HOW TO PREPARE FOR AN INTERVIEW

The job interview process can be quite long. It can involve a combination of phone calls, video calls, on-site interviews, and tests that evaluate your skills and knowledge. Although the interview process varies from employer to employer, there are some standard steps that most organizations follow during interviews.

1. Screening call/chatbot or video prescreening or on-site interview

Typically, the first round of interviews is a prescreening call with a recruiter. The recruiter will verify your basic requirements for the job and your language skills and find out more about your availability and salary expectations.

Chatbots or video prescreening rounds could replace the prescreening call with a recruiter. This is a preferred method in companies that hire hundreds of people every week, companies like Amazon.

If you apply to a smaller company or startup, the first round of interviews is likely to be an on-site interview, as there is only one decision maker. In most cases, this is a hiring manager or company owner.

2. Technical interview

A technical interview is a type of interview specifically for jobs in the technology industry. In this interview, you will need to demonstrate your experience and skills related to the job. You may be asked technical problem-solving questions, behavioral questions, and situational questions, or the interviewer could give you various brainteasers that you need to solve.

The interviewer during this round will assess your technical knowledge, skills, and abilities as they relate to the needs of the specific job you are applying to. In many companies, the technical interview is the first part of an interview done with a technical team, and if you pass the technical round, you move on to an interview with the hiring manager.

3. Homework (take-home assignment)

When you are progressing through an interview process, you may be asked to do a take-home assignment. For hiring managers, this is the best way to evaluate your knowledge on a practical task, see how creative you are, and discover how well you are able to communicate and present your results.

The interviewer will also be focusing on the quality of your work and your turnaround speed. These assignments are often used in software development, graphic design, and marketing. Because you may not be compensated for completing homework assignments as part of your job application, think carefully before investing the time whether you really want to work for that company. If you're applying to multiple jobs, completing multiple homework assignments could take up a lot of your time.

4. Another round of interviews/last round

After the prescreening call and technical interview, there may be one or more additional rounds of interviews. These could include a meeting with the hiring manager or another decision maker within the organization. Although additional rounds of interviews are typically the final steps in the interview process, some organizations may try to conduct all interviews in a single visit.

Keep in mind that every company has a different approach to interviewing. The more senior the role you are trying to get, the more interview rounds you should expect. These rounds may involve on-site interviews and phone/video calls. Hiring managers use these interviews to get assurance from others in their organization that the candidate is compatible with company culture and has the right experience.

5. Offer

One of the final steps in the interview process for many companies is a job offer. This offer may be divided into two parts: pre-offer and offer.

Pre-offer negotiations are often verbal. During the pre-offer stage, you have your last chance to negotiate your salary and terms before they are sent for official approvals.

During the offer stage, you will receive written confirmation of the offer, including all details such as the job description, salary, benefits, paid leave, and other terms related to your offer. The offer is usually connected with a deadline, by which the company expects your answer. The offer may be extended based on your discussion with a recruiter or hiring manager.

6. Background check/pre-employment screening

A background check is the final stage of the interview process. A company will start this process right after you accept their offer or even prior to the offer. In some cases, it happens between the pre-offer and offer stages.

A background check typically covers past employment verification, criminal history, and credit history. What is included depends on the country.

You should not give notice at your current job until you pass the background check. If you fail the background check, the offer may be withdrawn; you don't want to be put into a bad position at your current place of employment by giving notice and then needing to beg to get your job back.

In most countries, the employer must obtain consent from the applicant to conduct the background check.

FINAL THOUGHTS

Today, many companies have an involved interview process that can include screening interviews, technical interviews, and in-person interviews. Some employers may require a pre-employment test to see if your skills match the requirements of the job description.

The job interview process can vary from company to company. Some companies may only require one on-site interview with an offer at the end. Others may require a series of phone or video interviews followed by several on-site interviews. The process can be quite lengthy, so be prepared for a long wait.

To get a better understanding of what the interview process will be like, ask the recruiter or hiring manager at the beginning of any communication. This will help you understand how much time you will need to devote to the process and how you will need to prepare.

23. How to Ace Your Chatbot Interview

Chatbots have been around for a while and are commonly used by companies to improve customer interaction and satisfaction as well as to answer basic customer queries. In a recruitment world, the goal of a chatbot is to improve the candidate experience. Some people see automated interviewing as dehumanizing, but it can help companies remove unconscious bias from their recruitment process. In addition, the chatbot interview can prescreen hundreds of candidates in a few hours, whereas humans need days or even weeks to manage such a workload.

Don't be surprised if you have to go through a chatbot interview for a job you're interested in.

If you think that an interview with a chatbot is easier than with an actual human, think again. You need to get ready if you really want to pass this interview round.

WHAT RECRUITING CHATBOTS ARE

A chatbot is an artificial intelligence software that can simulate a conversation (or a chat) through messaging applications, websites, or mobile apps. You may encounter a chatbot right after hitting the *Apply* button on a company's website. Or you might be given a link to a chatbot interview after finding out you were selected for prescreening.

Employers use the chatbots to narrow down the number of candidates for a particular job. The chatbot will get certain information from the candidate, such as experience, availability, certifications, and language skills.

Chatbots are also able to provide the candidate with information such as about the company culture, benefits, company perks, and job specifics. Sometimes the chatbot is the only contact a candidate has with a company after applying for a job.

YOUR CHATBOT INTERVIEW

When you first start talking to a chatbot (the chatbot may even have a name), you can expect some small talk. This is the bot's way of putting you at ease and making you feel comfortable. This small talk serves as an icebreaker and helps to build rapport. It also allows the chatbot to gather information about you so that it can better serve your needs.

However, don't be surprised if the conversation quickly turns to business. After all, chatbots are designed to help you with your tasks, not just chat with you. So, while the small talk is nice, don't be afraid to get down to business.

After the chatbot asks for your name, surname, and email, it will start with its first question from the list of preset questions. Very often there is a pause between questions when you will see the chatbot "typing." The pause has only one purpose: to create the impression of an interaction.

Most chatbots will consider any questions you ask part of your answers to their questions. You will not have a chance to correct your response, so any question you might ask at this point could be evaluated as an incorrect answer that will influence your overall score.

If you want to ask questions, wait until the end of the interview.

Following are several guidelines for succeeding during an interview with a chatbot.

Be professional

Even if you are talking to a robot, stay professional during the interview. Treat this interview the way you would treat a job interview with a human being. The reason is that everything you say to the chatbot will be recorded and stored in your file. All your answers will be analyzed and evaluated.

Try to avoid colloquial phrases and abbreviations in your texted answers. Spell out words; don't abbreviate. Use correct punctuation. Avoid emojis. Abbreviations, emojis, and errors may be misinterpreted by the chatbot and evaluated as incorrect answers. Even if the chatbot gets stuck or stops responding, try to be polite in your texts.

Even unfinished answers will likely be reviewed by a company representative, most likely a recruiter.

Be brief

Don't forget that you are talking to a robot, so being concise is recommended. Don't waste your time elaborating too much because the robot is just looking for relevant information (keywords and phrases).

In fact, chatbots may not even be able to handle complex answers, which can raise issues for your application. To make sure there are no errors and everything goes well, keep your answers short, simple, and relevant to the question you are answering. Right before your interview, research keywords for the job and use them when providing your answers. When your answers are evaluated, you might get a higher score if you have the right keywords in your answers. And this will help increase your chances of being selected for the next round of interviews with a recruiter or hiring manager.

Don't see the interview as a threat or sign of disrespect

Some may see a chatbot interview as some sort of test. Others might feel intimidated by the interaction. Still others might be irritated that no human is paying attention to their application. Try not to look at the experience in any of these ways. Don't worry that the chatbot will not understand you well enough. Chatbots have experience handling many interactions, and the people behind the technology will be able to make sense of your answers as long as you follow the previous guidelines. In fact, try to see the experience as a positive: You can relax and feel more comfortable interacting with a nonjudgmental bot than with a human.

Think about the fact that most people never get an answer when applying for a job. The chatbot is there when a human cannot be. And thanks to them, your application will not get lost in a pile of materials from other candidates or in the ATS system. Now you have a shot to excel so you can get invited to the next round.

Check your responses before you hit send

Chatbot interviews are usually on text. That is why you should proofread your answers before you submit them.

Double-check for grammar errors and typos because a clean answer makes a better impression than one that looks like it was written in haste. If your answers are full of typos, the chatbot may not be able to understand and might evaluate your answers as errors. That could lead to rejection.

Even if the chatbot can make sense of a message full of errors, you don't want a recruiter or hiring manager reading over your answers to find such careless mistakes. Show your potential employer that you care about details, quality, and your image when presenting yourself to others.

Follow up

Chatbots can be an immensely helpful tool for any recruiter team. Nevertheless, technology is not flawless. If you encounter any error, don't hesitate to follow up with a recruiter to inform them about it. It is better to do this than to be eliminated from the recruitment process because of a mistake that is not yours.

FINAL THOUGHTS

Chatbots are not perfect and taking an interview with a robot may sound weird, but it is something that will happen more often in the future. Chatbots already provide assistance on a wide range of websites, so it's no wonder they ended up being used for recruitment purposes as well.

They can easily create a bad candidate experience if they do not know how to respond to what a job seeker is saying. For this reason, you would be smart to keep your answers brief and clear and to include in them the keywords the chatbot wants to find. If you ask questions, the chatbot may not be able to answer them. Don't ask questions until the end of the interview so the chatbot won't mistake your questions for answers. If you get frustrated, don't show it as your interview is being recorded. All of your own unanswered questions will be checked by a company representative and answered so next time when somebody asks a similar question their chatbot will have the answer ready.

24. How to Ace a Phone Interview

Many companies start the recruitment process with a phone call to screen candidates. This call, usually done by recruiters, checks your experience, language skills, and salary expectations. The goal of this call is to determine if you are qualified and to weed out those who are not. If you are qualified, you will be advanced to the next stage of the process.

A prescreening call is often a good indication that the recruiter saw your resume and considered you a potential fit for the role.

The time it takes to interview a candidate can vary depending on what the interviewer needs to know and whether they are just checking your basic information or trying to see if you would be a good fit for the company. This phone interview is a fast way to check out candidates and narrow down the talent pool of applicants.

TYPES OF PHONE INTERVIEWS

There are two types of phone interviews: scheduled and unscheduled.

Unscheduled Interview

During unscheduled interviews, recruiters often try to find out your salary expectations. If it is just a quick call, try not to be too specific about the salary you are expecting and provide the salary *range* instead. This will push the issue to a future discussion about it during your next rounds, especially when you learn more about the role and company.

When you hear, "Do you have a few minutes for a quick call?" but you are busy or distracted, do not be afraid to ask the interviewer to call you later. Offer them a time when you are going to be free and focused. If the recruiter forgets to call you, you can always call them back on the phone number they called you from. Better yet, ask them how to reach you before you hang up.

Unscheduled calls never work in your favor. That is why you should always ask them to call you back or ask them when you might call them. This will give you time to find a comfortable environment without any noise at a time when you are ready.

When you get an unscheduled call, you can always ask the interviewer to send you an SMS and email with their name and contact details. This small "interview hack" will get you not only the name of the recruiter but also the name of the company the person is working for.

With that information you can learn about the company before the scheduled call and prepare questions. Questions indicate you are an interested candidate, something recruiters like and may share with their hiring manager.

Scheduled Interview

A scheduled phone interview is a conducted by one or more interviewers. As you progress through the interview process all of your interviews will be scheduled.

Before your scheduled interview, confirm all the details: from the date to the time to who is going to conduct it. If the interview is a phone interview, make sure to ask who should call whom. Whether it's a phone call or a Skype call, join the call on time. If the call is via an application like WebEx, MS Teams, or Zoom and you have never used the application before, try to log in a few minutes before your call. Make sure you have enough time to install any plugin or program required.

STRUCTURE OF THE PHONE INTERVIEW

There are three parts to the phone interview.

1. Get ready for the call

Be ready five to ten minutes early so you do not sound rushed. Take the time to calm down and focus. Gather your notes with your questions or have a notepad ready for taking notes. Have a copy of your resume handy, either in paper form or on your computer, so you can answer questions about your experience. Even though you know your experience, when you're nervous you can blank out on key information. Having a glass of water ready is also a great idea, especially if the interview will take an hour or more.

If this call is on your computer keep in mind that keyboard clicks might be distracting for the interviewer. Try to keep them to a minimum and turn off all other applications or distractions. Frequent Facebook message pings or email dings will be distracting. Also, don't check your social media or email during the interview.

If the interview is on your phone, put the ringer on silent—but don't miss your interview call as a result! If you are expecting any interruption, like a package delivery, alert the interviewer in advance. If you have dogs, try to keep them from barking.

2. The call

There is one rule that you should follow no matter what during the call: **Listen first. Then speak**. I know it sounds simple, but interviewers always start with their intro, sales pitch, and requirements. The part about their requirements is an especially important part for you as it will give you some idea of what they are expecting, so listen carefully. Then, when it's your turn to speak, you can point out how your experience matches those expectations.

Ask the interviewer how much time you both have to talk. That way you can make sure you have enough time to convey the most crucial information. If you have something you have to do following the interview, like take a call or have a meeting, let the interviewer know at the start so that the interview doesn't run long.

3. The end

Toward the end of the interview, try to ask at least two or three questions. This will signal your interest in the company. You can ask about the scope of the job or the company mission, for example. But be sure to ask something that you couldn't easily have answered yourself such as by looking at the website. Avoid specific questions about benefits, company shares, and salary during this interview as asking about them at this stage in the process will signal that what you get out of the job is more important to you than what you give to it.

Of course if you are not interested in the job opportunity, this will be the time to share that with the interviewer. You can also share your concerns about the job scope if you think this job is not going to match your career goals.

If you are interested, end the call on a positive note. Say thanks for the opportunity and for the interviewer's time. Express your ongoing interest and ask what the next step will be.

When you get to the interview, you will still likely have several competitors. Differentiate yourself by sending a thank-you note. If you have an email address for the interviewer, email your brief thanks. Make sure before ending the interview to find out how you might contact the interviewer with your follow-up note.

PHONE INTERVIEW TIPS THAT WILL LAND YOU A SECOND INTERVIEW

To increase your chances of making the first cut, here are some tips on how to prepare for your interview.

Do your research

Although a phone interview may seem informal, it is important to prepare for it just as you would for an in-person interview. Research the company and the job you are interviewing for, review your resume, and practice answering common interview questions.

To get a better understanding of the role you applied for, you should review the job description and the requirements and scope of the job. If you were contacted by a recruiter about the job, ask them for a link to the job opportunity or find it on the recruiter's career website. This will help you ask questions related to the role.

Practice

Phone interviews can be tricky because you don't get any non-verbal cues. You can't read the interviewer's facial expressions and body language. To offset this disadvantage, before you answer each question, take time to compose your thoughts. And when you do answer, speak slowly, carefully, and to the point. These are habits you need to practice in advance of the interview.

Make a checklist of common phone interview questions and practice your responses to them. Record your answers so you can listen to them after you practice. That's when you'll notice any problems in your communication, like filling up empty space with ummmms or not fully answering the question. In addition, practice the interview over the phone with a friend.

Prepare questions

Create a list of questions for the interviewer. By posing the right questions, you can glean firsthand information about the company. When your questions are interesting and informed, the interviewer will see your commitment and enthusiasm.

Employers know that the best candidates are those serious about knowing whether they will fit into the corporate culture and eager to know what an average day in the organization looks like.

Prepare for curveballs

It's hard to prepare for a curveball. They are notoriously difficult to hit and you can't tell they're coming until the last second. But if you go up to the plate knowing you might get one and if during practice you try to hit them, you'll generally do better when the pitcher throws one at you. During an interview, a curveball question is intended to weed out the candidates who aren't a good fit.

Make sure you don't get weeded out this way by expecting a curveball question, anticipating what that question might be, and practicing answering. Even if the interviewer doesn't throw you a curveball now, you might get one in the face-to-face interview, so your practice will still be worthwhile.

Typically, curveballs are behavioral questions that require candidates to share examples of specific situations they've been in during which they had to use specific skills.

Examples:

- What do you consider your biggest success in your career?
- Can you describe a time when you faced a challenge and how you overcame it?

Do a mock interview

You can conduct a mock interview with a family member, friend, or career coach to help you improve your interviewing skills. This will allow you to hear what you sound like over the phone, replay your conversation to see your strong and weak points, and pinpoint answers and speech patterns you need to improve upon.

I know that many people don't want to hear their voice or spend time listening to their answers from recordings, but listening to recordings of conversations can be a valuable tool for learning.

Find a suitable space

Select a quiet, comfortable, and private space for the interview. Clear the room, remove every possible distraction, and close the door. Get some water to ward off thirst and stay hydrated. Remember to let your voice echo energy and enthusiasm.

Unexpected things can happen during an interview. Your neighbor might start drilling into your common wall, or a series of fire trucks might tear down your street. Control what you can. Alert the interviewer about what you can't control but know is happening or will happen. And don't worry about the stuff you can't control and don't know about. If something unexpected happens, apologize.

If you can't find a quiet place, try to use headphones during your call.

Keep a notebook and pen handy

Are there certain skills and experiences you want to emphasize? Are there certain interests you would like to share with the interviewer? Note the most critical points you want to make with your interviewer. Refer to your notes as needed during the interview. If you don't see another opportunity to bring up these points, raise them when the interviewer asks you if you have any questions (or anything to add) at the end of the interview.

Charge your phone

This one may seem obvious, but during my career I have had many interviews during which the candidates' phones died.

Dress properly

It may seem silly to wear a suit in the comfort of your home. However, from a psychological standpoint, caring for your appearance as you would for a normal interview sets you in the right frame of mind. You will not be on your A-game if you're lying in bed in your pajamas. Standing up or sitting straight during the interview might help you feel more confident and help you project your voice better.

FINAL THOUGHTS

Phone interview etiquette is just as important as face-to-face interview etiquette. A successful interview will shoot you to the next stage of the hiring process, and a bad interview might get you cut. Prove you are the best person for the job by nailing the phone interview with a top-notch performance.

Remember that even though you are being interviewed over the phone, it is important to smile. Smiling over the phone interview makes your voice sound warm and engaging, and it also makes you sound excited and happy to be talking about your qualifications. Smiling can also calm your nerves and make you feel better.

25. How to Ace a Video Interview

Employers have increasingly turned to video interviews as a low-cost and efficient way to screen job candidates, and the COVID pandemic has helped accelerate this trend. During the pandemic, video was the primary method for interviewing candidates. Thanks to the advancements in video and web-based technology, video interviews are easy to set up and conduct.

For some people, the video interviews bring new challenges. Some candidates are uncomfortable being on camera. Others lack the technology to manage this type of interview.

LIVE VIDEO VS. PRE-RECORDED INTERVIEWS

There are three types of video interviews.

Live Video

Live video interviews are often done through applications like Skype, Zoom, WebEx, FaceTime, Microsoft Teams, and Google Hangout. You won't need an account to use most of these applications. In most cases, the recruiter will send you either a link to the meeting or a calendar invitation with the link embedded.

For Skype, however, you will need to share in advance your Skype ID with the recruiter or hiring manager. Be careful what Skype ID you share. Don't use the one that you created as a teenager (Skypeid: joemegasuperkiller*47*). And do not forget to upload a professional photo to your Skype profile.

If you have never used any of these applications before, visit YouTube and check out the related "How To" videos. Install the application before your meeting and test it with your friends. You need to know how to operate it when it is time for your interview.

Live video very often starts with some pleasantries or icebreakers to set a less formal tone.

Pre-Recorded

There are two types of pre-recorded interviews. The first one is done via a simple system. You see a question on your computer screen, and you have several minutes to record your answer and submit the video.

The second version of the pre-recorded interview is the video interview conducted through a platform, like HireVue.[73] This is an algorithm-based interview using video and artificial intelligence (AI). During this type of interview, the assessment is done by AI, and recruiters get the results of your performance along with a recommendation.

When you talk to a camera during a pre-recorded interview you don't get any feedback from the other side. For this reason, you need to adopt a different approach. Get directly to the point with your answers. The things you say during the interview will be analyzed by AI looking for the right keywords. Enunciate carefully and make sure to include keywords from the job description in your answers.

Some companies also use AI tools to analyze your facial expressions and how you say things in addition to what you say. After the interview, your answers are accessed and your performance is evaluated against that of other candidates or against a profile of the ideal candidate created by the company. This methodology might be banned in the future as some governments see it as a discriminatory practice.

There are several things you need to consider when you are being interviewed. Make sure your room is well lit, so your face is visible. Also, consider what you're going to wear. You can find more information on what to wear later in this chapter. Remember to smile, nod, and use gestures to make yourself appear more relaxed during the interview. If you're going to use gestures, make sure that your upper body is visible on camera so that your gestures will be seen.

If you've never done a video interview before, record yourself during practice. Look for sample questions in this book or Google examples.

Practice makes perfect. Even though most of us do not like to see ourselves on video, practice will give you an idea of how to improve. You'll notice awkward hand gestures or if you repeat particular words too often.

One last point: Some companies hire psychologists to evaluate recorded interviews.

In-Office Video

You may be invited to an on-site interview conducted via video conference. This is similar to a video interview, but the camera will usually capture the

---

[73] https://www.hirevue.com/

entire room, so you should maintain good posture and think about your body language throughout the entire interview.

PREPARE FOR THE VIDEO INTERVIEW

An interview is an interview, whether it's in person, via text, on the phone, or on video. Don't forget your basic interview prep. Research the employer, prepare responses to typical interview questions, and formulate a few questions of your own. Try not to skimp on reviewing the job description, your resume, and supporting materials. Some job seekers might be tempted to use the video interview to show off their quirks and creativity. Remember that your responses to questions will also be evaluated against a traditional set of metrics.

1. Prepare the equipment

Decide which hardware to use

The first step in preparing for a video interview is making sure your technology is ready to go. You can use most devices for video calls: computers, tablets, or smartphones. My recommendation is to use your computer or laptop. That way you won't need to hold anything in your hands, you'll look better on camera, and you'll be prepared if the interviewer shares their desktop screen with you.

Set up your webcam

When positioning your webcam for your video interview, be sure to place it so that you can look directly into the lens, not your screen. This will ensure that the interviewer sees your entire frame, from the waist up, and not just your face. This will also present a more polished and professional appearance. Be sure to have the camera at eye-level; you don't want to appear awkward by looking down or up at the interviewer.

If you are using a laptop with an internal webcam, you may want to consider getting an external one. Not every laptop on the market has a good quality camera; if yours is low quality, invest in an external camera with high resolution, especially if you'll be working remotely.

Check the camera's resolution and clean the lens before your interview.

Set up the lighting

You don't need a Hollywood-sized budget to achieve proper lighting. Illuminate your face by putting a light source behind your computer; avoid casting shadows on your videos with overhead lighting. Do a test run to see whether the lighting flatters you.

Lighting is incredibly important; you can look like a weird character sitting in shadows waiting on prey or like a movie star. You can buy a cheap ring light with a stand or get more professional lights from a company like Elgato.[74]

Set up the audio

Although not mandatory, the use of a headset is recommended. A headset is better than your computer's built-in microphone at reducing ambient/background noise and carrying the tone of your voice.

You can also use wireless earbuds and their built-in microphone but test them in advance and charge them before your interview.

If you are going to use a headset, try to find one that will not only help your voice sound clearer but will also cut down on extraneous noise. You will better hear the questions from the interviewers.

If you are using a headset that needs to be charged, do that before the interview so your call will not be unexpectedly interrupted.

Check your Internet connection

If you have a bad or unreliable Internet connection, it will ruin your chances of having a successful video interview. Test your Internet speed and make sure it meets the minimum bandwidth required to run a video interview. This is especially important when you are using Wi-Fi, as a poor signal could be a deal-breaker. If you have a slow Internet connection, you may also need to ask your family members not to use streaming services during your interview.

2. Set up your location

Choose a quiet and private room for your video interview. Make sure the room has controlled lighting and no auditory distractions.

Posters, photos, and mirrors can be background distractions during an

---

[74] https://www.elgato.com/

interview. Make sure your location is clean and free of distractions. Check your background to make sure there is nothing inappropriate behind you. Do not be misled by the seeming informal nature of a video interview: Your background must be presentable.

If you decide to use a background cover for your Zoom or MS Teams interview call, choose something neutral that will not be distracting. Make sure not to choose virtual backgrounds that have colors that clash strongly with your clothing, hair, and skin. The best option is to choose something plain with only a few elements, like an old bookshelf with books, a white wall with plants and clocks, or a painting.

3. Select your wardrobe

Clothes might be the last thing on your mind when preparing for an interview, but they are an especially important consideration when you're going to be on camera. After all, you want to make sure you look professional.

Dress to Impress

Like you would for any traditional in-person meeting, be professional with your dress. Do not wear the old t-shirt that you usually wear at home. When it comes to clothing, it is always a good idea to dress in a way that makes you feel comfortable and confident.

Do not forget to wear pants even if you're going to be filmed from the waist up. You might need to stand during the interview to get something.

Choose the right colors

When it comes to video, the color of your wardrobe requires serious attention for the best outcomes. Wear clothing that is in a warm color. Purple, cobalt, teal, and coral are all colors that are warm and associated with comfort and relaxation. They are also popular choices for clothing because they can make a person look more elegant.

Avoid the wrong colors

There are some colors that should be avoided on video because they can cause technical issues. Bright red, white, and black look too dark when the exposure of the camera is adjusted for a light-skinned face. White will also reflect lighting.

If you wear a black shirt, people may be able to see your dandruff on your shoulders. If you're shooting on a green screen, don't wear green clothing or your body will disappear.

Avoid wardrobe distractions

Avoid patterns and stick to solids when dressing for a video audience. Patterns can be a distraction away from your face. You want your audience to focus on you, not your outfit.

Simplicity is key when selecting your clothes. Try to avoid lots of buttons and frilly collars, as these will distract your audience. Your clothes should follow the contours of your body or be well-fitted. Avoid baggy clothes, which make you look bigger.

If you are going to wear a t-shirt under a jacket, avoid ones with logos, inappropriate pictures, or slogans.

Avoid distracting accessories

If you wear glasses, consider using contact lenses for a video interview. Glasses reflect light, which can make it difficult for your audience to see your eyes, or they can create glare during your video call, especially if you are using a light ring. The reflection of the light ring will be visible in your glasses.

If there's not enough light in the room, the interviewer might also be able to see a reflection of your computer monitor in your glasses. And they can easily spot when you are not paying attention or Googling your answers.

Try to wear small and simple accessories whenever possible, like soft bracelets and simple necklaces. Anything flashy or reflective will create more glare. Bracelets can be noisy.

Consider the image you are conveying

The overall image that you want to present also matters when deciding on which outfit to wear for a video shoot. The outfit you choose for a video shoot should make you feel confident and comfortable in your own skin. It should also reflect your unique personality and style. If you have a video shoot coming up, use the tips mentioned to help you choose what to wear.

Also consider the context. If the company interviewing you is a casual place, like many technology companies are, don't overdress. On the other hand, if you're applying to a financial firm that emphasizes security and professionalism, dress it up. The general rule is to dress like someone who works at the company that is interviewing you.

Bonus tips

- Use natural fabrics that can breathe. You will be sweating, so wear an undershirt or bra.
- Avoid shiny fabrics and complicated patterns.
- Try not to wear short sleeves.
- Do not wear heavy fabrics.
- Do not wear neckties with tight patterns.
- Keep your jewelry simple.

THE VIDEO INTERVIEW

Log in for your interview a few minutes early. This will give you extra time if you need to install a video application or set up an account for using the software. You can also use this time to calm down a little bit before. Conduct one last check of your surroundings and turn off distractions, silence your phone, and pour yourself a glass of water.

Once your interview starts, say hello to the interviewer and thank them for meeting with you. The first few minutes will likely be dedicated to introductions. The interviewer will also likely talk briefly about the company and the vacancy. During this part, listen more, talk less, and do not interrupt.

Think of the interview as a conversation with another person. During the interview try to smile, and when you are asked to answer a question, give yourself a moment to think before answering.

If you couldn't hear the question or want to be sure that you heard correctly, you can always ask the interviewer to repeat it.

In general adhere to the following guidelines during the interview.

Maintain eye contact

Balancing good eye contact and looking into the webcam can get awkward. Practice with a partner or a mirror. Eye contact should be neither too aggressive nor too weak. Your eyes shouldn't dart around nervously. Use a smooth and natural gaze.

One thing that might help is to add a sticky note with an emoji or photo close to your camera. Instead of looking at the camera lens, you can talk to the emoji or photo.

Smile in moderation

You want to come across as approachable and friendly. A warm, confident smile will show that. Don't look overly enthusiastic or nervous by overdoing it. Let your smile project confidence and enthusiasm.

Maintain good posture

Having good posture projects confidence and strength. Avoid leaning left or right. So that you don't appear too high or too low, properly adjust your chair and sit up straight with both feet planted firmly on the ground.

Control your nervous energy

If you tend to twirl your hair, use animated hand movements, touch your face, tap your fingers, or cover your mouth whenever you get anxious, practice controlling these impulses. Remember that every slight movement becomes more magnified on screen during a video interview.

Verbal ticks such as saying "uh-huh," "you know," or "like" are annoying and distracting. The more time that you invest in conducting mock interviews, the more at ease you will become during the real ones.

Don't Google

Do not Google answers during your interview. The interviewer will be able to tell either because you'll be looking away from the camera lens or because they'll hear your keyboard or because they'll see your computer screen reflected in your glasses.

If you want to take notes during your interview, use a notepad and pen. You can prepare several questions before the interview and read them from your notes at the end of the interview.

You might need to share your desktop during the interview to show your portfolio for example. Just in case, have everything ready. You don't want an interviewer taking a look at your screen and seeing a mess or inappropriate files. Open tabs in Incognito mode. Then, if you need to search for something when you are sharing your desktop, your interviewer will not accidentally see your search history.

AFTER THE INTERVIEW

Most scheduled interviews are set for thirty to sixty minutes. But if you end sooner than the scheduled amount of time it does not mean that you failed and won't be selected for the next round or for that job.

At the end of the interview, you should always ask when you should expect any feedback and what the next step is. An interviewer should be able to give you a specific time frame for feedback or even give you feedback on the spot.

Try to stay calm even if you receive negative feedback. Thank the interviewer for the opportunity. If you were not selected for the job or were rejected, it is not the end of the world. Company representatives could still consider you for a different role that better matches your skills and experience.

Although it's normal to feel nervous, anxiety can sabotage all your hard work. Practice and proper preparation are all you need to give a stellar performance.

26. The On-site Interview

If you are lucky enough to be selected for an on-site interview, don't let luck be the only thing that gets you through. Prepare thoroughly so that you have the best chance of succeeding and getting the job you want.

The on-site interview is an important step in the hiring process because it's your first opportunity to meet your potential employer in person. It usually takes place at the company office, but it can take place in other locations as well like a coffee shop, restaurant, or hotel lobby.

Making a good first impression is important as it gives both sides a chance to see if there is good chemistry. The employer can also gain a more in-depth knowledge of how well the potential employee would "fit" with the company's work environment and culture. In other words, you only have one chance to make a good impression, so make sure you play your cards right.

If the on-site interview is your final chance to make a good impression, you need to make sure you ace it. Even if there are subsequent rounds of interviews (phone, video, or on-site interviews), the impression you leave during the on-site interview will have a major impact on the overall evaluation.

Some candidates find on-site interviews to be a stressful experience. It can be uncomfortable to navigate, but it's not impossible. With the right planning and positive attitude, you can win people over and find your next job.

Following are some tips on how to do well at an on-site interview.

BEFORE THE INTERVIEW

As with any kind of interview, you need to prepare.

Carefully Read the Job Description

Before you attend an on-site interview, read the job description of the role you are interviewing for one more time. This will remind you what skills and qualities an ideal candidate should provide, and then you'll know to look for a way to incorporate them in your interview.

From the job description, you will also learn about the responsibilities that the employee working in this role will have. And this will give you fodder for preparing several questions to ask during the interview.

Learn About the Employer

I've said it before and likely will again, but too many candidates fail to take this point seriously. Never attend an interview without doing some research about the company first, especially when it is an on-site interview.

During an interview, you will need to prove that you know the company and, more than this, that you are interested in becoming a contributor to its success.

If possible, try to learn who the interviewers are. You should receive their names from a recruiter before the interview. If you don't, contact the recruiter to ask. Once you have their names, dig up information about these people on LinkedIn. Acquiring such information can provide great advantages during an interview, so do not miss the chance to turn the odds in your favor.

You can find out a lot about your interviewer by researching them online. If they have a LinkedIn, Twitter, or Facebook profile, you can learn about their work history, education, and interests.

You can use this search string to find something about them on the web:

"Full Name" Company

Or

(filetype:pdf OR filetype:doc OR filetype:docx) "Full Name" Company

Keep the name in quotations marks and always start with the first name. Add the company name at the end. If they are working for a company with two words in their name include both words in the quotation marks: "United Airlines."

Familiarize Yourself with Interview Questions

A great way to prepare for an on-site interview is to become familiar with the most used interview questions. Once you have formulated answers, you will relax, which will enable you to think better during the interview.

Most interviews start with the question "Tell me about yourself." How you answer will make your first impression. The best way to answer it is to prepare an elevator pitch. This short, pre-prepared summary of yourself should not be longer than a few sentences but it should be longer than thirty to sixty seconds.

During the interview, you might be asked, "Why are you looking for a new job?" At the end of the interview, you will be asked questions like, "What are your salary requirements?" and "What is your availability?" It is good to be prepared for those questions before the interview so you will sound more confident when you are answering them.

Prepare a Set of Questions

Although the interviewer will ask most of the questions, do not participate in an interview without having a set of questions of your own ready as well. Doing so will prove that you are genuinely interested in the available job. Just make sure to ask pertinent questions and formulate them in a polite manner.

Questions regarding the company, the work environment, what a regular day at work looks like, potential opportunities, and the interviewer's favorite part of working for that company are good ones to ask during an interview. Wait your turn to ask questions and don't interrupt the interviewer, no matter what.

Even if you find out, during the on-site interview, that the company is not a place where you want to work, try to ask at least two to three questions at the end. It is better to make a good impression because you never know when you will have a chance to meet the interviewer again.

Asking questions in an interview will take you to the front of the queue. If there is very little time, ask one question that matters the most to you.

Prepare Some Stories

During the interview, you will get some behavioral questions asking you to share examples of your teamwork, initiative, or even leadership. It is good to think of these examples ahead of time so you don't freeze in the moment.

When you practice retelling these examples, make sure they show what value you bring to the table and the impact you will make in the company's future.

Prepare Materials to Take to the Interview

There are some items you will need to bring to the interview. A general rule is to bring along a copy of your resume, even if you already submitted one.

Take a notepad and pen with you and write down ideas during the interview. Some information provided by the interviewer you may want to remember and need to jot down. If you have business cards belonging to your past employers, having them during the interview will be good proof of previous working experiences.

If you apply for a role for which a portfolio is important, take it with you. If your portfolio is digital, do not assume that you will be able to access the Internet at the interview so download the portfolio onto your device.

Dress Properly

The way you look and present yourself is very important during an interview. This is your first in-person contact with a company representative, so you should create a good first impression. Choose clothing items that make you look like a professional. You should have a mature, capable, and trustworthy look.

A business-casual attire is what you are looking for unless you have been instructed otherwise by your employer. Get your clothes ready in advance, making sure they are clean and free of wrinkles. So, yes, ironing them is a good idea. Pick clothing that fits the climate if you are traveling for the visit because you do not want to arrive with sweaty armpits.

Be conservative and don't show too much skin.

Arrive Early

When it comes to on-site interviews, it is never a good idea to arrive late. In fact, it's not even a good idea to arrive on time. As a general rule, you should be at the set location earlier than the interview. How early is early enough? It is ideal to be there around ten to fifteen minutes before the interview start. This will give you sufficient time to find the right office for the interview, go through security check-in, and even use the restroom. Also, if you have some spare minutes review your notes.

If you feel anxious, try some square breathing to calm down and relax. Square breathing consists of rhythmic breathing based on a count of four. You inhale for four counts, you hold your breath for four, you exhale for four, and you pause for four before starting up again with inhaling for four. Repeat this process to circulate oxygen through your body and into your brain. It will help you stay alert, calm, and focused.

To get to the location in time, do some prepping. First, know the location and the route. Next, make sure you have adequate transportation to get you there. Regardless if you are driving yourself to the interview or opt for public transportation, calculate the time required to reach your destination well. Take potential traffic or service delays into consideration. You can use an application like Waze[75] to find your way easily and anticipate traffic problems.

Make sure to have the number of the recruiter or interviewer on hand so if you are late for reasons beyond your control (such as a traffic accident blocking the road), you can call to alert them.

Adopt a Positive Attitude and Remain Calm

Your attitude and state of mind count as well during an on-site interview. Even if you are enthusiastic and full of energy, being too nervous or agitated could make the interviewer think you are a person hard to handle. Also, if you are too dull and calm, the interviewer may suspect you are getting bored or you're not too interested in the job.

Try to stay positive, attentive, and engaged but also calm and relaxed. Get rid of the fear of being rejected and focus on playing the game right. Not getting the job after the interview is not the end of the world. If this happens, at least you gained another valuable experience in participating in an interview.

It is normal to feel nervous. Just make sure not to allow these feelings to overwhelm you. Remember that you are talking with another human and you have no reason to be afraid, nervous, or anxious. If you have all the skills and requirements suitable for the job, you should feel positive and confident.

Do not walk into every interview thinking you're going to impress everyone. That is too much pressure. Some interviews will go well, and some will not, and that is completely okay.

DURING THE INTERVIEW

Once you arrive on site and the interview starts, adhere to the following guidelines.

Observe Interview Etiquette

Interview etiquette is important, so be sure to greet everyone with respect when you arrive at the company. Smile and shake hands firmly with your interviewer

---

[75] https://www.waze.com/

to make a good first impression. Nothing will ruin the first impression like a sad face and limp handshake, signaling that you are nervous.

During the interview, be aware of your body language, make eye contact with the interviewers, do not interrupt them, and focus on the conversation. Remember to silence your phone so the interview is not interrupted by incoming calls and messages.

If you cope with pre-interview anxiety by chewing gum, throw it away before you enter the building.

Present Well

In today's world, it is more important than ever to make a good first impression. Whether you are meeting someone for the first time or continuing a conversation, using the first thirty seconds to your advantage can help you build a lasting impression and achieve your desired outcome.

Make Yourself Comfortable

Before the interview starts, you will be asked if you want anything to drink. I always recommend water, but tea and coffee are great too. If you don't feel thirsty, ask for water anyway so you don't have to interrupt the interview when you need it. If the interview takes a while, you won't be sitting there with a dry throat.

Address the Compensation Package

At the end of the interview, you will be asked about your expectations about the compensation package. You should be ready for this question. In your preliminary research you should have found out the typical salary range for the job.

Close the Interview

At the end of the interview, ask the interviewer what the next steps are. They will let you know if there will be another round of interviews and about how long they will need to make a decision. When you have your answer, it is time to say goodbye.

Most people end their interview with a simple "Goodbye" instead of using these last few moments to their advantage. I suggest you end the interview by saying, "Thank you for this opportunity to meet with you and learn more about your company." Not only will you be showing gratitude but you will also show your interest in their company.

AFTER THE INTERVIEW

When the interview is over, you're still not done with the process. Use the following strategies to keep your momentum going.

Send a Thank-You Note

It is always a good idea to follow up an interview with a thank-you note even though most people don't. Make sure to follow up with your thank you within twenty-four to forty-eight hours. Send the note via LinkedIn as a LinkedIn message or as a message attached to the LinkedIn connection request or via email.

Even if you know you did not land the job or you don't want to work for the company, it's important to show that you have the right attitude. Every interaction you have could have an effect on your future. The interviewers could be your next interviewers at another company. They could decide to recommend you for another job. You never know.

That is why you should keep in touch, no matter what. Leveraging LinkedIn for that is the perfect way to stay in contact with the interviewers and decision makers you met during the interview. They will also see any of your posts and activity, and some of those things could attract their attention in the future.

If this is the company where you want to work, even if you do not get the offer, continue to express interest. You never know when the next position will crop up, the position for which you are the perfect candidate.

Don't Stop Your Job Search

Even if you think that you nailed your interview and you expect an offer, don't stop your search until the moment you sign a contract. This is always a good idea, even if the recruiter contacted you with a pre-offer and told you it was a done deal. It is never a done deal until the offer is signed. Hiring decisions and job approvals, especially at larger organizations, are complex processes, and things can change at the last minute.

FINAL THOUGHTS

An on-site interview is more personal. This means you'll be under closer scrutiny and you'll have the chance to make a stronger impression and a deeper connection.

No matter what you do, try to enjoy the experience and make the most of it. I always say that every interaction we have with other people is like a small interview. We're leaving any people we meet in our daily lives with an impression of us. When you're prepared, your chances of leaving a good impression are much higher. Even if you don't get the job or an invitation for the next round, don't be discouraged. Try to find out why you didn't succeed, learn from it, and move on.

27. The Salary

One of the questions that people often find difficult to answer is, "What are your salary expectations?" This is because they are afraid that if they answer it with a number that is too high, they will be removed from consideration. If they answer with a number that is too low, they won't get as much as they could have.

Be prepared for this question when you go for a job interview. In addition to rehearsing your regular interview responses, make sure you have a good answer ready for your salary expectations. All employers will want to get your answer on this question. They will want to see whether they can afford you and how much will make you happy and motivated.

WHY COMPANIES ASK THE SALARY QUESTION

The majority of recruiters ask the question early on to save the time of their hiring managers and other people involved in the interview process. They want to know if you are within their budget and if they can afford to hire you before they invest any more time and resources in you.

If you ask for a salary that is higher than what the employer has budgeted for the position, the employer may be willing to negotiate and go beyond their budget, but the budget is a reality, and they can't use it all up on one employee.

What you have going for you in this negotiation is the value you will bring to the company. If the company perceives you as highly valuable, they may be willing to go higher. If the company cannot pay as much as you'd like, then seriously consider if it is worth accepting the offer. Remember: If multiple high-value candidates ask for a number exceeding the budgeted amount, the company will realize they need to revise their budget. They may even re-contact you with a better offer after telling you they can't meet your price. That's why it's important not to burn bridges and act badly when the first proposed offer is not what you are expecting.

The question serves multiple purposes besides quickly ruling out candidates they can't afford:

- The question is meant to check your level of self-worth. If you don't think highly enough of yourself, maybe you're not the right person for the job. After all, if you don't believe in yourself, why should anyone else?
- There are still employers who will try to get away with paying as little as possible even if the market demands more. When you answer the question with a number lower than the interviewer expected, they might see you as an opportunity to save money.
- The question also checks whether a candidate is at the right level for the available position. If you're overqualified, the company may decide it's not worth investing in you for that particular position.
- Finally, the question can also rule out inexperienced candidates. If a candidate answers with a number lower than the one given by other candidates, it can be a sign that they don't know their worth, which may be because they are inexperienced.

Taking into account your education, training, and skill set, research how much you are worth. Come up with a real value and be confident in what you have to offer.

HOW TO RESEARCH SALARIES

Never answer salary questions without doing your research! You can't answer a question about salary expectations if you don't know what the market is like. Even if you know how much you have been able to earn in a particular position, it's still worth researching to see if the market has changed.

Several websites offer information about salary ranges, but none of them is 100 percent accurate. Nevertheless, they will at least give you an idea of the going rates. Try Payscale.com, Indeed.com, Glassdoor.com, or Salary.com. You can also use search phrases like "PayScale alternatives" or "Salary.com alternative."

These websites can give you a personalized pay range based on factors like your experience in the particular field, your location, and the company you're applying to. They collect their data from various sources like previous job advertisements and site users who submit their data anonymously.

If you're willing to relocate for a job, research the cost of living in the job location. What may seem like a good salary for where you live may not go nearly as far in the new location. Also take into consideration the income taxes of the new location.

HOW TO ANSWER SALARY EXPECTATION QUESTIONS

When you are interviewing for a job, you may be asked what your salary expectations are at least once or twice. The first time you will hear this question is during a prescreening call, when a recruiter is trying to see if you are in the salary range they have for their open position. You will hear this question the second time at the end of the interview, when the hiring manager wants to check if your salary expectations have changed.

During a Prescreening Call

If you are asked about your salary during the prescreening, don't respond with a question: "What budget do you have for the role?" "What is your salary range?" The first call with a recruiter is often an introduction call, and from my experience answering the question with a question lowers your chance of getting an interview. The impression is either that you don't know the answer (which means you're unprepared) or that you simply want to get as much as you can (not necessarily an amount equal to what you're worth).

If your answer is that you don't know, expect the recruiter to push a little to get an answer.

If the recruiter insists on a number, share a salary range that is comfortable for you or that is 15 to 20 percent higher than your current salary.

You should know your value on the market. If you do, your answer can be something like, "Based on my previous experience and qualifications, I am looking for between $X and $Y as a base salary plus benefits. But I am open to discussion."

During an Interview

Expect the question again at the end of the interview with the hiring manager. The hiring manager will also double-check how your stated salary expectation has changed from what you told a recruiter during the prescreening.

If this is the first time when you are asked this question during the whole process, bear in mind that expressing your desires is not wrong, as long as you keep your expectations within a realistic range and you have good arguments for them, such as experience and skills. And that is why it is important that you spend some time on salary research.

SALARY NEGOTIATION TIPS

When you are negotiating your salary, use the following guidelines.

State a Range of Pay

Sometimes it is hard to determine a precise figure and it may feel uncomfortable to do so. Mentioning a range will be more comfortable for you and give the employer a bit of wiggle room, which makes negotiations easier. However, even if you opt for a range, make sure the difference between the minimum and maximum values is somewhere between $5,000 and $20,000, depending on location and currency. The idea is to restrain the wiggling area of the employer, so you can get closer to what you want.

Try to avoid too broad a range like $80,000 to $150,000, as this will create too much space for an employer and create the impression that you do not know your real value on the market.

You should also try to avoid saying, "My absolute minimum is . . . ." Not only will you be telling the interviewer what your lowest salary is but you will also be disclosing that you are willing to accept the minimum. In addition, you're not giving yourself any room for negotiation.

Make Room for Negotiation

Obtaining certain benefits and perks from the employer, besides a salary, is also a good way to increase the value you receive from the company. Look to benefits when the employer doesn't have the budget to fit your salary requirements. In this case, you might say, "I am looking for a job that can pay within $90,000 and $95,000 per year, but I am open to negotiating based on the availability of benefits, bonuses, stock options, and other options and opportunities."

Avoid Answering the Question

When you are asked about salary at the beginning of the recruitment process, you probably do not know that much about the responsibilities of the job. Because you don't have enough information about the role, you should postpone the discussion to the end of the interview process.

Use diplomacy to postpone an answer to this question. Give them a range but say you'll have a better answer when you know more details about the job.

You can always turn the question around. Without simply asking what the employer is offering, say, "Since I don't yet have all the details about the job, I'd love to hear about the budget for this position as well as any other types of compensation and benefits your company offers."

Not only you will avoid answering this question for a moment, but you'll be tossing the ball to their side, and you'll have bought yourself some time to learn more about their compensation structure before you give them an answer.

How to Answer Questions About Current Salary

Questions about your current salary are not polite, and in some locations they are illegal. Check the local regulations in advance so you know how to handle the question if you get asked.

Employers who ask this question want to know how to hire you by offering you a little more than you're currently making. They also want to find out what their competitors are paying their employees.

You do not have to answer this question when you are asked, because the information is not relevant to the job you will be doing. If the interviewer insists on knowing, you have several options.

The first option is to politely explain that you will bring your skills and experience to the company, and you want to focus on that more than how much you are or were earning. Say, "I would prefer to focus on what value my experience, knowledge, and skill set could bring to your company rather than my current salary."

The second option is to tell the interviewer that your current contract prevents you from sharing your salary. At the very least, this answer will show that you are a trustworthy and loyal employee. Say, "My contract prevents me from sharing my current salary with anyone, and I am a loyal employee."

The third option will help you understand the company's compensation structure. Say, "It would be very difficult for me to compare my current salary with any salary I might get for this position as I do not have enough information about benefits. If you can first share with me more about how the compensation structure looks like, I would love to answer your question."

Answers to Avoid

There are several things you should avoid when talking about your salary expectations.

Ranges of other companies

Do not bring into a discussion the salary range of the company's competitors. Many companies on the market have different compensation structures. You will only hurt your chances if you compare the company interviewing you with others.

Negative reactions

If the offered salary range is below your expectation or even below what is typical on your market, try not to react impulsively. Always act like a professional. Don't insult the interviewer by laughing, scoffing, or expressing negativity.

You never know if the company will offer you a different role, decide to go above the salary range because of your skills and experience, or reach out to you later when they have an opportunity that matches your salary expectations.

You can say this: "Thank you for sharing your range with me. I appreciate your being transparent with me so I will be transparent with you too. This amount is below my salary expectation. Based on my experience and knowledge, I am expecting between $X and $Y, with benefits."

FINAL THOUGHTS

Be prepared to negotiate and show flexibility. By showing flexibility in your answer, you will demonstrate that you are not rigid and demanding.

But it's okay to be thinking about yourself and your needs when you answer the question. Offer a range you would be happy to get and that would make you feel that you were being fairly compensated.

If you want to find out how much people in the same position or in higher positions than you are earning, you can run a simple search on Google.

Visit Google and type, **filetype:pdf "Salary Guideline" Year Location.**

Example: filetype:pdf "Salary Guide" 2022 Germany

This search string will help you find PDF files that contain the phrase **Salary Guide**, the year you added, and the location as keywords. If you want to use a more complex string that will narrow your search even further, add an intitle operator. You will need to add **intitle:term** to restrict results to documents containing the term in the title of the web page.

Example: filetype:pdf intitle:"Salary Guide" 2021 Germany

This string will help you find all PDF files that have the phrase Salary Guide in the title of the webpage and include two keywords (**2021** and **Germany**). You can replace the location with the name of the industry too.

You can also replace the phrase **Salary Guide** with the phrase **Salary Survey** or **Salary Benchmark**. These are common phrases used in salary guides published by recruitment agencies. By replacing the year and location, you will be able to find salary guides from previous years and also from other locations.

I have found that the published salary ranges are often one year behind the reality of the market. Nevertheless, they tend to be more accurate than the information on sites like PayScale and Glassdoor.

HOW TO ANSWER SALARY EXPECTATION QUESTIONS AS A FREELANCER

When you're applying for a job, one of the things you'll need to negotiate is your salary. If the job is a freelancer job, the company will likely ask you what your price is. So how do you answer this question?

The first thing you need to do is figure out what the going rate is for the work you'll be doing. You can research this online or ask people in your network who are familiar with the industry. Once you have a good idea of what the market rate is, you can start to think about what your bottom line is and what the ideal rate looks like.

Negotiating rates with a new client is never easy, and it can be even more daunting when you're trying to find work as an independent professional. You want the best price possible so your worth will show, but you don't want to scare away clients.

When it comes to negotiation, the key is always to be confident and understand your worth. If you go into a negotiation unsure of yourself, it will show, and you're likely to end up with a lower rate than you deserve.

Instead, do your homework ahead of time so that you know what other people in your field are charging for similar services. Then, when it comes time to negotiate, be prepared to argue for the rate that you believe you deserve. If you can do that, you'll be in a much better position to get the rate that you're after.

When negotiating rates, there are a few key things to keep in mind:

- Know your worth as a freelancer.
- Research the going rates for your skill set and experience level.
- Be clear about what you are willing to work for.
- Prepare to compromise.
- Remember that you can always say no if an offer is unfair.
- Remember that there are infinite clients.

The following three tips will help you get started with negotiations.

Do Your Research

Know your worth by researching what others in your field are charging for similar services. This will give you a good starting point when negotiating rates with potential clients.

As a freelancer, it's important to know your worth. If you don't value your own time and skills, no one else will. That's why it's crucial to have a bottom line, the lowest equivalent hourly rate you are willing to work for.

This is called Minimum Acceptable Rate (or MAR). Once you know your MAR, you can enter into negotiations with confidence, knowing that you will never work for less than you are worth. When setting your MAR, be sure to consider all of your costs of doing business, such as overhead, your need for benefits, and taxes. By knowing your bottom line, you will be able to stay afloat financially and avoid becoming undervalued and taken advantage of.

It's so important as a freelancer to think about the long game. So often when we're just starting out, we are driven by what we need to get by. We calculate our monthly available revenue based on our current quality of life and the bare minimum that we require to maintain that. But if we take a step back and think about where we want to be, we can begin to make decisions that will help us get there.

Our MAR should be driven by our future goals, not by our current situation. When we think about what we want to achieve, we open up new possibilities and new opportunities. We may be surprised at what we're able to accomplish.

You can research the cost of similar service you are offering via Google or sites like Upwork.com. There are many resources that can help you with negotiating rates with a new client. The Freelancer's Union[76] has an excellent guide that covers everything from setting your rates to dealing with difficult clients. There are many other helpful posts and articles that cover some of the basics of negotiating rates.

Be Confident

Remember that you are providing a valuable service and believe in the worth of your work. This confidence will come through in your negotiations and help you secure the rate you deserve.

However, it's also important to be realistic. If you're just starting out, you may not be able to command the same rate as someone who's been in the business for years. But if you provide high-quality work and build a strong reputation, you'll be in a much better position to negotiate higher rates in the future.

Be Prepared to Walk Away

When it comes to negotiating freelance rates, there are a few things you should keep in mind. First, don't be afraid to walk away from a deal if the other party isn't willing to meet your rate. Don't get upset; there's no sense in accepting less than what you're worth. It will only devalue your work in the long run.

Second, be prepared to compromise. If you're flexible on some aspects of the deal, you may be able to reach an agreement that works for both parties. However, make sure that you do not undervalue yourself or your skill set. It is also important to remember that you can always say no if you do not feel like the offer is fair.

Finally, remember that sometimes the best deals are the ones you don't make.

---

[76] https://www.freelancersunion.org/

If a potential client is being unreasonable, it may be better to walk away and look for another opportunity.

Negotiate Based on The Client's Perception of Value

Your opinion isn't particularly important when it comes to negotiating rates. What matters is what the client thinks. If you want to be successful in freelancing, you need to understand that it is all about providing value to the client.

If you don't provide them with enough value, then you will have to accept a lower price. It's as simple as that. If you want to be successful in freelancing, focus on providing a lot of value to your clients and forget about what you think your services are worth.

As a freelancer, one of the most important things you can do is to think about the value of your work to the client. How will your work benefit the client? How will it affect their bottom line? The answers to these questions will help you decide how much to charge for your services.

For example, if you're doing a web design project for a small business, you may want to consider how much money the client stands to make as a result of your work. If you can show that your work will directly increase profits, then you can justify charging a higher rate.

On the other hand, if the project is more of a "nice to have" than a "need to have," then you may need to lower your price in order to win the job. Ultimately, it's up to you to decide what value you bring to the table and how much you're worth. But by taking the time to consider both your client and the nature of the project, you'll be in a much better position to set a fair and reasonable price.

How to Ask for a Raise

If you're not getting paid what you think you deserve, it's time to have a serious discussion with your client about value-based pricing. This means focusing on the quality of your services and the value you bring to the table, rather than simply asking for a higher rate because you need the money.

When you negotiate from a place of confidence and transparency, it's much more likely that you'll be able to reach an agreement that reflects the true worth of your work. So put your clients' needs first, communicate your value clearly, and don't be afraid to ask for what you deserve. With a little effort, you'll be on your way to getting the prices that reflect your true value.

FINAL THOUGHTS

No matter what you're selling, there will always be someone who thinks it's too expensive. And that's OK! Your job is not to try to convince them that your service is worth more than they're willing to pay. Your job is to find the clients who see the value in what you're offering and are willing to pay what you're asking.

No matter what price you set for your service, some clients will still tell you no, whether it's $10 or $10,000. Your job is not to persuade the $10 clients to pay you $100. Your job is to find the ones who think $500 for your service or product is cheap and target them instead.

28. Types of Interviews and Interview Methods

You may experience different types of interviews during your job search. Each type has its own methods, styles, and techniques and its specific questions: Chatbots typically don't ask too many open-ended ones while video conferences usually do.

The type of interview hugely depends on your industry, business, and advertised position. Although I will describe these interviews separately, your interview may be a combination of types. Having prior knowledge of the nature of the job interview could help you know how to prepare, which will give you an advantage.

TYPES OF INTERVIEWS

There is a variety of methods that employers can use when conducting interviews. Some employers prefer to use a combination of methods.

Remember that for any job opening, the company needs candidates who meet the basic qualifications, which are usually screened for in the first interview. The next interview(s) is (are) usually more rigorous.

There are several types of interviews you might come across during your job search.

Video, Phone, and Online Interviews

Phone

There are two types of Phone interviews: prescreening phone interviews and regular phone interviews. The prescreening interview is usually a stepping-stone to further interviews or in-person interviews. It is cost-effective and time-saving for both the employer and the candidate. Prescreening interviews are usually short, a few minutes to half an hour long.

Prescreening calls with recruiters may be unscheduled. Recruiters may call a candidate right after reviewing their profile.

During the prescreening call, a recruiter will introduce the company, share basic information about the role, ask several questions about the experience of the candidate, and verify that the candidate possesses relevant experience for the role. At the end of the prescreening call, a recruiter will usually ask about availability and salary expectations.

Questions during a regular phone interview can range from questions about skills and experience to behavioral questions. One great thing about phone interviews is that they reduce the chances of bias since the interviewer cannot see the candidate, and candidates are more likely to perform well on them because the phone interview seems more casual.

Before your phone interview, find a quiet place to take the call, and have your resume and other credentials nearby. Take a few deep breaths and compose yourself as if the interviewer is in the room with you.

These phone interviews usually take between thirty and sixty minutes.

Video

There are two types of video interviews: one-way and two-ways. For one-way video interviews, the employer sends text-based or video prerecorded interview questions to candidates and asks them to record their answers via webcam or phone. In most cases, candidates are given a time limit for each answer. The video answers are reviewed by a recruiter, hiring manager, or external partner after candidates submit them.

One advantage of these types of interviews is that candidates can take them anytime and almost anywhere. However, there are some disadvantages too. For example, if the candidate is not sure what the question is asking, they can't get anyone to help them.

Many companies use a two-way video interview as the next step after the prescreening call with the recruiter. The two-way interview can be done via Skype, Microsoft Teams, WebEx, Zoom, or any other recording application.

This type of interview is often the preferred method for interviewing candidates remotely, especially when the candidates are located in a different area. They were the only and preferred interview option during the Covid pandemic.

When you are invited for a video interview, you should join the call a few minutes before it starts. Since you probably won't have the company's application installed on your computer, showing up early gives you time to install all necessary applications. These interviews usually run from half an hour to an hour.

Chatbot

Some companies use chatbots to prescreen candidates. The system is supposed to be faster and less biased than other types of interviews, but some candidates say it's just like filling out a registration form.

The interview process is simple. You will be sent a link with an interactive window (chat room) after you submit an application online or after your resume is prescreened by a recruiter. You may be sent an email with step-by-step instructions on how to start the interview.

When you are interviewed by a chatbot, you will be asked to respond to several prescreening questions. It is important to be aware that your writing skills will be evaluated since you will be texting your answers, so make sure to proofread your responses for mistakes and use proper grammar. Making too many mistakes or using too many abbreviations could hurt your chances of being invited for the next round of interviews.

Chatbot interviews do not have specific time limits.

Portfolio-based interviews

Portfolio-based interviews are mostly connected with job positions in the communication, design, digital, art, or architecture industries. You will be asked to provide or show your portfolio and answer questions related to that portfolio. In most cases, you will share your portfolio ahead of the on-site or online interview. If the interview is online, you might be asked to share your portfolio during a video call.

Make sure that your content and presentations are up to date, and always try to start with the work that is most relevant to the job and the company you will be interviewing with. You may be unable to share some of your previous work because of nondisclosure agreements. If you do share that work, do it by creating a password-protected page on your website. That way Google will be unable to index it and your current employer will not discover that you are trying to get another job.

Phone, video, and portfolio-based prescreening interviews usually take between ten and thirty minutes. Regular interviews run between twenty and ninety minutes.

ON-SITE INTERVIEWS

On-site interviews are usually held in the employer's office. They can last anywhere from half an hour to several hours. During the on-site interview, candidates can expect to meet several representatives from the company and to be asked several types of interview questions via different interview styles.

The company may invite the candidate for a coffee, lunch, or short office tour after the main interview. This is also part of the interview process, as company representatives want to see how the candidate interacts with potential colleagues.

When you are invited for an interview, always try to research on LinkedIn the people you will be meeting with. This will help you understand their seniority and roles in the company.

Different types of on-site interviews serve different purposes. Knowing what to expect can help you present yourself in the best way possible and increase your chances of getting the job.

Informational interviews

An informational interview is a form of one-on-one conversation in which a candidate collects information about the desired job and checks expectations. Performance pressure and interview-related stress are usually absent from this method of interviewing as it gives candidates the chance to interact freely with current employees in similar roles. Candidates can use what they learn to make a decision about whether to accept a job offer.

During this type of interview, you can meet company representatives (not just the recruiter or hiring manager) and obtain information about the company and its process, products, and culture. Keep in mind that even though this is just an informational interview, the employer could still use it to assess your fit for the job. One reward of informational interviews is the opportunity for candidates to focus and plot their career paths and aspirations. The interview might give you an inside look at what a regular day in the company or industry looks like.

Dress professionally as you would for a formal job interview. If you have a work portfolio, bring it with you so you can discuss it during your meeting and even ask for feedback on it.

Prepare the questions you would like to ask, questions about the corporate culture, the typical workday, industry trends, and management style. Also prepare your responses to likely questions about your skills, work experience, and career plans. Perform deep research on the inner workings of the organization and industry trends so you can pose insider questions that can't be answered easily by visiting a website.

When in an informational interview, getting an immediate job offer isn't really the goal. Your primary objective is to learn more information and build some sort of relationship with the interviewers. You need them to get to know you and see your enthusiasm for their company.

Even if after the informational interview you no longer have interest in pursuing a position with a company, remember to follow up with a simple email or thank-you letter. It will go a long way toward cementing the great impression you made during the interview.

These interviews are in most cases less than half an hour, but they can run longer if you're having a discussion over coffee, for example.

One-on-one interviews

A one-on-one interview—sometimes called an *individual* or *traditional interview*—is a common type of interview with just one interviewer and a candidate. This interview type is easy to set up and offers the chance for the candidate and employer to build rapport.

Indeed, rapport building is the goal of such interviews. The employer gets to know you and you get to know them and the company.

Expect questions about your resume and your previous experience. Because you have a limited amount of time to make an impact on the interviewer, you need to emphasize the qualities the company requires. The interview will likely take between thirty and sixty minutes.

For the company there is a risk of making a wrong selection when relying on the one-on-one interview since only one person is getting to know you. This is why most companies use multiple interview rounds or panel interviews.

Panel interview

A panel interview is conducted by a group or panel of interviewers. The objectives of such interviews are to gather multiple perspectives concerning the candidate and to save time.

The panel will have already prepared a set of questions for each candidate. Each panel member may be involved with posing questions relevant to their position in the company. As each panel member takes a turn asking prepared questions, an interviewer may also interject on-the-spot questions. The decision about the candidate is reached through consensus.

You need to be clear and accurate with your answers. Remember to make eye contact with each interviewer.

Since numerous people are involved, each with specific questions to ask, expect the panel interview to last anywhere from sixty to ninety minutes.

Serial interviews (sequential interviews)

A serial interview requires a candidate to meet with multiple interviewers in succession, not all at once. The first interview is to gauge whether the candidate meets the basic requirement for the position. The candidate may then be passed on for a one-to-one or panel type of interview or tested with a behavioral or task interview method.

Companies usually prefer to conduct serial interviews in a single day. Because the interviews require candidates to clear a series of levels to prove their competence and efficiency in multiple areas, the serial interview helps the employer hire with precision.

The key for the candidate in a serial interview is to provide good and *consistent* answers. After the interviews, interviewers will meet to deliberate, uncover inconsistencies, and reach a consensus on whom to hire.

One disadvantage of a serial interview is that, if done in a single day, it may be very tiring for even the most capable candidates as it can take several hours.

Group interview

Group interviews involve one or more interviewers and a group of candidates. A company may conduct a group interview with the aim of quickly prescreening candidates for the job opening and also giving said candidates the opportunity to get a feel for the company.

Typically, a group interview starts with a short presentation regarding the company. Next, the interviewer may speak individually to candidates, asking each a few questions.

During a group interview, the interviewer is particularly interested in observing your interaction with the other candidates, checking if you are a focused task finisher or an emerging leader with delegation skills. You will want to demonstrate the skills required by the particular role. These interviews typically last for one to two hours.

Behavioral-based interview

This method is popular among interviewers because it goes way deeper than other interviewing techniques. This type of interview takes into account candidates' performances in past experiences to predict future behavior. By focusing on past performance, the employer gets a glimpse of the candidate's abilities, skills, and personality.

Behavioral-based interview questions focus on areas such as communication, teamwork, problem-solving, dealing with stressful situations, and organizational skills.

The best framework for answering any behavioral questions is the STAR technique. The STAR method is a technique of answering behavioral interview questions in a structured manner by describing a specific Situation, Task, Action, and Result of the situation you are discussing.

While you can use the STAR method for any interview question, it's most useful for answering behavioral interview questions.

Behavioral-based interviews usually take between thirty and ninety minutes.

Case interviews

Another common type of interview method is the case interview. In such interviews, a scenario is presented to the candidate and the candidate is expected to provide a proper solution to the question, alternative answers, or more suggestions.

Used mostly by tech companies, investment banks, and management consulting companies, a case interview assesses analytical skills in real-time and in a pressure-filled environment.

In some case scenarios, the interviewer may be in search of a candidate capable of executing long-term strategies. And in other case scenarios, the interviewer may be looking for a calm and composed candidate ready for any emergency. Critical thinking and planning are at the heart of these interviews. The questions may include anything from estimation exercises and business problems to logic questions and arithmetic.

Remember that getting it right is not the primary aim of the case interview. Often, in fact, there are no specific answers to the case questions. Instead, the task is meant to showcase your ability to handle stress and the way you think and reason.

Because the employer wants to place you as a potential colleague who can work with an engagement team, the interviews are quite interactive. You should be able to seek clarification, ask questions, and exchange ideas.

Usually, case interviews are one-on-one engagements. As the interviewer may begin the task by presenting a lot of information, you should take notes. You will also likely be given tools for brainstorming and calculation. After the interview, some firms will collect your handwritten notes to assess your performance.

To ensure that you are on the right track and have a common understanding of the question's requirements, be sure to seek clarification on the details. The interviewer may step away to give you space to think, but they will be on hand to give additional information, answer questions, and provide guidance through the problem.

Try to remain relaxed and confident, whatever the scenario. It is natural to feel anxious or flummoxed during a case interview, but part of the test involves keeping your cool, no matter what.

Case interviews range from about thirty to sixty minutes. The case question itself can last from about twenty to forty minutes.

Task-oriented or testing interview

During this type of interview, candidates are asked to complete a task that will demonstrate their abilities—usually their problem-solving ability.

Sometimes candidates are asked to take a short test. For example, if the role requires a good knowledge of Excel, candidates might be asked to solve a task that involves Excel to demonstrate their knowledge of the program.

Some companies conduct these tests by sending candidates an assignment to do at home.

On-site tests usually take between ten and sixty minutes. At-home assignments can range from one hour up to several days.

Lunch interviews

Lunch interviews are usually the last stage of the interview process. Their goal is to test the social skills and fit of candidates. One or more interviewers take the candidate to lunch or coffee to get to know the candidate better. As the interview is very much unstructured, the interviewer is prepared to observe candidate behavior in an informal atmosphere, like a restaurant, where both parties are at ease.

In lunch interviews, candidates have the opportunity to ask the interviewer questions concerning the firm or the job. Lunch interviews are a good platform for showing your industry smarts through impressive questions, so prepare in advance.

Remember not to order very expensive items or choose food that is difficult and messy to eat. Don't ask to take your leftovers home with you.

Brush up on your table etiquette if necessary. Sometimes, it's the small stuff that counts in lunch interviews. Because the interviewer could ask a question while you have a mouthful of food, eat small bites and chew as quietly as possible.

Lunch interviews veer on casual: Jokes and banters may fly in such a neutral environment. But do not be too playful or even too stiff. Show the employer your best qualities by emphasizing the characteristics the company is looking for. Stay calm and polite.

Since the candidate is not expected to foot the bill for the launch interview, you do not need to offer to pay. If you offer to pay your bill, your request will be rejected but it might earn you a few extra points.

Even when company representatives take you to lunch to meet the team, and the experience doesn't seem to be part of the interview process, it is.

Lunch interviews usually take between one and two hours.

Stress interviews

This type of interview is not as popular as it was in past, yet some employers still use it to assess their candidates. Stress interviews are designed to see how a candidate will respond to stressful situations. In such interviews, the interviewer may suddenly ask an out-of-the-blue question without giving the candidate sufficient time to think. The interviewer may even interrupt your response jut to throw you off.

The goal is to see if you would perform well under stress. Candidates may be tested on how they handle argumentative-style questions, long awkward silences, or even sarcasm.

Knowing that you are in a stress interview is the key to beating it. Do not take the questions personally. Measure when to hold back and when to push back. Remain focused and calm and do not be tempted to react hastily even though the interviewer is. When you need clarification, ask for it.

This interview type does not work well for all jobs. In addition, the employer might miss out on a potentially capable candidate just because they did not perform well on a mock stress test.

Luckily, this type of interview is not very common.

The stress part might take only ten to thirty minutes of an hour-long interview.

The Career fair interview

You can expect this type of interview at career fairs. They are designed to prescreen as many candidates as possible during the event. Employees will conduct short one-on-one interviews with candidates. These interviews are usually announced ahead of the event, with recruiters reaching out to potential candidates via LinkedIn and via their resume databases.

These interviews are not very long, usually between ten and twenty minutes.

Mock interviews

A mock interview gives you an opportunity to practice for a real interview and get feedback on your performance and your answers. You can involve a recruiter, career coach, family member, colleague, or friend to help you.

Career coaches and agency recruiters use mock interviews to prepare their clients for a real interview.

FINAL THOUGHTS

The ways companies interview candidates are always changing. The type of interview that is right for a company depends on the job position, the interviewer, or the company's principles.

Whatever the interview type, the best put the candidate and interviewer at ease, so that both parties can have a transparent and honest conversation to pave the way for a quality hiring and long-term association.

The best way to prepare for an interview is to do your research and to try to understand what the company is looking for in a candidate.

29. Types of Interview Questions

If you have interviewed before, you know that most recruiters ask similar questions. They have a set of questions that they find effective, and they use them year after year. During an interview, you will likely be asked behavioral, situational, competency, and case-related questions. Your answers to these questions must show the interviewer that you are the best fit for the job and the company.

To prepare for a job interview, it is best to research the types of questions that are commonly asked by interviewers at the company. You can find this information on sites like Glassdoor, where people share their interview experiences and the questions they were asked.

If you don't have any friends or acquaintances working at the company, try researching the company online and see if they have posted any blog articles about the interview process.

Following are the most common types of questions and tips on how to handle them.

Classic Interview Questions

The following are some questions that employers typically ask during interviews. If you have interviewed with several different companies, you will likely recognize many of them. These questions are usually asked at the beginning of the interview (such as questions about your background) or in the middle (such as questions about your strengths and weaknesses). They are meant to help the employer learn more about you and your motivations, strengths, weaknesses, passions, and working style.

Here are some classic questions:

- Can you tell us about yourself?
- What motivates you?
- What are your strengths?

- What are your weaknesses?
- Why did you apply for this job?

The interviewer may also ask about other aspects of your LinkedIn profile or resume in order to get a fuller picture of you as a candidate. They want to see if you can talk in detail about your experiences and qualifications. When answering these classic questions, you have an opportunity to share more about yourself as a person.

Behavioral Questions

Some employers may be looking for candidates with particular behavioral traits, such as being able to handle stress or resolve conflicts. Behavioral questions help employers predict how an applicant would behave in a certain situation and also to learn how they handled challenges or duties in their previous jobs. Many recruiters and hiring managers find these questions valuable, so I am going to share more information about them in the next chapter, including examples of the questions and how to answer them.

Situational Questions

Situational interview questions are related to the situations that you may face while being in the workplace. They are similar to behavioral interview questions, but situational questions are hypothetical and not based on your actual experiences. Situational questions generally involve finding out how you would handle tough and complicated issues in the workplace.

Competency Questions

The interviewer will ask you questions about your skills and abilities in order to find out if you are competent for the job. They will ask you about your abilities in specific areas and will want to know how you have used these skills in the past to achieve results.

You can demonstrate your competency in any area of your life. Competency-based questions are often asked in interviews for entry-level jobs. This is because for those jobs practical ability is more important than qualifications, experience, and achievements.

One way to prove that you have the qualities and skills mentioned in a job description is to provide specific examples of times when you have demonstrated those qualities.

Character Questions

The interviewer may ask you about your values and character. There may also be questions about your behavior. Your answers to questions about your character will help the employer make judgments about your morals and integrity.

Here are a few typical examples of such questions:

- Tell us about your core values.
- What was the last time you got angry and why?
- Tell us about a time when you handled a difficult person.

There are several ways to answer character questions successfully:

- Learn about the company values before the interview.
- When you are answering the questions, tie your answers in with the company values.
- Show that you can work well with others as a team.
- Appreciate the positive work ethic. Remove any negative comments from your answers.
- Emphasize the point that you are fully capable of doing the job.
- Demonstrate your capability to handle tough situations and show that you are flexible and coachable.

Character questions are very often part of behavioral questions when the interviewer is trying to learn about you from your past experience.

Career Goal Questions

These interview questions are typically aimed at candidates who are changing careers or have recently graduated. However, that doesn't mean they can only be asked in those circumstances.

The employer asks these questions to learn about your long-term career plans. They want to know where you are at present in your professional life and where you are aiming to be in the future. The employer wants to know if this job is just a stepping stone for you to achieve your professional goals or if you are planning to stick with this job for a long time.

Here are a few examples of career goal questions:

- Why do you want to work for our company?
- What is your dream job?
- Where do you see yourself in the next five years?

The question "Where do you see yourself in the next five years?" was popular among interviewers before 2015 as a way to identify if a person would stay with the company. Some people believe that this question is no longer relevant, because the answer can change and companies should focus on the present skills of the applicant.

To answer such questions effectively, it is important to know about the company and its future goals. This is because your answer should reflect that your future goals align with the company's future goals. Therefore, be sure to do some preparation on this topic before going for your interview.

Many interviewers ask this question to understand your career ambitions. If you are expecting fast career progress and planning to seek yet another job soon, they might feel threatened by your answer and not move forward with your application.

That's why it is always good to answer something like, "It would be great to stay in this company for five years and learn new things while helping my team with anything related to my job position."

Interpersonal Skills Questions

Almost every job out there involves working with people. There are very few examples of jobs that don't require any human contact. So knowing how to interact with people of all kinds and personalities is extremely important, regardless if they are your colleagues, managers, customers, or collaborators.

The interviewer will likely try to ensure that you have the required interpersonal skills. They will likely ask questions about your interpersonal skills, regardless of the level or type of job you are interviewing for. No one wants to hire someone who doesn't have good people skills because they are difficult to work with and tend to develop a negative reputation.

Questions Specific to the Job

When applying for a job, be prepared to answer questions about your skills and abilities that are related to the specific job. For example, if you're applying for a job as a salesperson, you may be asked about your negotiating skills and selling abilities. If you are looking to get hired as a manager, the interviewer may ask questions about your experience, management style, and past accomplishments.

Communication Skills Questions

Having great communication skills is important in any profession. No matter what you're doing—whether you're working with a team, collaborating with coworkers and other departments, or solving customer problems—good communication skills are essential.

The employer will want to see how well you can communicate in difficult situations. If you don't understand a question or are unsure how to answer it, take a few extra seconds to check with the interviewer to make sure you are on the same page. You can say, "As I understand it, you want me to talk more about ____. Is that correct?"

Creativity Questions

Creativity questions are often asked in interviews for jobs that require a high level of creativity. This type of question is also common in group interviews. Because the interviewer wants to know how you think on your feet and how you handle pressure, the questions will be designed to put you in a slightly uncomfortable situation. By asking such questions, the interviewer also wants to assess your creativity in solving a situation.

Here are a few examples of creativity questions:

- If you were a dessert, what dessert would you be?
- If you could only read one book for the rest of your life, what would it be?
- What would you title your autobiography?
- Who is your role model and why?
- Sell this pen to me.
- What was the last great idea you had?

To answer such questions, it is recommended that you take a deep breath and think about why the interviewer is asking you the question. Keep in mind that the reasoning skills and creativity you show are more important than your actual answer.

Some questions might sound irrelevant to you. That's because employers want to learn if you're capable of answering hypothetical questions on the spot, so be prepared for that.

Questions Regarding the Company's Culture

Many companies these days embrace and promote a particular culture at the workplace. You can often find more information about their cultures on their career websites and social media. When these companies are looking to hire new employees, they ask questions to determine whether the candidate being interviewed is a good fit for the company culture. For example, in a company with an open floor plan in which people don't have their own offices and spend a lot of time collaborating at each other's workstations, an interviewer might ask you questions about how well you work with ambient noise and distractions.

To prepare, research the company's culture and ask yourself if you could work in those conditions.

Location Questions

If you are not located in the same city or country as the hiring company, expect questions regarding your location:

- Are you open to relocation?
- When are you moving to our country/state/city?
- Are you moving with your family? (This one is quite tricky since the interviewer shouldn't be asking, but sadly it is still happening.)

In several countries, questions about location are illegal. Your answers could bias employers against you. For example, if the interviewer asks you if you will be relocating with your family, and you say, yes, you will be bringing your six kids, the company may decide not to hire you because they're afraid your kids will be a distraction. Or if the company asks where you live and you say that you live in a rural area but are excited to relocate to the city, the company may decide you couldn't possibly have enough relevant experience in tech if you've been working in a rural area.

Management/Leadership Interview Questions

In interviews for jobs with a management role, you will be asked questions about your management skills, past management experience, and managerial accomplishments. They will also want to know about your leadership style.

Brainteaser and Problem-Solving Questions

Questions like "How many golf balls would fit into a Boeing 747?" or "How many windows are in New York City?" are very popular among Silicon Valley tech companies.

If you encounter this type of brainteaser, the best way to approach it is to break it down into smaller pieces and describe how you would go about solving it. These brainteaser interview questions often don't have one solution; the recruiter or hiring manager is trying to see how you would solve it and how you think through problems.

You should always stay calm and not start arguing with an interviewer if they ask a nonsensical question. Don't worry about the question; focus more on finding a method for achieving a solution. Describe the way you would solve it.

Informal Questions

With informal questions, the interviewer is trying to find out more about your personal interests and how they might fit with the company culture. They may ask about your hobbies or things you like to do in your free time. This is common for smaller organizations or startups.

That is why it is important to learn about the company and its activities before the interview so you can better understand their company culture.

 Some companies use informal questions as a way to find out if you have a family (kids). If they are looking for somebody who will be working 24/7 for them and you have a child, they will likely look for another candidate who will have more time. Be careful not to give that kind of information; it is illegal in many places to ask you directly so you should be able to answer the question without giving too much away.

Questions About Leaving the Job

If you are interviewing for a new job or company, the interviewer will likely ask you questions about why you're leaving your current job. They want to understand your motivation. Your answer will help them understand if there is a possibility that you will leave them suddenly for the same reasons you are leaving your current workplace.

If you have left your job, the interviewer will want to know why. If you were fired or laid off, they will want to know why as well. If you have been between jobs for several months, you may be asked about your activities during that period and why you were not successful in finding a job so far.

It is very important not to talk badly about your last employer at this stage! This could build mistrust and show a side of yourself that you may not wish to show at this point, so keep it professional.

> If you are between jobs for several months and you don't know how to explain that gap in your resume, there are several ways to answer this question. My recommendation is not to say that you've been out of a job because you haven't yet found anything good or you haven't had luck. Even if it's true, this will put you in a bad light. Instead, talk about taking a career break or time to learn new skills.
>
> Some people explain that they took a career break after a long time working so they could travel, spend time with their family (or take care of a family member), or just rest and learn new skills. They explain that the career break has given them a chance to recharge their batteries and come back with a fresh perspective.
>
> One of my friends didn't have luck finding a job. He kept saying that to employers when they asked about the break in his career. Once he started saying that he was taking care of family members, nobody questioned this answer and he found a job within two weeks.

Salary-Related Interview Questions

The interviewer will usually ask about your current salary and salary expectations toward the end of the interview. How can you ask for a salary that's fair to you without pricing yourself out of a job opportunity?

When you are asked to provide your salary information, always give a range and never just a single salary. For example, say, "I am looking for between $X and $Y." Do not mention that X is your minimum, and it shouldn't be the real minimum that you need anyway. The X should be at least 10 to 15 percent above your real minimum.

If you don't know how much you should be asking for, try to find out what people in similar positions are making. Most companies have a salary range for their roles, so if you're not sure if you're asking for too much, you can say, "My salary expectation is between $X and $Y. Is this within the salary range/budget for this role?"

When you are asked, be honest, not greedy, and take your experience, training, and qualities into account. Do your research about the salary for a job you are interviewing for.

In several locations in the world, asking about salary is prohibited. But even if it is permitted, you don't have any obligation to reveal your current salary. If the interviewer is pushing you to reveal it, the best way is to mention that based on your contract you can't share your salary. This will not only show that you are somebody who is following rules, but it will stop those types of question.

FINAL THOUGHTS

Job interviews can be nervewracking, especially if you're not sure what to expect. One of the best ways to prepare is to familiarize yourself with the most common types of questions and how to answer them. For example, many interviewers will ask about your experience and qualifications.

Be prepared to talk about your relevant work history and explain why you're the best candidate for the job. Another common question is about your strengths and weaknesses. Be honest about your weaknesses but focus on how you're working to improve them. And be sure to highlight your strengths that are relevant to the job you're applying for.

Finally, interviewers often ask behavioral questions designed to gauge how you would handle real-world situations. Be ready with examples of times when you've demonstrated the skills they're looking for. If you go into an interview armed with this knowledge, you'll be more likely to impress the interviewer and land the job you want.

30. Behavioral Interview Questions

Most job interviews will include behavioral questions. These are questions that ask you to describe how you have handled certain situations in the past. For example, an interviewer might ask you to describe a time when you had to deal with a difficult customer. Behavioral questions are designed to give the interviewer a sense of how you would handle similar situations if they were to arise in the job.

Knowing how to answer behavioral questions can help you stand out from other candidates and increase your chances of getting the job. When preparing for your interview, take some time to think about how you would answer common behavioral questions. This will help you feel more confident and poised when it comes time to answer them in the interview. With a little preparation, you can ace the behavioral portion of your interview and increase your chances of getting the job you want.

These questions are popular among recruiters and hiring managers regardless of the size of the company or industry. The aim of behavioral questions is to assess the thoughts, skills, and attitudes of candidates. The questions are based on the idea that past behavior is a good indicator of future behavior.

In today's job market, interviewers want to know how you have handled difficult situations in the past and how you would approach similar challenges in the future. Your answers can help them predict how you will work for them.

The questions are typically scenario-based.

The interviewer may ask how you approached a situation.

HOW TO PREPARE FOR A BEHAVIORAL INTERVIEW

There are several ways to prepare yourself for these questions. One of the best ways is to use the STAR technique. Instead of trailing off-topic or rambling your way through each question, you can follow the four-step STAR framework to formulate your answer in a thoughtful and thorough manner.

STAR stands for **S**ituation, **T**arget/**T**ask, **A**ction, **R**esult:

- **Situation**—Describe the situation in which the event took place and provide some high-level context.
- **Target**—Identify the goal and barriers to achieving it.
- **Action**—Describe what action you took to complete the task or solve the problem you were describing.
- **Result**—Describe the outcome of your actions.

If possible, always provide specific examples of how your effort has had a positive effect and share a quantitative result, such as a 25 percent cost saving or $2 million in revenue.

Let's look at some tips for how to answer behavioral questions.

Don't Forget to Prepare

Preparation is the key. That's why you should do a deep review of common behavioral interview questions before the interview. Practice and review your answers, ensuring that you will have ready answers to any behavioral-based interview questions thrown at you.

Don't Be in a Hurry to Answer

Never jump into replying to a question; there is nothing wrong with taking a moment to gather your thoughts. Take a deep breath or just pause for a second or two to calm your nerves and ruminate on an appropriate example that answers the question.

Get Inspiration from the Job Description

Always check the job description! If the job description explains that the role requires a person who will bring creative solutions to problems, you should prepare several examples of you bringing creative solutions and how those helped your employers. Job descriptions are full of clues about what is important to the company and what interviewers may be asking during their interviews.

Remain Optimistic

Sometimes behavioral interview questions ask you to talk about a past failure or problem at a workplace. Nobody wants to start out by remembering their failures. But try to be optimistic, don't talk only about negatives, and explain the issue or problem you tackled and how you addressed it and what the result was. Even if you didn't solve the issue at the end, don't highlight the negative. Do a quick shift to talking about what you learned from the situation and how you applied that learning to a subsequent situation with a successful outcome.

Have Some Great Stories to Talk About

Some behavioral questions will ask you to recall a tough situation at work. Prepare in advance by listing difficult workplace situations you faced. Then create a list of steps that you took to help resolve each problem. Assemble some tales you can tell briefly.

Then expand your list to include occasions when you have been able to tackle challenges or help drive a fruitful workplace partnership. Think about how open you are to fresh concepts, how skilled you are at trying to fix problems, and what insights you can draw on.

Imagine the interviewer asks you, "How do you manage to convey your feelings when you profoundly disagree with team members?" You've certainly already experienced a dispute with a boss or colleague. How did you handle it? Maybe the difference in opinion spurred you on to come up with a different solution agreeable to everyone. Maybe you were able to calmly state your opinion and then accept that you weren't going to get your way. Share your thinking process and communication process. Tell how you helped resolve the difference in opinion positively. Hiring executives want to hear about your job experiences in actual situations because they are searching for clues to how you will act when you're working for them. So help them find those clues.

Quantify When Possible

Another standard behavioral interview question is, "Explain how and when you established an achievable work project and were able to accomplish your goal."

Did you boost the website traffic of your business, or find an innovative way to reduce quarterly expenses or hit gigantic sales numbers? When you talk about the approaches you used to achieve the outcomes, use numbers wherever possible to show your performance. Numbers give weight to your achievements.

Imagine Potential Work Situations in the New Job

Interviewers may ask you, not only about how you have responded to problems in the past, but also about how you might react to new challenges in the future. It is difficult to prepare for such questions because they require you to talk about something that hasn't happened yet. But you can prepare somewhat by imagining situations that might arise in the new role.

Take some time to picture what might happen and how you might respond. For example, imagine you have a managerial background, but the new job will differ in that part of what you will be managing is use of a key technology in the company. What would happen if one day the technology broke down and the employees were unable to use it? How would you respond to that situation? Think through a process for addressing the imaginary problem. When you answer a question about a potential instead of experienced situation, make sure to show the interviewer your process for approaching it. That will matter more than the specific solutions you can invent on the spot.

Here's a question from a mock situational interview: "How will you react to a customer who claims that you made a mistake?" Whether or not you have made an error is not the right focus. Instead, concentrate on the solution. The interviewer needs to know not that you never would have made the error in the first place, but how you will handle an upset customer who believes you have made a mistake. Talk about the steps you might take to deal with the situation.

Here's another example: "How will you deal with a task assigned to you for which you lack the necessary abilities or experience?" A successful response is one that highlights your effort, resourcefulness, and desire to succeed. This could mean pursuing leadership development, finding an informed colleague, or collecting the necessary information systematically to complete the task.

BEHAVIORAL INTERVIEW QUESTION EXAMPLES

What follows are some popular questions you might be asked in a behavioral interview along with suggested answers. Review the questions and think about how you would respond if asked.

Remember that interviewers, whether they are hiring managers or recruiters, want to learn about your real-life work experiences. They are looking for clues about how you'll behave in the future based on your past actions. Always try to be specific and provide concrete examples.

If you come across a challenge, how do you handle it?

What they want to know: Problems occur. You cannot altogether avoid them. So how will you respond when they do?

Response: My leader had to leave town due to a family emergency, and at that time we were stuck in the middle of a difficult discussion with a new investor. From the little bit of information she had written before leaving and with some guidance from our leadership, I was entrusted with bringing together a PowerPoint presentation. Even though I did not have all the necessary information, I worked with my team and we were able to put together a presentation that made a positive impact. We got the funding, and I was also recommended for the company management award.

Question: Give an example of a goal you have recently achieved and how you did it.

What they want to know: The interviewer wants to know if you have the skills and mindset to pursue and accomplish a specific goal. They want to make sure you are determined enough to set goals and achieve them.

Response: I decided to win the Employee of the Month award when I began working for X Company. It was a challenge even though it was not taken that seriously by all the staff. The reason I wanted it is I wanted to understand what it takes to be an exemplary employee. I provided exceptional support to my boss and clients. I looked for ways to go above and beyond and followed through. Throughout, I made sure to keep enjoying the job and the people with whom I worked to make sure that I demonstrated the right attitude. I received the award in the third month I was there. It was great to accomplish my goal, and because of my good outlook and persistence, I eventually ended up progressing into a management role there fairly fast.

Question: Can you share an example of how you were able to motivate a coworker or your team?

What they want to know: Your answer will give the interviewer an idea about your leadership skills. Also, this will show them the strategies you used to achieve your goal and the results of your actions.

Response: My team member was struggling to achieve their KPI. Their motivation was quite low due to a series of declined projects by our client.

I offered to analyze why their projects were rejected more than the projects of other colleagues. We had several late-night meetings and identified a few key issues. We also quantified the results and in so doing discovered that the number of unsuccessful projects was still quite small compared to the number of successful ones. We set goals and milestones. And it worked like a miracle. Within the next two months the project acceptance doubled from that of the previous two months.

Question: Explain how you have managed to work well under pressure.

What they want to know: The interviewer wants to know about your work efficiency. They want to know if you can perform well if you are given a high-pressure job.

Response: I was working on a project expected to be delivered to the customer within sixty days. One day my boss said that I had to submit it in forty days. I met with my employees to divide up the remaining work in the time that was left. By approaching it this way we essentially added only a few hours to each person's plans, and we completed the job in thirty-eight days. The efficient task assignment made a big difference, and I had wonderful individuals to collaborate with.

Question: How have you handled your mistakes?

What they want to know: No one is perfect, and we all tend to make mistakes. The interviewer is not looking to hear you say that you never make mistakes. Instead, they want to know how you respond when you do.

Response: One time, I misinterpreted the club's charges for one type of membership. When I discovered the error, I told my boss about it. He told me to refund the new member's application fee. Despite my error, the new member was happy with our resolution, my boss knew that I was honest and conscientious, and although I felt bad that I had made a mistake, I learned from it to pay careful attention to the membership specifics. In addition, I proposed a change to the employee training manual to highlight the potential for this error so that future employees wouldn't repeat my mistake. My boss happily updated the manual.

Question: Half of your team is sick. You're in the middle of an important project for your client that is close to a deadline. How would you handle this situation?

What they want to know: Interviewers are trying to find out how creative you can be in your approach to this situation. They'll want to know if you are going to act as a team player and involve the rest of the team or if you will decide to handle the problem yourself.

Response: I will call a meeting with the healthy half of the team so we can evaluate what we need to finish to deliver the project to our client. Based on that analysis, I will decide what to do next. If we need to add a few extra working hours, I will assign this work to myself and several members of my team. I will also reward them with a bonus after the project is delivered. If the project is going to require more work and is impossible to deliver on time, I will contact our client to explain the situation and discuss options.

Question: Tell us about how you set goals.

What they want to know: The interviewer is trying to assess how well you are able to prepare and set your targets and goals in your work life. They'll want to know how you set them up, whether and how you track them, and if you focus on short-term goals, long-term goals, or a combination.

Response: I thought that within several months of starting my initial job as a sales associate in a shopping mall I needed to be part of the fashion industry. I figured that I could surely make my way up to shift supervisor, and by then I would have made enough money to be able to attend a full-time design school. I did this alone, but through an internship I secured the summer before college, I was also able to land my first job.

FINAL THOUGHTS

Interviewers formulate questions to assess how successful an applicant would be in a specific role. Based on answers and examples from the candidate's career, the interviewer makes a decision.

If you're not sure how to answer behavioral questions, start rehearsing with your friends, ask a career coach or recruiter for help, and use the STAR method. You can also find out what hard and soft skills companies want for the job from the job description, and use actual examples and scenarios from your career to demonstrate both types of skills.

31. Most Common Interview Questions

Different interviewers have different question styles, but most ask common questions, looking for specific answers. Although they will ask behavioral questions as they can provide insight into your personality traits and how you handle situations, most interviewers will use other types of questions as well.

THE MOST COMMON QUESTIONS

The questions you are asked during an interview are heavily dependent on your skill set and the position you are applying for. But what follows are the most common questions. I have also added the one question that most candidates hate so much, that many recruiters have finally stopped asking it.

Question: What do you know about our organization?

This is often the first question you will hear during an interview. The aim of this question is to find out how serious you are about your application. If you are serious, you will have taken time to research the company.

Finding out things about the organization, values, goals, size, and culture gives you basic knowledge you should acquire before you attend the interview.

Question: Tell me a little about yourself.

When an interviewer asks this question, you might be tempted to go all out by telling your life story and history, but what the interviewer is interested in is if you are suitable for the job. So in your answer focus on the qualities that relate specifically to the job. Connect the dots on your resume and describe what led you to make decisions about your career.

Ensure your response is short and straight to the point and tailor your response in a way that proves why you are the perfect fit for the job. As usual, only make positive statements about yourself.

Question: What do you consider your greatest strength?

This is one of the trickiest questions you will likely have to face during an interview. The question is the perfect opportunity to share your most impressive success story. Focus on a strength that is crucial for the job. Don't make false claims and don't focus on a strength that is completely irrelevant to the job.

For example, if the advertisement for the job specifies an individual who is easy to work with, teachable, and goal-oriented, you could list your greatest strength as flexibility and adaptability to new environments and situations.

Question: What Are Your Weaknesses?

This question is one of the most commonly asked questions. Most candidates fear this question because they don't know how to answer it. They don't want to tell their real weakness, but they also don't want to sound too overconfident by saying that their weakness is that they work too hard.

The best way to tackle this question is to choose a weakness that is not related to a key requirement of the job. Also show that you have taken measures to improve in your area of weakness.

It is very important to show the interviewers that you have self-awareness. You need to make them understand that you can take responsibility for your actions and that you are always looking for ways to improve yourself.

Question: Why Do You Want to Work for Us?

Interviewers ask this question to find out the real motivation behind you wanting to join the organization. They want to see that your interest extends beyond seeking a bigger paycheck.

You will need to have conducted thorough research about the company's needs to show how passionate you are about meeting those needs. You can also try complementing the interviewers, but don't go overboard.

One possible answer is, "I like the company culture and your company mission, and this is the reason why I applied for this role and why I want to join your company."

Question: What Made You Leave Your Last Job?

This is a nerve wracking question for most candidates. If you were fired from your previous job, you need to be honest with the interviewers. You must show them that you have learned from your mistakes and addressed the issue. You may also need to explain why you were fired.

If you decided to leave your job voluntarily, provide an explanation. You might say that you are looking for new challenges. You could also say, "I left the company because I had been working in the same position for ten years and no longer felt satisfied" or "I left because my skills and knowledge were not used and because we didn't have enough work to keep me busy."

Don't lie. The hiring manager could look into your claims to make sure they're true.

Question: What can we expect from you in the first three months?

When employers ask you this, you need to show how your presence can add value to the company. Have a loose plan for your first three months. What do you want to get done? How will you help boost the enthusiasm and morale of your co-workers?

Question: Where do you see yourself in five years?

This is one of the most hated interview questions of all time. On the surface, it might seem like a fairly normal question. But, as you dig deeper, you will discover that there are several traps that could get you.

You need to show that you are an ambitious person, but you also need to make it very clear that you are focused on your job and won't be leaving the position right away. Having an ambitious mindset can be a major positive trait that interviewers are seeking, but you don't want to make it seem like the job is just a stepping stone on the way to something better.

If you answer that you want to pursue additional education, for example, the interviewer may hesitate to hire you because you might leave the job in the near future or you will not be 100 percent dedicated to it.

Question: Why should we hire you?

You hear this question mostly at the end of interviews. Fortunately, this question is not used very much anymore.

This question demands that you be specific about why you are the best suited for the job. It is your chance to elaborate on the unique set of skills that you have that might be beneficial for the company. You also get the opportunity to showcase how you would approach specific problems and solve them.

Avoid describing why you want the job. That is not what the question is asking. You should be defining why you are a perfect fit for the job.

A sample answer to this question could be that your experience, skills, training, and work ethic make you suitable for this job. Then list all the requirements in the advertisement that you possess.

Question: What is your salary expectation?

This is a very tricky question that could make you jittery if you are not well prepared for it. To answer you must know the acceptable salary range for your industry and the position you are applying for.

When asked, you can mention the range that is the industry standard. But don't be too specific or stubborn because, at the end of the day, you won't be able to dictate how much they offer you.

If you are speaking with the hiring manager, they already have the salary range you shared with the recruiter during the first prescreening or with the agency recruiter. Once you understand the scope of the job and you see that it is way harder than you thought before, you can say, "I already shared the salary range $X to $Y with a recruiter. But I understand now that the job requires more responsibility, so I would like between $A and $B."

Question: Do you have any questions for us?

This is among the most commonly asked questions when interviewers want to wrap up the interview session. About 75 percent of interviewees decline to ask a question. But this is a mistake. This question gives you an excellent opportunity to make your mark in front of the interviewers. With this question, you get the opportunity to express how passionate you are about the job and how you would like to be a part of the team.

You can ask about the organizational culture, training, or plans for growth, for example. You might ask, "What qualities would make a candidate ideal and suitable for employment in your organization?"

Not asking any questions could indicate a lack of interest in the job. That's why you should prepare two or three questions. Base your questions on the job description, if possible, and never ask a question that you could easily answer yourself.

HOW TO SELL YOURSELF

During an interview, you will be asked to tell more about yourself or why the company should choose you. If you get this question it is important to have the right pitch. You want to be confident without sounding arrogant, and you want to be honest without revealing too much.

The key is to focus on your strengths and how they align with the company's needs. For example, if you're applying for a job as a salesperson, you might talk about your ability to connect with people and your natural ability to close deals. If you're applying for a job as an accountant, you might talk about your attention to detail and your ability to stay calm under pressure. Whatever your strengths may be, make sure to highlight them during an interview so that the company knows why you're the best candidate for the job.

How to Pitch Yourself in Two Minutes or Less

In today's competitive job market, it's more important than ever to be able to sell yourself in a short amount of time. Whether you're networking at an event or meeting with a potential employer, you need to be able to pitch yourself effectively in order to stand out from the crowd.

Here are some tips for pitching yourself in two minutes or less:

- Keep it simple. Don't try to fit too much information into your pitch. Stick to the basics and focus on what makes you unique.
- Be confident. Believe in yourself and your abilities and don't be afraid to show it.
- Know your audience. Tailor your pitch to the specific person or group you're speaking to. What are they looking for? What do they need to know about you?
- Practice, practice, practice. The more you practice, the more natural and effortless your pitch will become.

With these tips in mind, you'll be well on your way to nailing your next job in a no time.

32. Illegal Interview Questions

Some questions during your interview may feel inappropriate. Some may be *illegal*. The ability to recognize these questions helps candidates protect themselves against discrimination. Employers want to find out as much as possible about you through their questions, but you need to know which questions they are not supposed to ask so that you know not to answer them.

If you are planning to apply for a role outside your country, you should always check via Google what interview questions should not be asked in that country. By typing in the Google search box, "Illegal interview question in" and then adding the location, you will be able to find out what questions interviewers should not ask wherever you are job hunting.

State and federal laws have been formulated to eradicate discrimination in the workplace. The Equal Employment Opportunity Commission (EEOC)[77] is the U.S. agency responsible for overseeing fairness in the workplace.

In the United States, the Equal Employment Opportunity Act[78] amended Title VII of the Civil Rights Act of 1964 to address employment discrimination against African Americans and other minorities. More precisely, the Equal Employment Opportunity Act protects people against discrimination during recruitment processes and discourages employers from asking discriminatory questions. The goal of this act is for everyone to be able to get a job, based on their set of skills, knowledge, experience, and training.

Unfortunately, there are still employers, whether they are aware of it or not, who tend to overlook the law. Wanting to find out as much as possible about a candidate is a good reason to conduct a thorough interview, but it won't protect a company from a discrimination lawsuit. If you feel you've been discriminated against or that your gender, race, or sexual identity are being judged during an interview, you should leave the interview and consider filing a lawsuit. A less time-consuming option is to share your concerns with other candidates on websites like Glassdoor.

---

[77] https://www.eeoc.gov/
[78] https://en.wikipedia.org/wiki/Equal_Employment_Opportunity_Act_of_1972

Any questions about details of your personal life fall into the illegal category. These include questions meant to reveal your age, ethnicity, race, sex, sexual identity, gender identity, country of origin or birthplace, religion, disability, marital status, pregnancy, family status, and salary history.

AGE

It's illegal under The Age Discrimination in Employment Act (ADEA) for employers to ask questions related to age. These questions can lead to discrimination and should not be asked.

Employers may know that it is illegal to directly ask candidates about their age, so they try to get the information by talking around it: "How long have you been working?" "When did you graduate?"

What is not illegal is a question concerning the years working in a particular industry, which is relevant to the available position. They can ask, "How long have you been working in the industry?" But if you don't want to answer it with a number of years, you can always say something like, "For more than ten years."

Illegal: How old are you? What year were you born?
Legal: Are you over eighteen?

MARITAL STATUS

Under Title VII of the Civil Rights Act of 1964, it is unlawful to discriminate against applicants or current and potential employees based on their marital status. Therefore, asking whether someone is married or has kids is forbidden. The majority of countries have similar laws in place.

Any question regarding your marital status is an illegal question. Employers want to know the answer because it gives them clues about how much time you will have or be willing to invest in work. If they're prejudiced, they may be trying to figure out if you're LGBTQ by asking if you're married. They might try to get around the law by talking about their own spouse in the hopes you will jump in with an anecdote about yours.

Illegal: Are you married? Where is your spouse employed?
Legal: Are you willing to relocate? Are you willing and able to put in the amount of overtime and/or travel the position requires?

FAMILY STATUS

It is illegal for employers to ask candidates if they are planning to have children or if they have children already. It is the right of every person to have children and to select when this will happen in their lives. If an employer wishes to find out more about your availability and work hours, they can ask about that directly. But they cannot ask you if you have a family or children.

Illegal: Do you have children? Are you planning to have children soon?
Legal: Are you willing to relocate?

CRIMINAL/ARREST RECORD

There's a difference between being arrested and having a criminal record. A criminal record means you've been convicted of a crime. A person can be arrested and released without a conviction. Employers may ask you, under some circumstances, if you have a criminal record, and in some states they may also ask if you've been arrested. In some states, they may ask you these questions but not until late in the interview process. Always find out what the laws are in your state before going to an interview.

If you do have a criminal or arrest record, it is illegal under *federal law* for an employer to treat you differently because of another characteristic, such as race, than they treat another person with a similar criminal or arrest record. In addition, an employer cannot try to find out if you have a criminal or arrest record if such information creates a significant disadvantage to people who are protected by Title VII, such as Black and Latino people. They also can't try to find out about your criminal or arrest record if such information would not be helpful in determining if you would be a "responsible, reliable, or safe employee."

Illegal: Have you ever been arrested?
Legal: We are going to run a background check; are you okay with that?

In some states, like Michigan, employers are not allowed to ask whether an applicant has ever been arrested or whether an applicant has been charged with any misdemeanors that did not result in convictions.[79]

Note: Federal law does not prohibit employers from asking about your criminal history. But federal EEO laws do prohibit employers from discriminating when they use criminal history information.

---

[79] https://www.goldstarlaw.com/can-i-be-asked-about-being-arrested-in-a-job-interview/

RELIGION

Questions regarding one's religion or religious preferences are illegal. When employers ask these questions, they're usually trying to figure what days you're going to want to take off from work. But biased interviewers could be trying to find out because they don't want to work with someone from a specific religion. To find out about your availability, an interviewer should simply ask what days you can work.

Illegal: What are the religious holidays you practice? What is your religion?
Legal: Can you work on weekends? (They should only ask you this question if the position requires working on weekends.)

VISA STATUS AND CITIZENSHIP

Does your accent suggest you're from another country? It's illegal for the employer to ask you if you are. The employer *is* permitted to ask you about your work authorization.

Illegal: Where do you come from? What's your country of origin? Are you a U.S. citizen? Where were your parents born? What is your native language?
Legal: Are you authorized to work in the U.S. (add any other country)? What languages do you speak (if relevant to the position)?

RACE

It's illegal to discriminate against employees based on their race under Title VII of the Civil Rights Act of 1964. Asking about a candidate's race or ethnicity, whether directly or indirectly (such as asking where they grew up), has no place in an interview. It's illegal to discriminate against someone based on their race.

Illegal: Are you Pacific Islander? I had a friend who was. Are you mixed race? Is it your mother or father who's Black?
Legal: There is no legal question in this category.

DISABILITY OR MEDICAL CONDITION

It's illegal to discriminate against an employee based on their disability under the Americans with Disabilities Act (ADA). You should not be asked any questions about whether you have a disability, nor should you be asked to explain any health conditions to a potential employer. However, if you have disclosed that you have a disability or if it is obvious that you do, the employer may ask you if you need a reasonable accommodation during the application process or if you will need one on the job. It is also legal to ask a job applicant to voluntarily disclose (they don't have to) whether they have a disability—the purpose is to keep track for the federal government of affirmative action hires.

Illegal: Are you disabled? Do you have an illness? Have you been through any rehab?
Legal: Are you able to perform this job with or without accommodation? Do you have any conditions that could affect your job responsibilities?

QUESTIONS REGARDING DEBT, PROPERTIES, OR WEALTH

It is illegal for employers to ask about your debt history, to try to find out if you own any property, or to pry into how much money you have. They need your permission to look into your debt history, just as they do to find out about your criminal record. Employers can't use such info to reject you unless it keeps you from performing well at work.

HOW TO AVOID ILLEGAL INTERVIEW QUESTIONS

Illegal questions can be a sign that the interviewer is not interested in hiring you. If you feel that an interviewer has asked you an illegal question, you can politely refuse to answer or you can leave the interview.

If you are asked any questions that could point to discrimination, it is important to know how to react. Do not act offended, upset, or annoyed; instead, politely and diplomatically decline to answer such questions.

You may be at risk of not getting the job if you decline to answer a question. However, you may also be saved from experiencing discrimination at the workplace or working for a company that does not take discrimination seriously. And, if you do get asked an illegal question, you can report the employer.

An employer might ask an illegal question at any time, such as during informal meetings or over lunch or coffee. These more relaxed situations are the occasions when an interviewer is more likely to get a candid answer from you because you will be feeling more relaxed and less guarded. Always be on the alert for illegal questions.

33. Questions You Should Ask in Your Job Interview

The job interview is a two-way street. Not only are you being interviewed by a potential employer, but you should also be interviewing them. After all, you want to make sure that it's a good fit for both parties. And one of the best ways to do that is to come prepared with a few questions for your interviewer. It shows that you're interested in the position and that you've done your homework.

SAMPLE QUESTIONS

Following are some of the best questions to ask during your interview.

What are the day-to-day responsibilities of the job?

The worst career nightmare is being asked to do tasks that are not in the job description. Asking about responsibilities also gives a strong impression and makes you look forward-thinking.

There are a few ways to ask this question and get more information:

- Are there future projects not displayed in the job description?
- How do duties change throughout a year? (You need to know the busy seasons that call for working extra hours at the desk.)
- What are the main priorities, and how do they change? (You will learn the overall goals and how they affect your work.)

Can you tell me more about the team I will be working closely with?

It is widely accepted that knowing your co-workers promotes strong working relationships. In addition, this question helps you know the company's structure and your department.

What are the training programs and advancement opportunities?

There is no doubt that employee training and professional development programs are vital for success. These programs provide opportunities for employees to improve skills, enhance productivity, and promote company culture. When asking this question, you're wanting to know if there are chances to grow in the job. You don't want to stay stagnant in a career without accessing new opportunities. Further, it will show the interviewer that you are committed to your career path and the company's future. You will also know whether there is a possibility for a long-term career with the organization.

Tell me about the performance review process.

Employees go through a performance evaluation to give them feedback on how they can improve.

The way an organization measures success is important to consider when interviewing for a job. You want to understand what the company expects from its employees and how it determines if the employees are living up to expectations. Knowing this information can help you assess whether the organization is a good fit for you.

What are the organization and employee culture like?

Workplace culture is important, seeing that it can affect employee productivity, happiness, retention, engagement, and recruitment. When you ask this question, you will be able to evaluate the working environment and values of the company as a whole. It will also give you a chance to assess if you'll fit in.

What do you see as the future of the company?

Most of us desire job security in a career. When you are sure about security, you can focus more on developing your career. Asking about the progression plan indicates that you are interested and committed to the organization.

Why do you love working here?

To avoid a toxic environment, you need to assess the job and interviewer. Individuals who love the company and enjoy their jobs will help you feel good about accepting a job there. If the interviewer hesitates to answer, this could be a red flag.

Is there anything on my resume that makes you question if I am the best fit for this role?

This query is best to ask after the process. It shows that you are highly interested in listening and growing. In addition, this question will allow you to address any concerns the interviewer may have. This can help ensure a smooth interview process and that all bases are covered.

What is your budget for this role?

This is a tricky question, but you want to get the highest salary possible. Before salary negotiation starts, ensure you take time to show your professional values. Demonstrate your experience and accomplishments. Once you've done that, you can turn your attention to salary and compensation.

Here are tips to start this conversation:

- Delay the conversation. Push this question until the end of the interview.
- Turn the question to the interviewer: At the end of the process, try to get the interviewer to tell their ideal salary range for the role first.

QUESTIONS NOT TO ASK

Avoid any questions like the following:

- *What does the organization do?* By asking this, you're showing that you didn't bother to do your research.
- *When can I get time off?* Asking this question shows that, even before getting the job, you're already thinking about when you'll get a break.
- *Can I change my working timetable?* If you have specific schedule needs, save questions about your schedule until after you've been offered the job. When you ask this question earlier, you're showing that you're going to require special conditions, which might make you less desirable as a candidate.
- *Did I get the job?* First of all, the interviewer doesn't know yet if you got the job so there's no point in asking. Second, asking shows impatience and a lack of familiarity with the ways things work in a company.

GUIDELINES FOR ASKING QUESTIONS

When preparing a list of questions, follow these guidelines:

- Do away with "me" questions such as questions about vacation time, work hours, and health insurance.
- Avoid "Yes" or "No" questions: Choose ones that can create a dialogue.
- Don't ask personal questions about gender, race, religion, and family.
- Ask questions on a range of topics. You don't want to appear single minded and you want to show your curiosity in all aspects.

FINAL THOUGHTS

There is no definitive list of questions to ask in a job interview, but the questions shared in this chapter are generally good ones. You might also consider the following:

- What are the company's core values and how do they align with my personal values, which are X?
- What are the company's goals and how will my skills help achieve them?
- What are the company's biggest challenges and how can I help solve them?
- What is the team culture like and how would I fit in?
- How do you evaluate success and what defines a successful employee within your organization?

In order to make a good impression and find out if the company is a good fit for you, ask questions that focus on what you can offer the company, rather than on what the company can offer and do for you, such as questions about salary, benefits, and working hours. Instead, ask about the company's mission and values. Additionally, be prepared to discuss your own skills and experiences in depth.

Lastly, avoid questions with yes or no answers because you can find those answers yourself on the company's website.

34. Why You Didn't Get Picked for an Interview

You spend a lot of time writing a perfect resume and replying to job offers, but you don't get any responses. And when you do get a response, it's usually a rejection. It's discouraging to learn that you weren't even considered for a prescreening call with a recruiter. It would be helpful to know why your application was rejected, but there's usually no specific reason given.

Didn't the company like my experience? Wasn't I senior enough for a role, or was there some other reason behind not getting the job? Was it the way I conducted myself during the prescreening?

Following are some of the most common reasons candidates are rejected by companies. This information will help you understand what you can do differently next time.

YOU APPLIED TO EVERY OPEN ROLE IN THE ORGANIZATION

Many recruiters still use the "Spray and Pray"[80] method of contacting candidates on LinkedIn. In this approach, recruiters run a LinkedIn search based on the job title and location. And when they get their results, they contact every single candidate that matches their keywords without checking their profiles.

The majority of candidates do not like this approach, and I don't blame them. Candidates sometimes do the same to us recruiters. They visit the career page, create an account, and apply for every single position that is close to their current job title without even reading the job descriptions. They hope that recruiters will match their profile against any opportunity the company has.

If you submit your resume to every single position, hoping for a positive outcome, you will be disappointed. Even if one of the positions is a match to your skills, a recruiter will likely overlook you after rejecting your resume for a variety of other positions that you applied to. The recruiter will likely find your

---

[80] When recruiters spray their message on LinkedIn to as many people as possible, praying the right ones see it and respond.

approach annoying. They will also get the impression that you don't really know yourself, what you're looking for, and what you're good at.

Irritated recruiters may even assign a poor rating to your profile in their ATS so when other recruiters check your profile they will not want to pursue you.

YOU DIDN'T MEET THEIR CORE REQUIREMENT

It can be difficult to find a candidate who meets every requirement for a job, especially if the hiring manager is looking for someone with the same skills and knowledge as a previous employee.

If you're not sure which requirements are most important for a role, try to focus on the core skills that are necessary. The most important things are usually the top three or four requirements listed in the job description. If you don't match those, don't consider applying.

Some career coaches recommend applying for a job even if you do not meet all the requirements, as not every requirement is important. It is true that you often don't need to meet all the requirements, but you still have to meet those requirements that are considered most important by the hiring company.

My recommendation is that if you match three core requirements and are at least 70 percent qualified for a job, apply. If you're less than 70 percent qualified, reconsider spending the time to fill out the registration form. Your chance of getting the job is quite low.

YOU ATTACHED THE WRONG COVER LETTER

If you never got to the interview stage, it might be because your cover letter was not good enough. You may have sent a cover letter for a different role or attached the wrong document. Maybe you stressed the wrong things about your experience and background. Maybe you sent the wrong message, like feeling negative about your current employers or being insecure about your skills.

Maybe you simply forgot to proofread your cover letter. The result could be numerous typos, the wrong company name, the incorrect job title.

YOUR RESUME IS POORLY WRITTEN

If you want to make sure your resume catches the recruiter's or manager's attention, make sure you include all the information they need to see quickly if you are a good fit for the job. This includes highlighting the skills, qualities, abilities, experiences, and achievements that fit the available job the most. Poorly written resumes that do not have enough information will lose the attention of the reader very fast. Bear in mind that recruiters or managers are very busy and are not keen on reading resumes that are not well-made.

The formatting of your resume is also important because it can help or hinder the reader's ability to understand and remain interested in what you have to say. If everything is presented as one block of text, the reader may not read it all or may have trouble making sense of it. This is why it is important to use formatting to break up the text and make it easier to read.

You would be surprised how much formatting and highlighting the important parts in your resume could improve your chances. I have helped hundreds of people with their resumes. People who were previously rejected outright, were invited for interviews after making the suggested changes to their resumes.

THE RESUME FORMAT MADE IT HARD FOR ATS TO INTERPRET

More and more companies are using advanced applicant tracking systems to help them save time. Unfortunately, if your resume is uploaded in the wrong format, the software may reject it because it can't read or scan it correctly.

If you're looking to apply for a job online, it's best to use a clean, standard resume file format like PDF or Word (DOC, DOCX, RTF). Submitting your resume in a graphic format like PNG, JPG, or BMP could create problems for the company's ATS, and your resume content may not be scanned and analyzed properly. Additionally, recruiters may overlook your resume if it is unreadable by the system.

YOU APPLIED TOO LATE

If you want to increase your chances of being invited for an interview, apply as soon as the job is posted. Recruiters often screen candidates and present the best ones to the hiring manager in the first two to three weeks. If there are already fifty or more candidates, say, applying for a role, the interview process is likely already underway and your application will not be considered. Recruiters generally do not want to add more candidates to the interview process and lengthen the job search.

THE COMPANY ALREADY KNOWS WHO THEY WANT TO HIRE

In some locations, companies are required by law to publicly advertise all positions. But sometimes the employer already knows who they want to hire. So they post the job ad, you apply, and they ignore you and all the other applicants except for the one they invited to apply.

YOU DON'T HAVE A GOOD REPUTATION

If you never received a call back from a recruiter, it may be because your reputation precedes you— and not in a good way. If the hiring manager who received your application for review finds out from a colleague—somebody who worked with you before—that you're not a good fit for the job, you will not be hearing from them. Alternatively, if a recruiter sees something not so great about you posted online—even something you posted—you're not going to get an interview.

YOU FORGOT TO FINISH YOUR REGISTRATION

Did you attach your resume to your application? It may surprise you, but quite a few applicants forget to do this step. If you don't complete the online registration, your application won't be processed.

Always check before you hit submit. Even after you think you've registered, check your spam email folder occasionally; an ATS system might have sent you an automated email telling you that you need to upload or re-upload your resume.

YOU'RE NOT IN THE SAME LOCATION AS THE JOB

Despite the increase in remote job opportunities, many companies still require their employees to come into the office and some jobs can't be done remotely. The reason your home address might be a factor in whether you're considered for a job is that many companies prefer candidates who are located near their offices.

If you are located in a different place than the job, it's always a good idea to mention in your resume and cover letter that you are willing to relocate. If you live a good distance away from the job but are willing to make the commute daily, mention that fact in your resume and cover letter.

YOU REQUIRE A VISA OR PERMIT TO WORK

If you are seeking a job in a new country or continent, you may need a visa and work permit to work there legally. Even if you are planning to get the necessary documentation, however, you may still be rejected simply because the company doesn't want to hire anyone in that situation.

Many companies are unwilling to incur the extra costs associated with hiring international candidates. Even if you are willing to cover the costs of a work permit, visa, and relocation, they may still say no. The administrative tasks associated with hiring a non-national can be time-consuming and costly, and many companies are unwilling to shoulder the extra work and wait the extra time needed. That is why it is always a good idea to reach out to recruiters before you apply to ask if their company is open to candidates who require a visa.

If you are already living in the country where the job is located and already have a visa and work permit, it is easier for the new company to transfer your existing permits to their company. Make that clear in your resume and cover letter.

THE EMPLOYERS ARE BIGOTED

Sadly, racism and sexism are still alive in the 21st century and your application might not be selected just because the hiring manager is looking for a "specific type" of candidate, and you don't fit the bill. Companies that make hiring decisions based on gender or race are not healthy places to work.

It can be difficult to prove that your application was rejected based on discriminatory practices. But if you feel this was the case and you can prove it, contact your local authorities.

YOU APPLIED TO A HIGHLY POPULAR COMPANY

Major companies like Google, Meta, Twitter, Spotify, Tesla, and SpaceX receive a high volume of applications, so they are very selective in who they choose to interview. They only interview the best of the best because they have many qualified candidates to choose from.

If there is only one open position and hundreds or thousands of candidates are vying for it, there are many things that could work against you, such as your location or experience.

YOU ARE OVERQUALIFIED

If you are applying for a Senior Accountant role and you are currently a Manager of Accounting, your application might be rejected because the recruiter or hiring manager sees you as overqualified for the role. They may also think that you will be asking for a salary that is too high for their budget. Finally, they may worry that you will feel unchallenged and dissatisfied and want to leave or be promoted quickly.

FINAL THOUGHTS

There are dozens more reasons your application might not be considered for a role. Even if you do everything right, checking all the requirement boxes, you still might not receive any feedback or invitation for an interview. Sometimes there are simply too many candidates for a role, and the people who get invited to interview were recommended personally. The company might have already filled the role. They might even have decided not to fill the role at all because they're restructuring.

You may never know the reason because many companies still don't inform candidates when they're passed over. One reason is that the company may not even have enough recruiters to inform all the candidates. Another reason is that recruiters who have a bad experience with a candidate, such as when a candidate threatens to sue when they don't get hired, may not want to engage with rejected candidates.

Although you may have some things working against you, like a lack of experience or education, don't be discouraged from applying for jobs that are a good fit for you. Keep developing your skills and knowledge so you can become a more valuable employee and keep applying for jobs that interest you.

35. What to Do During an Interview

The first impression you make is very important when you're meeting someone for the first time. In most cases, you won't get a second chance to make another impression.

People form an impression of you very quickly. Everything from your attire, your way of talking, and your appearance, to your facial expressions, your posture, and your bearing, can contribute to this impression. The impression generally forms before you even speak. That is why it is important to be prepared for the first thirty seconds of any job interview. Let's learn how to create the best impression during those important first seconds.

BODY LANGUAGE

Nonverbal communication can influence the evolution of a meeting. If you want to win those first seconds of your interview, then keep in mind that your body language is a stronger source of communication than your mouth. Even before you say the first words to a recruiter or hiring manager, you must apply the art of body language.

Even the way you present and hold your body can influence the way you are perceived by others around you. What do you think of someone standing with their shoulders dropped and eyes focused on the ground? You'll probably think they're sad, feel hopeless, or have low self-esteem.

The interviewer will be paying attention to your body language in the first few seconds to see if you're nervous, tense, or worried. Your body language can also say a lot about your confidence, so try to remain calm before the interview starts.

Even when you're waiting in the interview room, it's important to be aware of any gestures that might convey anxiety or fear, like biting your nails, fidgeting, pulling your hair, or looking down a lot. If you know you do any of these when you're nervous, try to remain conscious of your body language.

If you want to stay calm, use this time to breathe deeply and slowly. Remind yourself that you are not going into an exam but a conversation. You will survive this.

Following are several body language tips that will improve your chances during the interview.

Online

Look at the camera

When speaking during an interview, it is important to make eye contact with the interviewer. Look directly into the camera to make eye contact and don't make faces. Be natural.

Not making eye contact can make you come across as untrustworthy. If you are struggling with this, try your best to make eye contact as much as possible.

 If you are wearing glasses your screen will be visible in them as a reflection. If you are not paying attention or if you're answering messages or Googling your answers, the interviewer will know.

Maintain good posture

It can be difficult to maintain a posture for a long time. Sitting up straight during an interview for a long time can be hard, especially if you have several interviews in a row and your body is tired. Sometimes, our body language can reflect that we are feeling overwhelmed.

Sit up straight and relax. Sitting up straight gives the impression of confidence and reliability, and relaxing shows that you are interested and engaged. Bear in mind that you should not be too relaxed, or you might start slouching, which could be a sign of being anxious or bored.

Avoid touching your face

It is common to touch our faces an average of sixteen to twenty-three times an hour, but you should try to avoid touching your face when you are answering the interviewer's questions. Many people believe the myth that when you touch your face you're lying, and hiring managers and recruiters are not exempt from this belief.

Maintain a genuine smile

Smiling genuinely is necessary while talking to someone. When you smile, people tend to feel connected to you and are likely to pay more attention to what you are saying. If the interviewer says something funny, there's nothing wrong with smiling and laughing a little.

Limit your hand gestures

During an interview, it is okay to use some hand gestures. But making too many hand gestures will make it hard for the interviewer to focus on what you are saying. Also, try not to play with your face, chew your hair, or bite your nails during the interview.

Avoid crossing your arms

During a virtual interview, crossing your arms indicates that you are uncomfortable opening up or feeling uninterested. Sit up straight and keep your arms in a comfortable position so you look engaged during the interview.

Mirror

Mirroring is a technique used to create rapport with someone. It consists of reflecting back what the other person is saying, through your words, phrases, and gestures. When we're speaking with an interviewer, and they wave their hands around, we tend to do the same. The same goes for when they smile—if the other person smiles, we smile too.

Some people use mirroring unconsciously as a method to garner sympathy from others. Career coaches often recommend mirroring the interviewer in order to build rapport and create the illusion that you are similar to them.

Pay full attention and nod

Always pay full attention to the speaker while they are speaking and do not interrupt unless necessary. Nodding at the right times will help keep the interviewer engaged.

Be in a good mood and try to relax during the interview. Worrying about the interview will only make it harder to focus. It's important to pay attention to show that you are interested and so you don't miss anything important.

If you will be sharing your screen with the interviewer, become familiar with the tool you will be using so you can share only your browser or the specific application. If you plan to use an Internet browser during your online interview, try opening it in incognito mode so you will not be sharing your browser history when you start typing.

On-site

Sometimes, people send out messages about how they feel through their body language, without even realizing it. Employers are used to looking for any clues that may betray how someone is feeling, both verbally and non-verbally. So, if you're feeling anxious or nervous or lack self-confidence, your body language will give you away.

Pay attention to your entrance

Walk into the building with your shoulders back and your head up, so that you appear confident. This will help you during interviews.

It is important to read the room and adapt your behavior accordingly. If the interviewer seems stressed, stay calm. If the energy in the room is formal, be formal. Your goal at this point is to fit in without contributing to any dysfunction.

Give a firm handshake

A weak handshake can make the other person feel insecure or afraid, and a forceful handshake can be interpreted as intimidating. The best way to shake someone's hand is firmly without bone crushing, offering your entire palm and not just your fingers.

Before you shake hands, make sure your palms aren't sweaty. Take a handkerchief with you to the interview so you can wipe off your hands right before greeting your interviewer. Arrive on time, visit the restroom before the interview starts, and do some breathing exercises to calm down—this will help your hands stay dry.

If you're sweating, don't worry about it. The interviewer was once a candidate too and knows that interviewing is stressful.

Mind your posture when sitting

Don't slouch when you're seated. Sitting sloppily, hunching over the table, or leaning too far forward are not good options. Instead, make sure your feet are firmly on the ground and your shoulders are pulled back and keep your head up. When listening to the interviewer, sit straight or lean forward a little. When it's your turn to ask questions, you can lean against the back of the chair, as long as you don't slouch.

Make and maintain eye contact

Retaining suitable eye contact is among the most critical skills to learn for a work interview. In a report,[81] nearly half of the 2,500 hiring managers evaluated said that the top facial expressions error job seekers make is the inability to make eye contact.

You don't have to stare deeply into your interviewer's eyes the entire time, but it's important to maintain eye contact for much of the time and show that you're listening.

Avoid fidgeting at all costs

Ideally, during an interview, you'll be calm and patient enough to sit still. Fidgeting can transmit bad messages to the interviewer. If you are fidgeting or playing with your hair, it may come across as boredom or impatience.

One strategy is simply to put both of your hands together in your lap. This will allow you to provide yourself with the opportunity to fidget out of the interview's view.

Don't cross your legs

Leg crossing comes off as too casual in formal settings. In addition, it tilts your body back, making it harder to sit up straight.

Smile when appropriate

Smiling during an interview is okay. Everyone enjoys seeing a smiling face, but you should only smile if it is the right time. Don't keep a fake smile plastered on your face during the entire interview. Smile readily and openly when it's appropriate such as when you're greeting or thanking the interviewer.

---

[81] https://www.prnewswire.com/news-releases/new-careerbuilder-survey-reveals-top-body-language-mistakes-candidates-make-in-job-interviews-99451339.html

Use a variety of tones

Use a variety of tones when speaking to avoid sounding monotonous and boring. Monotones can make the interviewer miss details and think that you have no emotion.

Small Talk

After you have won the recruiter or hiring manager over in the first ten seconds, it is important to make the next few seconds fruitful as well. The next second should be used for small talk, as the interview will not start immediately with questions about your experience. This is the point at which many people fail.

Small talk should not be serious. Your interviewer also knows this and will not bombard you with questions as soon as you shake hands. This is the time when you will be asked about the traffic and whether you managed to find the office easily.

Although these questions may seem mindless, you must know how to answer them. Follow these guidelines:

- Answer every question asked of you positively. Don't give off negative or hopeless vibes.
- Smile and be friendly to the person in front of you—they're a human just like you and nobody dislikes a friendly person.
- Try to speak in a normal tone and remember not to make the interviewer's job difficult by being too loud or too quiet.

If you did your research about the interviewer, you probably already know what you have in common. You can use this moment as an opportunity to talk about that. For example, if you have a dog and the person also has one, you can say "I'm doing great, thanks! I started the day by walking my dog early this morning and it is always a great way to start a day." People like other people with the same interests, so this might give you a better start to your interview.

If you don't know how to start your small talk, compliment the offices: "This office location is amazing! Any good coffee shop around that you would recommend?" You can always talk about the weather, location, or travel.

CLOTHING AND ACCESSORIES

The clothes you wear for the interview are important in terms of making a good first impression. You should wear smart clothes that are appropriate for the job you are interviewing for. If you are not sure about what to wear, it is better to dress in business attire.

The clothes you wear also play a role in the impression you make in the first seconds of an interview. Your goal is to look like someone who could work at that company. Try to match the existing dress code.

If you have no idea what that is, opt for business-casual attire, consisting of clean clothes that were ironed well. Avoid clothing that is too revealing and try to cover up tattoos.

When choosing accessories for an interview, stick to simple items instead of flashy ones that will make you stand out.

MANNERS

It is important to have good manners when meeting someone for the first time. Make eye contact, shake the person's hand firmly but without hurting them, and say please and thank you. Don't sit down until you are invited to take a seat.

VALUES

Companies look for employees who are capable of following rules. One of the most important rules is arriving on time. Show you are capable of being there on time for your interview.

Some other things to remember that are related to discipline and respect are not interrupting the interviewer when they are speaking, waiting for your turn to answer or speak, and making eye contact. Eye contact is very important during a conversation as it shows that you are paying attention and that you care to listen.

If you want to make a good impression on your interviewer, give them a strong handshake as soon as you meet them. A good handshake will show that you are positive and confident, which are both great qualities to have during an interview.

JOKES

If you're in an interview, avoid making any jokes. Especially when you are interviewing with someone from another country. Everyone has a different sense of humor, so it's safer to not joke around at all.

FINAL THOUGHTS

The best way to get through an interview successfully is to prepare some talking points in advance. If you have some prepared things to talk about, you can relax, and a relaxed interviewee creates a better first impression. Talking points will help you keep the conversation running and avoid any odd silences. It is important to engage and be engaging.

Remember to shake hands when meeting someone new—it's a gesture that is universally accepted. Be aware of your body language and avoid using your phone. It will make you seem uninterested in the conversation.

You have only a short amount of time, so make those first thirty seconds count!

Your body language can affect your interview, whether you like it or not. If you want to improve your chances, try practicing with a friend or career coach to get feedback on your body language. Maybe the feedback will help you realize that you are unconsciously playing with your hair or moving your hands too much. When you improve your body language, you'll also be improving your communication.

WHAT NOT TO DO OR SAY IN A JOB INTERVIEW

The way you behave and present yourself during an interview is important because it helps the interviewer determine whether you are the right candidate and a good fit for the company and culture.

You need to use the job interview to convince the hiring manager that you are the right person for the job. To accomplish this goal, as we have seen, there are things you need to do during the interview. But there are also some things you definitely want to avoid doing or saying.

WHAT NOT TO DO

Never be late for a job interview

Arriving late at a job interview will make a bad impression and affect your chances of getting hired, especially if you are dozens of minutes late. Make sure to plan well ahead, giving yourself sufficient time to get ready and arrive at the set location in time.

There are situations that may throw your schedule overboard such as a family emergency, a really bad weather situation, or even a car accident that blocks traffic. If you know that you won't make it to the job interview for reasons out of your control, call the employers to reschedule. If you know that you are going to be five to ten minutes late, call the interviewer ten minutes before the interview time. Calling is way better than sending a text or email. If you can't reach the interviewer, reach out to the recruiter who set up the interview for you. If you can't reach the recruiter either, send an email to inform them that you will need to reschedule.

Don't arrive too early

To make sure you won't be late, you may be tempted to leave home very early. But arriving too early can create a bad impression. When the hiring manager hears from reception that you have been waiting for thirty minutes before the interview, they'll feel pressure. They don't want to have you wait, but they won't be happy that they need to rush with their meeting either.

If you arrive too soon, you might end up waiting in a room with another candidate. That wait will seem like an eternity.

If you find yourself arriving early to your interview, don't worry! Grab a cup of coffee or tea nearby to relax and refine your plan for the interview. Just make sure to watch the clock so you don't spend too much time at the coffee shop. Drink your coffee carefully to avoid stains.

Alternatively wait outside. Look around the neighborhood. You'll get a good idea of what is nearby. You might even discover another company that is hiring.

Don't lie

It is important to put your best foot forward during an interview, but don't lie.

Sooner or later your lies will be discovered and that will have a negative impact on your reputation. A background check could reveal your lie. So could a person who knows both you and the hiring manager or recruiter.

Avoid an arrogant attitude

Confidence and arrogance are two different things. Confidence is good; arrogance is not. If you mistake one for the other, you'll do poorly in an interview. No one says you should behave in a humble way, but having an "I know it all" mentality won't get you anywhere. A good manager will appreciate a candidate who is confident, comes with strong arguments, and is open to new ideas.

Companies are looking for confident, well-prepared candidates—not candidates with big egos.

Don't eat or chew gum

No matter how long the interview is, bringing a snack to the interview is a bad idea. The same goes for chewing gum whether the interview is on the phone, via video, or in person. During my career, I have experienced gum chewers every year, and sometimes the chewing is so loud I can't focus on what the candidate is saying.

Don't check your phone

Do not check your phone or answer any calls during the interview. Turn off your phone or put it on silent to avoid distractions. Fidgeting or constantly checking your phone during the interview could be very distracting and leave a bad impression.

If you turn off all notifications, you will limit the urge to check your phone or think about who sent the message and what the content is. This can be very distracting—instead of paying attention to the interviewer, you might be thinking about the message you received.

Avoid looking at your watch

If you have a watch, try to avoid looking at it during the interview. Constantly checking your watch may send the wrong message to the interviewer. For example, they could think you're not interested in the job or that you're in a hurry to leave.

WHAT NOT TO SAY

Don't mention your bad relationship with your former boss

Would you want to hire someone who talks badly about their former boss during an interview? Probably not. If the interviewer knows your former boss, they may ask you about your relationship. In that case, you can say that the relationship was challenging at times.

Don't express negativity about your previous job

Although you may not have had the best experience with your previous job, it is important not to speak badly about it during an interview.

When discussing your previous job, focus on the positive aspects of your experience and all positive interaction you had there and how many things you learned. Discuss how the job helped you develop as a professional. Avoid disclosing private information about previous deals or customers.

Don't say you're willing to do anything if you get the job

When managers are hiring, they're looking to find people who are passionate about the job. Those people are likely to give more effort to their work. But this is different from being "willing to do anything." Employers don't even want people who can do "anything." They want people who can do the job.

If you'll say that you'll "do anything," you may give the impression that you are desperate and even that your have questionable judgment.

Do not admit to a lack of professional experience

No one expects you to know everything, especially if you just graduated or are embarking on a second career. But admitting that you lack experience is a very bad move. When you do this, clearly stating that you don't have too much experience, it's like admitting that you're not such a good hire after all or you're not a match for the available role within the company. Instead, focus on your qualities and strengths, avoiding talking about your weaknesses. And even if you are requested to name a few weaknesses, as a part of your job interview, avoid saying you lack experience.

During my career, I have often heard from candidates that they lack the required experience. Sometimes candidates will say, "I just need a month or two to learn this thing and then I will be on the level where you need me." This is always a red flag to me—why would I want to hire someone who is going to need two months to get up to speed if I can hire someone who already knows what to do?

Don't say that you are overqualified

You may have more experience than required for this role, but avoid saying that you are overqualified. If you say this, you'll likely be seeking a promotion within the first few months. This is reason enough to be rejected.

Don't rely on your resume

If the interviewer asks you about information that is included in your resume, don't simply say that it's already in your resume. Answer the question. The interviewer wants you to elaborate on what they can read in your resume. They want to know what you've done, what you've seen, and what you know. This is an important part of the interview process, as it allows the interviewer to get a better understanding of who you are and what your skills and abilities are.

Avoid filler words

When communicating during a job interview, it is important to provide clear answers and statements that show your self-esteem and confidence. Avoid words and sounds like "like" or "um." They are distracting and make you seem unprofessional. You may even come across as having difficulty organizing your thoughts and communicating effectively. This is not the image you want to project during a job interview.

Don't say you desperately need a job

You could be out of work for several months, desperately seeking a job. But it is best not to mention this during an interview. Companies may use this information to offer you a lower salary. In addition, there is no purpose to saying it because the employer doesn't owe you anything; they're not going to hire you simply because you need them to.

Don't talk about money at the beginning

If you don't want to seem like you're only interested in the job for the money, don't bring up the salary until the end of the interview. If you've already talked about salary with the recruiter, wait until the hiring manager brings up the topic or you can discuss it at the end.

Most hiring managers I've met during my professional career see candidates who bring up money right away as people they don't want to have on their team.

36. Psychometric Test

Psychometric testing is a commonly used interview type for giving context. Psychometric testing establishes a person's psychological profile, which can help identify any potential weaknesses or strengths. This information can then be used to make better hiring decisions.

WHAT IS PSYCHOMETRIC TESTING

The term *psychometry,* derived from the Greek word *psyche* (mind) and *metron* (measure), literally means "measuring of psychological traits." The goal of a psychometric assessment is to better understand a person's skills and knowledge, abilities, attitudes, personality traits, and mental models. Things like personality, motivation, reasoning, integrity, and general mental ability/intelligence are what most psychometric tests in recruitment are being used to assess.

A test can be called "psychometric" as long as it is standardized and has been the subject of scientific validation studies, which means in the most simple terms that they meet OVR standards (objectivity, validity, and reliability): (a) they measure what they say they are going to measure (validity), (b) they do so consistently (reliability), and (c) different evaluators assess the performance or results the same way (objectivity). In contrast to assessments based on subjective perceptions, psychometric tests make it possible to study the characteristics and differences between individuals or groups of individuals, based on an objective statistical approach and sound science.

In other words, the Reddit quizzes probably do not go through the same OVR[82] rigor (see "Grain of Salt" section at the end of this chapter).

According to meta-analysis from Schmidt, Oh, and Shaffer (2016),[83] the

---

[82] Objectivity-Validity-Reliability
[83] Schmidt, Frank (2016.) *The Validity and Utility of Selection Methods in Personnel Psychology: Practical and Theoretical Implications of 100 Years of Research Findings.*

top five KPIs[84] when hiring for future job performance are general mental ability, interviews, peer ratings, job knowledge tests, and integrity tests. General mental ability (GMA) is the most predictive of employee performance and, when combined with integrity tests and structured interviews, offers measurable benefits. In any case, when hiring, one should not rely on age, years of experience, graphology (handwriting analysis), or references. These have basically not much to add in terms of being able to predict job performance.

This may seem a bit mind boggling as years of experience, age, and references are common tools used in hiring. But you and I are not going to change that. Let's dive deeper into the areas that really do matter when it comes to psychometric testing in recruitment.

These tools are also used in internal evaluation to better predict a person's behaviors, job success, and potential.

The key here is that the assessments used (usually there is a "battery" or a series of them) need to be relevant to the requirements for the specific job, and the results delivered must be relevant for success in that job or type of work.

According to the JDL group,[85] "at least 82% of employers use some form of pre-employment assessment as part of their hiring process with research indicating those organizations using predictive, pre-employment assessments are 24% more likely to have employees exceeding performance goals. Unfortunately, there is a difference between 'some form of an assessment' and 'predictive assessments'—a highly important distinction much of the buying public does not make in these scenarios. In fact, the majority of Fortune 100 companies use personality assessments such as the MBTI and DISC, with no real predictive validity. As such, they neglect to establish a link between a candidate's test results and their job behaviors, meaning they are of little predictive value regarding job performance."

So this is why it is important, whether you are a candidate, recruiter, HR manager, or hiring partner, to understand a bit more about what a psychometric test is, why it is being used, and what happens with your results.

PSYCHOMETRIC TESTS AND RECRUITMENT

Tests are used at different stages of the recruitment process, sometimes when the candidate is applying online but also during the first job interview, in assessment centers, or at the end of the recruitment process to confirm previous results. Many employers use them to judge candidates more fairly, regardless of their

---

[84] KPI stands for key performance indicator, a quantifiable measure of performance over time for a specific objective.

[85] https://www.thejdlgroupllc.com/bad-hires-are-bad-news-pre-employment-assessments-prevent-hiring-mistakes/

training or background. Although, again unfortunately, many psychometric tests used by companies are non-standardized, you can still prepare for them in advance.

How come psychometric tests made their way into the recruitment sector? Until not so long ago, the candidate evaluation was based primarily on a submitted resume, but this method fell short when companies were trying to find the ideal candidates for given positions. As Elizabeth Lembke (Founding Director L&D Cares)[86] says, this is the fallacy of CVs being common practice—but not necessarily good practice when it comes to predicting job performance. In Bas van de Haterd's[87] words, " A resume tells me what you have done, for how long, and for whom—not how well."[88]

To fill in the gaps left by resumes, psychometric testing has become more prevalent over the years.

PSYCHOMETRIC TESTING AREAS

There are three common psychometric testing areas: aptitude, personality traits, and interpersonal skills.

Aptitude

Tests regarding one's aptitudes target the person's cognitive abilities. When it comes to cognition, these tests are most often focused on numerical and verbal reasoning but often also include concentration, abstract reasoning, and physical and mechanical understanding. Basic numeracy and literacy skills are assessed as are more advanced skills and abilities, such as analysis and interpretation of data.

Aptitude tests include the following:

- Verbal reasoning tests: timed tests that measure the candidate's ability to perform verbal analysis. These are written documents in which the candidate must summarize the most important points as quickly as possible.
- Abstract reasoning tests (or conceptual reasoning tests): non-verbal tests that use shapes to measure the fluid intelligence of the candidate.

---

[86] https://www.linkedin.com/in/elizabethlembke/

[87] https://www.linkedin.com/in/basvandehaterd/

[88] van de Haterd, Bas. (2018.) *A Free White Paper on Modern Assessment Tooling.* https://www.recruitmenttech.com/a-free-white-paper-on-modern-assessment-tooling/

- Numerical reasoning tests: timed tests that analyze the candidate's ability to process numerical data, including charts and tables.
- Spatial reasoning tests: timed tests that measure the candidate's ability to manipulate objects visually, such as in organizing space or identifying potential hazards.
- Mechanical reasoning tests: timed tests that measure the candidate's ability to understand mechanical concepts in order to solve problems.
- Inductive reasoning tests: often used for positions in computer science or engineering, tests in the form of multiple choice questions (MCQs) or tests on the correct order of a sequence of images.
- Deductive reasoning tests: tests used to evaluate logical thinking and problem solving, usually consisting of an observation period after which the candidate must establish a theory and solve a problem.

Bear in mind that proofreading and spelling tests can also be used to evaluate your aptitude.

For internal promotion or higher pay-grade positions, analysis is often done via cognitive complexity/capacity interviews. These are conducted to see how well a person is able to identify concepts and links, weigh those against each other by making connections to a broader context (e.g., a business market situation), and then draw conclusions on how to move forward.

Personality Traits

Depending on the type of job, the recruiter will want to find candidates with particular personalities that increase the probability for role success. For instance, it may be more difficult for an introvert to work in sales, which has a high degree of interaction with people. One of the main goals of recruiters is to identify the candidates that best meet the ideal candidate's profile in terms of personality and behavior.

When it comes to assessing a candidate's personality, the recruiter can choose among several options: personality tests, leadership tests to check motivation, and tests requiring the candidate to make judgments based on given situations.

Personality tests

In general, personality tests are used to provide insight into individuals' needs, attitudes, motivations, and behavioral tendencies. Most personality tests have the so-called "Big Five" at their core, the most widely accepted personality model for the elements that influence behavior.

The Big Five personality traits are as follows:

Extraversion	Degree to which a person is active, gregarious, sociable, talkative
Agreeableness	Degree to which someone is cooperative, courteous, flexible, forgiving, good-natured, soft-hearted, tolerant, and trusting
Conscientiousness	Degree to which an individual is achievement-oriented, careful, hard-working, organized, planful, persevering, responsible, and thorough
Emotional Stability	Opposite of emotional instability, which is the degree to which a person is angry, anxious, depressed, emotional, insecure, and worried
Openness to Experience	Degree to which an individual is artistically sensitive, broad-minded, cultured, curious, and original

* How the Big Five personality traits in CPSQ increase its potential to predict academic and work outcomes[89]

In terms of predicting actual job performance, personality tests are and only ought to be one element in a broader assessment process, as they are fairly low in terms of validity (r = 0.0 to 0.25; a correlation coefficient of r = 1.0 represents perfect validity) if just used on their own. That being said, in terms of how the Big Five play out in terms of job performance, conscientiousness is the most strongly linked, followed by emotional stability and extraversion, with agreeableness and openness having the lowest validity.

In other words, just because you have an introvert applying for a sales role doesn't mean you should immediately put their resume on the "no pile." It just means that it can be more challenging for them to get their energy re-charged if they are dealing with a lot of people at once. They may, in fact, be better listeners and understand your customers better. It is important not to make blanket assumptions based on assessment of the Big Five.

The purpose of assessment tests is to assess the candidate's potential to learn the new skills they will need for the position in question. These tests are timed, under exam conditions, and often in the form of multiple choice questions or true/false questions. Normally, the recruiter will then compare your results with those of a demographic segment, such as with the results of candidates who were previously hired by the company.

The most commonly used test is the personality questionnaire, which is meant to show a candidate's weaknesses and strengths by creating a profile.

---

[89] https://www.admissionstesting.org/images/419493-the-big-five-personality-traits-in-cpsq.pdf

Leadership tests

Another type of test you may come across, particularly in leadership potential assessment, is the fluid intelligence test, otherwise known as *learning agility*. Learning agility is the willingness and ability to learn new competencies in order to perform under first-time, tough, or different conditions. In other words, how do you figure out what to do when you do not know what to do? It is considered less static than the Big 5 for predicting job performance and the ability to interpret and respond in a complex environment.

Situational assessments

If the recruiter chooses tests of situational judgment, then the aim is to see how the candidate reacts to various situations that may occur at work. They can be in two forms:

- Quizzes on the company's website that allow young graduates to self-assess to determine if they fit the company.
- Assessments integrated into job interviews to determine how the candidate works.

 It is important in personality assessments, to be yourself (or the best possible version of yourself)! Try to be as honest as possible, make sure you understand the scenario, and use only the information provided by the recruiter. The purpose of these personality traits tests is to better match candidates with the demands of the role.

Interpersonal skills

Assessment centers are based on the fact that humans interact at work and they need to do so in order to be successful. Assessment centers measure a variety of job-related skills and abilities mainly focusing on interpersonal and social competence, communication, planning and organizing, and analytical skills. The tests also measure individual qualities including the g-factor, which is general mental ability/intelligence, social competence, achievement motivation, self-confidence, and dominance.

The exercises at assessment centers are based on human interaction and usually run by psychologists. Usually, time constraints are applied to see how the candidate behaves and reacts when working under pressure. The test consists of a variety of group exercises and role plays.

The tester will be on the lookout for certain characteristics depending on the position in question. If it is an HR position, for example, the recruiter will be looking for a candidate who has excellent interpersonal, organizational, and listening skills.

Don't try to impress the recruiter by saying what you think they want to hear. Being professional and honest will serve you much better. By tailoring your answers to match what the recruiter wants to hear, you might get the job but you won't necessarily be a good match for it, which could lead to failure and frustration.

OTHER TYPES OF PSYCHOMETRIC TESTS USED IN RECRUITMENT

Although they are less common, you might encounter these additional psychometric tests.

Wonderlic Contemporary Cognitive Ability Test (formerly Wonderlic Personnel Test)

This is the grandaddy of psychometric tests. It has been around since 1937 and is still in wide use. Its latest iteration, an online version, is known as WonScore. The Wonderlic Personnel Test is made up of four categories: General Knowledge, Abstract Reasoning, Verbal Reasoning, and Numerical Reasoning. It is used to measure the cognitive ability and problem-solving aptitude of prospective employees for a range of occupations.

California Psychological Inventory

This personality test measures individual differences, such as socially observable qualities around how one engages and interacts with others, internal values and controls, achievement-seeking needs, and approaches to problems. It is also used to assess managerial potential and creative temperament.

Caliper Profile

The Caliper Profile is a scientific instrument for in-depth personality assessment. Its primary purpose is job matching. The Caliper Profile, which has been validated by nearly half a century of research and measures more than twenty-five personality traits related to work performance, is usually used during pre-employment assessment. It adjusts for faking (e.g., lying and under- or overreporting) and social desirability.

Although it is not time-limited, the average Caliper test time is between sixty and seventy-five minutes.

The Caliper Profile is based on the Minnesota Multiphasic Personality Inventory (MMPI),[90] a psychological test that assesses personality traits and psychopathology and is primarily used to test people who are suspected of having mental health or other clinical issues. It was not originally designed to be administered to non-clinical populations and is considered a protected psychological instrument, meaning it can only be given and interpreted by a psychologist trained to do so. If you are subjected to this test, be wary of the employer as (a) what this test measures is none of their business and (b) the test is not appropriate.

16pf Questionnaire

The Sixteen Personality Factor Questionnaire (16PF, sometimes called *sixteen personality factors*) is a personality assessment tool that provides a complete picture of the person, unlike other personality tests that only assess the individual's work abilities. It was created by statistician Raymond Cattell, who notably participated in the creation of the Big Five model.

In order to integrate use of the 16pf for recruiting, the employer must carry out a two-day training on how to use and interpret this test in the recruitment process.

Predictive Index Behavioral Assessment

The PI Behavioral Assessment is a personality test that categorizes and assesses the motivations of employees and candidates. Published in 1952, it is one of the most widely used pre-employment tests—more than 6,500 companies use it—and has been translated into seventy languages. It is divided into four basic behavior scales: dominance, extraversion, patience, and formality.

The Hogan Personality Inventory (HPI)

The HPI is a well-constructed and validated tool that hones in on normal or "bright side" personality traits, qualities that describe how we relate to

---

[90] https://psychcentral.com/lib/minnesota-multiphasic-personality-inventiry-mmpi

others when we are at our best. Basically, it focuses on one's reputation in the eyes of others even though it is a self-report. The HPI is linked to on-the-job performance and can be used for hiring and personal and leadership development.

The HPI was refined by the authors on the basis of performance-related validity research in an effort to "capture excellence" across a wide range of jobs. They started by identifying the facets of personality that differentiate the best from the rest. The result is a 206-item questionnaire that identifies the individuals most likely to be effective in any role and the roles in which individuals are likely to be most effective. It is the first normal range personality questionnaire based on the Big Five model that was designed specifically for occupational assessment.[91]

If you are given this assessment, you can fairly safely assume the organization is taking a responsible approach to pre-employment assessment.

Widely Used Invalid Instruments

Two tests you may run across that shouldn't be used in recruitment are the Myers-Briggs Personality Indicator and DISC Profile. After more than fifty years of psychologists saying these tests feel good but have no scientific validity, you will still find both in practice almost everywhere, so it is important for you to be aware of them.

The MBTI or Myers-Briggs Type Indicator personality test was developed by Isabel Briggs Myers and Katherine Cook Briggs, based on the psychological types theory of Carl Gustav Jung. Psychologist Lisa Feldman Barrett describes it best: "The MBTI and various other personality tests have no more scientific validity than horoscopes. Years of evidence show that the MBTI does not live up to its claims and does not consistently predict job performance." The problem with the MTBI is that it uses vague, broad statements with which test-takers either do or do not self-identify.

Nevertheless, the MBTI is currently the most widely used corporate reference tool for working on individual or collective personal development topics. It allows the taker to identify their own profile from among sixteen types and to identify strengths and weaknesses, improve relationships within a working group, and identify areas for improvement.

The DISC profile, published by Wiley, analyzes personality along four scales corresponding to communication style: dominant, influent, stable, and conscientious.

---

[91] https://www.psychological-consultancy.com/products/hogan-assessments/Hogan-personality-inventory/

In academic psychology no work has been done using the DISC model since it was first developed in the 1950s. Also, the model was never intended to be used as an assessment. Nevertheless, the DISC system is used in companies either as an employment or team-building tool. And you will probably come across it.

Most companies do not know how invalid and unreliable the MBTI and DISC are, so do not judge an employer too harshly for using either or both. Large consulting companies have been built around the tests, so there is an assumption that they are reputable. Both tests help folks feel seen and find language to help others understand their perspective. These are fine outcomes, but they do not form a reliable basis for making personnel decisions.

HR Tech Assessments

As the business world becomes increasingly digitized, human resources departments are turning to technology to help streamline their operations. HR tech assessments are one way that companies are using technology to evaluate job candidates. By using algorithms to analyze a candidate's experience, skills, and personality, HR tech assessments can provide a more objective assessment of candidates. In addition, by considering a wider range of factors, HR tech assessments can help to identify candidates who may be a good fit for a role but who may not have been considered using traditional methods.

Dr. Juliya Golubovich wrote in the American Psychological Association's *Psych Learning Curve*, "According to a *Washington Post* article, in the last five years, more than 700 companies have used AI to evaluate close to twelve million video interviews automatically. Providers of this type of technology promise to greatly reduce the amount of time it takes an employer to screen candidates (by automating the interview) and to recommend the best hires, such as by identifying the candidates whose personalities most closely resemble those of the company's current star performers. This trend has outpaced related psychological research. Louis Tay and Louis Hickman saw an urgent need for research that would evaluate the accuracy and fairness with which AI can judge job candidates' personality." Juliya Golubovich[92].

As the use of HR tech assessments becomes more widespread, they are likely to transform the way that companies hire employees. No longer will candidates be judged solely on their resume or interview performance; instead, their ability to excel in a role will be determined by data. This shift is sure to increase the accuracy of hiring decisions and help companies find the best possible candidates for open positions.

---

[92] http://psychlearningcurve.org/can-ai-predict-your-personality-in-a-job-interview/

This is an unfortunate but real challenge right now in the industry. "With investment into new assessment companies and technologies at an all-time high, and many end users of assessments largely choosing to focus on short-run efficiencies over a long-term strategy based on sound science, there is cause for concern. 64% of firms offering any form of AI do not employ an I/O psychologist[93]."

Robotic Process Automation (RPA) Technologies, Artificial Intelligence (AI), and Chatbots

RPA is used for CV prescreening, monitoring of a candidate's experience, and automated communication. Essentially, RPA is meant to replace the more routine recruiting processes like managing meeting logistics and making job ads.

Chatbots are text-based dialogue tools that simulate interpersonal communication.

FINAL THOUGHTS

Psychometric tests are increasingly becoming a part of the recruitment process for many organizations all over the world. If you are looking to increase your chances of getting hired, it is worth exercising your skills for undergoing psychometric tests. Getting familiar with these tests will help you be more comfortable during the recruitment process and allow you to perform better. The most common types of psychometric tests used in recruitment are aptitude tests, personality tests, and intelligence tests.

Aptitude tests assess your skills and abilities in areas such as mathematics, verbal reasoning, and spatial awareness. Personality tests aim to measure your suitability for a role by assessing your character traits and work style. Intelligence tests focus on your memory, problem-solving abilities, and general knowledge. By familiarizing yourself with these different types of tests, you can develop strategies for how to best approach each one. Psychometric testing is becoming more common in the recruitment process, so it is worth taking the time to brush up on your skills. With a little practice, you can maximize your chances of impressing potential employers and landing the job you want.

Psychometric tests can be administered online after you've submitted your resume for a job, they can be used during an assessment day, or they can be given after an interview with the recruiter. Psychometric tests can be found

---

[93] Rocket Hire, Talent Assessment Market Report 2021

online for free and some may be available for a fee. You can try out the free tests in advance.

FEEDBACK FROM A PRO

Dipl. Psych. Elizabeth Lembke[94], Chief Talent Navigator at Transforming Talent, has this to say about personality assessments:

"When used as part of a job-related approach to assessment, personality assessments increase compliance with guidelines for ensuring fair and non-discriminatory hiring outcomes that organizations are legally held accountable to. We do not advocate for the use of general personality assessments without proper methods to relate specific traits measured on the assessments to job requirements, and without proper validation evidence showing that they predict job-relevant outcomes. This distinction is what sets scientifically valid assessments apart from MBTI and others.[95] There is a dark side to personality assessments, or indeed any assessment, when they are not used responsibly or researched properly. However, there is also a bright side to personality assessments when used in an appropriate, evidence-based manner, by well-trained professionals."[96]

She continues: "In the US, there are Uniform Guidelines on Employee Selection Procedures (Equal Employment Opportunity Commission from 1978) that are supposed to be used as a quality control when creating the process for using psychometric testing. The guidelines state that employers must provide evidence that the data used in hiring decisions is job-relevant. The American Psychological Association (2018) has clearly defined outlines of what principles for the validation and use of personnel selection procedures are—but unfortunately, many companies do not know or perhaps choose not to know about the guidelines."

"As companies move forward with HR Tech and AI assessments, they will be asking more questions[97] like:

- How accurately do the AI supported assessments predict personality ratings from people's self-reports or interviewer judgments (validity)?
- When someone is interviewed on multiple occasions, are the personality scores produced similar over time (reliability)?

---

[94] https://www.linkedin.com/in/elizabethlembke/
[95] https://www.siop.org/Portals/84/PDFs/SIOP%20Response%20to%20HBO%20Max%20Persona%20Film.pdf
[96] This is from Lembke's address "Professional Grain of Salt" at the Transforming TalentSociety for Industrial and Organizational Psychology, March 2021.
[97] http://psychlearningcurve.org/can-ai-predict-your-personality-in-a-job-interview/

- To what extent do personality scores from automated interviews truly predict how well individuals will perform on the job (validity)?
- What are the demographics of the interviewee samples on which the algorithms are trained on? Are these samples representative of all applicants for a given position? (objectivity; addressing bias; reliability)"

"As a candidate, you do have the right to your test results - and an organization should also offer to take you through your results. This is part of the professional creed and practice of psychologists. As many folks do not tend to ask for this, many companies do not proactively offer. But if you are interested, do ask."

37. How to Ask for Feedback After an Interview

Requesting feedback after an interview will help you determine how you did and what your chances are. Even if you don't get the job, the feedback from the hiring manager or recruiter can help you improve for future interviews.

WHY YOU SHOULD ASK FOR FEEDBACK AND WHY IT IS IMPORTANT

The most important aspect of requesting feedback is that it can help you improve professionally. Although participating in an interview is often fulfilling and gives you hope for the future, an interview can also end in rejection and for almost all the people interviewing for a position it does. But it doesn't have to feel like a waste of your time, especially if you use it to make yourself a better interviewee.

Imagine that you're an inexperienced candidate. Your lack of experience is going to be a hindrance when applying for certain jobs. When you request feedback after an interview, you may receive suggestions about how you can improve this part of the application process and gain more experience. The next time you interview, you may have the same amount of work experience, but you will be armed with more interviewing experience. That alone can differentiate you from other candidates.

In addition to getting feedback, you will better understand what employers are looking for. This is important for your experience as a candidate so that you can build more effective strategies for future job applications.

Furthermore, if you ask for feedback after an interview, the employer might be impressed with your dedication to self-improvement and remember you for a job in the future.

If you're rejected for a position, don't be discouraged. Instead, use the opportunity to ask for feedback and grow from it. Implementing feedback effectively takes practice, so don't be afraid to ask for advice.

REASONS COMPANIES DON'T PROVIDE FEEDBACK

In order to learn about the best ways to ask for feedback, you first need to understand why companies don't automatically give you feedback in the first place.

They're Afraid of a Lawsuit

Although it can be helpful to receive feedback after a job rejection, some candidates use this information to sue. For this reason, many companies are unwilling to give specific feedback and instead provide a generic response when they reject your application.

They Don't Want to Argue with You

Many recruiters don't share more detailed feedback with their candidates because they know that some people will start arguing with them. The candidate mistakenly thinks that arguing will result in the interviewer changing their mind. In reality, it will make the interviewer even more confident they made a good decision.

They Don't Want to Tell You It's Because of Your Personality

Although you feel that you are the perfect candidate for the job based on the job description, let's say you were rejected because the company is looking for someone who will fit in with the company culture, and they don't think you're that person.

No one wants to tell you that you didn't get the job because of your personality. How would you even explain that? To avoid an uncomfortable conversation, they simply choose not to give any feedback at all.

The Recruiter Is Lazy

Some recruiters are lazy and don't follow company processes because they don't care about their jobs. This reflects poorly on the company culture, so if you don't get a proper reply, you may be better off.

The Recruiter Is Busy

Many companies have small recruitment teams that are often overloaded. If you don't get feedback it may be because the team just doesn't have time.

You Are the Backup Candidate

If you haven't received a response after a few days, the employer may have already filled the position.

If the feedback is delayed, one of the reasons could be that the primary candidate asked for more time to think about the offer, and the company doesn't want to lose you if the first-choice candidate rejects the offer.

People Are out of the Office

In larger organizations, the recruitment process can be quite complex, with several rounds of interviews. If one of your interviewers falls ill after your interview or goes on holiday and forgets to send feedback to the recruiter, you may not receive feedback from the company right away.

There's a Hiring Freeze

Companies go through changes and reorganization quite often. An internal upheaval could result in a hiring freeze, which will delay decisions about who to hire. Because the hiring manager doesn't want to lose you as a candidate, they simply delay giving you feedback until they know if they still have a budget for their open roles. Such a delay could last a few days or even weeks or months.

The Company Is Considering an Internal Candidate

If a company wants to hire someone internally but opened the role publicly to get more candidates in case the internal candidate doesn't accept, you may not get any feedback for a while.

The Hiring Manager Doesn't Provide Feedback

The recruiter may be unable to get feedback from the hiring manager if the hiring manager is busy or simply unresponsive. Even though the recruiter wants to give you feedback, they simply don't know what to tell you.

FINAL THOUGHTS

There are many reasons you might not get any feedback after an interview. Don't assume any single person is to blame. Sometimes the recruiter can't get feedback from the hiring manager, and sometimes the company has a "no detailed feedback" policy.

During my career, the one thing that always helped me get the feedback I needed was my good relationship with a recruiter. I advise my clients to maintain a good relationship with the recruiter for a number of reasons, including getting feedback.

HOW TO ASK FOR FEEDBACK

Asking for feedback may seem like a daunting task. For one thing, part of you doesn't want to hear how you did because it may make you feel bad. Try not to let your fear get in the way of self-improvement. Feedback is always your friend.

You should provide follow-up communication in every situation—after applying for a job and after going through an interview. Even if you are rejected in the end, it is still worth doing a follow-up. Saying "thank you" to the recruiter and politely asking for his or her thoughts regarding the interview will help you prepare better next time and develop a sturdier job-seeking strategy.

The way to request feedback is affected by the specific circumstances. We will take a closer look at each to see how to follow up in the best way possible.

You Applied for a Job, but You're Not That Qualified

If you recently graduated and you're not that experienced, you may not have all the qualifications necessary to land a particular job. If this is that case, there is no need to follow up with the company.

You're Qualified and You Applied for the Job

If you submitted an application for a job you're qualified for, then you can follow up on the recruiter's LinkedIn profile a couple of days later. Send the connection request with a message to the recruiter. Keep the message general, that you just want to connect or expand your network. Don't mention in your first message that you want to get an update. Recruiters are busy every single day, so when they see another work item for them, they will not rush to accept the invitation.

After they accept your LinkedIn invitation, you should thank them for accepting it and mention the fact that you submitted an online application for the available job. Write two or three good reasons you'd be a good fit for the position and end the message in a warm yet respectful manner. You will be able to see if the recruiter reads the message or not. If they read it and a week or so passes by with no news, there are high chances you were not selected for an interview.

You Interviewed with the Recruiter

Very few candidates take the time to follow up after an interview with a recruiter. That's a shame because this process can show your interest in the job while allowing you to establish a good connection with the recruiter. Send a quick message to thank the recruiter for the interview and ask one question about the job. There is no science behind this, but when the recruiter answers your question, they're essentially confirming that they're still considering you.

You've Been Rejected

A follow-up is still recommended even when you're rejected. If you do it right, you will impress the recruiter who will remember you if another position opens in the future. When you are rejected, never show your disappointment and bitterness in the follow-up message. Instead, say thank you for the interviewer's time, mention that it was a great experience for you, ask for feedback, and mention your desire to be remembered in case a position opens in the future that is more suitable for your training and experience.

Receiving an email or phone call that lets you know you have been rejected by an employer can leave a bitter taste and a good dose of disappointment. So the last thing you may think about is asking for feedback. Even if you do think about it, you may be tempted to respond bitterly or negatively. Avoid the temptation, swallow the bitter taste, and show your best self.

Prepare in advance for getting a rejection phone call, so you can ask for feedback then and there. You will need to take the news well and make the request in a calm and polite manner. If you do so, the employer will be willing to explain why you weren't their choice.

You Received an Offer

In the event you get an offer, follow up by letting the recruiter know that you are going to review the offer in the following day or two and return with an answer.

The idea is to make the recruiter see that you're seriously considering the offer and you're still interested in the job, but you need a bit of time to analyze the offer, making sure it is what you're looking for. At this point, you could negotiate the offer a little.

WHEN TO ASK FOR FEEDBACK

In the event of job rejection, you shouldn't wait for too long to ask for feedback. If you receive an email with the news, send an answer after a few hours but before twenty-four hours have elapsed. Wait a bit to send it so you don't sound panicked. Don't wait too long to send your feedback request because the employer may forget what happened.

If you receive a phone call, ask for feedback during that particular phone call. Try to remain calm and accept things as they are and politely ask for feedback. If you didn't manage to answer your phone and the employer left a voicemail, call them back. You could send an email as well, but it would be best to utilize the same means of communication chosen by the employer.

HOW TO ASK FOR FEEDBACK

Begin by saying thank you for the willingness of the employer to communicate his or her decision. It may be hard to do this, as you may feel aggrieved, but keep in mind that diplomacy and politeness are key in such situations. It is worth leaving an open door no matter how bad you feel, because opportunities may arise when you least expect.

Explain to the employer that you're continuously looking for ways to improve yourself, which includes job searching and career advancement. This will represent the ideal reason for your feedback request. The next step is to ask what skill or experience you lack, in their opinion. Also ask about the interview itself—what could you have done better?

If you send an email, thank the employer for their time and let them know you would appreciate any feedback on your skills, experience, and presentation.

If you're talking to the employer on the phone, make sure to take a pause after asking the feedback question. Give the employer the chance to offer an answer to your questions. If you do get feedback this way, pay a lot of attention to what the employer has to say. Resist the temptation to argue or deny whatever you don't agree with. Instead, write down the observations you receive, so you can reflect on them later on and use them to improve future performances. A kick in the back can be one step forward. Express gratitude for the feedback, even if it is hard to hear.

if you can't get any feedback from your request, move forward and stop pushing. Some employers don't want to give feedback and you need to accept that.

THINGS YOU SHOULD AND SHOULD NOT DO WHEN ASKING FOR FEEDBACK

Be Polite

There are a few things you can do to increase your chances of getting feedback and being considered for future roles. One of the most important things to remember is always to be polite, no matter what the feedback is. You never know who might see your angry or sarcastic email response and how it could influence your future career.

Don't Rush

After your interview, you'll want to know right away how you did. Relax and wait until the next day to ask for feedback from the employer. If you forgot to ask during the interview about the next steps, you'll just have to wait.

If you don't receive feedback after your interview, wait at least a day before reaching out. When you do, ask about the next steps rather than feedback. If you receive a rejection, feel free to ask for feedback then.

Don't Try to Make Them Change Their Decision

If the employer decided not to hire you, there was a reason. It's not worth trying to convince them to change their mind, and you may not receive feedback if you do.

If you decide to try to convince someone that their current decision is wrong, they will not like it. They may see your efforts as arrogant or presumptuous.

Show Gratitude

If you want to obtain feedback on the interview, be sure to be polite and show gratitude for the interview. Bear in mind that the employer is not obligated to respond to your feedback request.

Always begin your request by thanking the employer for the opportunity they gave you and for the time they spent with you.

Use a Positive Tone

If you received a rejection note, you may feel frustrated, upset, and even angry. If you feel this way when you receive the note, go for a walk or get busy doing something else. Do not reply right away, as you may regret what you say when you are angry.

Although it's unpleasant to be rejected, you should remember that there are other opportunities out there and you will eventually find a great job. Additionally, you can take advantage of the opportunity you just had to learn new skills and perfect the existing ones.

It is always good to leave a door open. You never know when you'll apply for another position in that company, so you want to be remembered as a nice and enthusiastic person. This is how you can adopt the appropriate tone: Feel gratitude for the opportunity to improve. Then, when you're in the right frame of mind, write your message to the interviewer thanking them and asking for feedback.

Do Not Beg or Seem Desperate

Although you may be between jobs for an extended period of time, you should not beg for a job. If you appear desperate, you could ruin any chance you have of being contacted again by the company. Even if they aren't hiring at the moment, they may be able to connect you with another company that is hiring.

Therefore, it is important to treat all interactions with the recruitment process as networking opportunities.

Accept the Criticism

When you receive feedback, it is important to remember that it will likely include some criticism. Accept the criticism and do not push it back. It is not a good idea to argue with the employer or disagree. Instead, thank them for their willingness to share their professional opinions and their time to explain what didn't go that well and express your gratefulness for the opportunity and feedback.

THE BEST FOLLOW-UP METHOD

When looking to follow up with a recruiter, should you call, text, email, or message via social media?

Before you leave the interview (no matter whether it's online or on-site), ask about next steps. This will give you a timeline for when you should expect your feedback. When you know the dates, ask the interviewer who to reach out to if you have any questions.

You can also simply ask the recruiter or hiring manager about his or her preferred communication means. This way, you'll know how to proceed when looking to do a follow-up.

In a study done by Robert Half,[98] 46 percent of recruiters and hiring managers preferred to be contacted by email. An email message will give a recruiter plenty of space to answer and find the best moment for it. And if you are using an email tracker, you can know exactly when the person reads your email.

SAMPLE FOLLOW-UP EMAILS

Following up after an interview can be difficult, but it's important to make sure you have the right approach. Here are several examples of follow-up emails that can help you get the conversation started:

---

[98] https://www.roberthalf.ca/en/the-art-of-following-up

Example 1

Hello, <NAME>.

I hope all is well.
I'd just like to check in on the status of the position that I interviewed for.
I'm excited to hear about the next steps and what the role will entail. The role seems like a great fit for my background and I'm looking forward to hearing more about it.

Thank you so much,
<NAME>

Example 2

Hello, <NAME>.

I hope all is well.
I'm following up to see if you have any updates regarding the <JOB TITLE> position that I interviewed for on <DATE>.
I'm excited to hear about the next steps, and the role seems like a great fit for my background based on what I learned! Any updates you can share would be great.

Best Regards,
<NAME>

Example 3[99]

Hello, <NAME>.

I thought I'd check in as, during our last interview, you mentioned that you'd be making the final recruitment decision for the <JOB TITLE> by <DATE>. Please, let me know if you have an update and if there are any additional details I could provide.

Best Regards,
<NAME>

---

[99] https://zety.com/blog/follow-up-email-after-interview

PHONE CALL FOLLOW-UPS

A phone call is the fastest way to reach out to anyone. But, before you call a recruiter, consider that they are quite busy and constantly on the phone. If they don't pick up, leave them a message. Don't hound them. If you wait a week and call them a second time and you still don't hear back, try a different follow-up method.

LINKEDIN FOLLOW-UPS

Since recruiters spend most of their time searching for candidates on LinkedIn, sending a LinkedIn message to a recruiter is one of the easiest ways to connect with them. Nevertheless, it's not the best way to get feedback since you'll be competing for the recruiter's attention with other candidates for other jobs. Your message could easily be overlooked.

HOW OFTEN TO FOLLOW UP

The best time to follow up is two days after the day you were supposed to hear back from the recruiter or hiring manager. Do one more follow-up if you still haven't heard from them in over a week.

If you have not received an answer after ten to fourteen days, you shouldn't expect to receive any feedback from them at all and you should assume they're not moving forward with your application.

FINAL THOUGHTS

If you're considering asking for feedback, it may take some courage, but it's worth it. Some hiring managers even give extra time to candidates seeking feedback.

No matter what your situation is, always remember to be polite. It doesn't matter if you speak to the recruiter or write an email; maintain a positive, grateful attitude.

THE MEANING OF GENERIC FEEDBACK

It would be great if employers could provide an explanation of why they reject a candidate. What can you improve so next time they will choose you and not someone else? Nevertheless, most of the time, you're probably going to get nothing more than an email or phone call informing you that you did not get the job. In the worst-case scenario, you may not get any answer at all from the employer, even if you do a follow-up and even though they promised to get back to you.

You Failed the First Impression

You have only one chance to make a first good impression, and if during the first thirty seconds you didn't create one, it will be hard to change it. However, this does not mean it is impossible to overcome a bad first impression once made. But because we are humans we create biases about people. That's why it is important not only to research the company but also to research the people before your interview.

If you wear shorts for the interview with an interviewer who never wears anything other than a suit, the impression you will make is not going to be good. Sometimes the chemistry wasn't there or you didn't pass their elevator test. In an elevator test, the interviewer asks themself, "How would I feel about being stuck inside an elevator with this person?" If they feel uncomfortable with you during the interview, they will probably feel uncomfortable with you at work. This test is a quick, thumbs up or thumbs down evaluation method.

Xero Australia managing director Trent Innes used a "coffee test." He offered candidates a drink. After the interview, he would check to see if "the person doing the interview want[ed] to take that empty cup back to the kitchen"[100]

You Were Not the Right Culture Fit

Companies are looking for candidates who are compatible with their culture and their values. Companies are not very open about this type of rejection because it is very hard to explain it and candidates have trouble hearing it. But if everybody in the company is crazy into sports and you never do anything, they will assume that you will not be happy at work. So make sure to do some corporate culture research to see how your social skills fit into the picture because you might be able to save yourself the time and trouble of applying.

---

[100] https://www.nzherald.co.nz/business/best-of-2019-xero-boss-reveals-secret-coffee-cup-test-and-that-he-wont-hire-anyone-who-fails/XSWYMWALIUCPOY5ZJPOWZFDLSE/

You Were Not Prepared

"What do you know about our company?" "Do you know our products?" "Who are our competitors?" If you answer questions like these with silence or incomplete answers, the employer is probably not going to hire you. The employer will assume that your lack of preparation means you don't care that much about the job.

You Lied During the Interview

When you were asked to state the reason why you were leaving your current job, maybe you said something that wasn't completely true. If the interviewer does good research, you will be found out. And you won't be hired.

It's important to admit when you don't know something and then show you're willing to learn it.

You Didn't Show Excitement

Employers are looking for people who truly want to work in their company and are not just looking for a job to pay their rent. Passionate and enthusiastic employees are the ones delivering the best results because they are willing to invest time and effort in performing well. So, besides being enthusiastic, you need to be ready to explain why you want the job.

If you know people who already work there, ask them what they enjoy about their jobs. This will show the employer that you care about the job and you're interested enough to do whatever it takes to increase your chances.

You Didn't Seem Coachable

If every answer and example you give during an interview demonstrates that you like doing things your way, the interviewer is going to decide that you would be hard to train. Every manager I know has had the experience of hiring somebody who was acting stubborn in the interview and then turned out to be a difficult employee.

All hiring managers want to see that candidates they are interviewing are able to adapt to new ideas because every business is evolving, and they can thrive only when employees continue to innovate.

You Didn't Show the Employer That You're a Long-Term Employee

Interviews help the employer get to know the candidates and assess their potential as long-term employees. Recruiting is a lengthy and expensive process, and companies don't want to have to do it frequently. Besides, once an employee is hired, the company spends more time and money training them. They don't want to see the employee walk away after six months.

So, if you want to land the job, you will need to get ready to answer questions regarding your plans for the next five or ten years. In your answer, focus on your career and professional life. The idea is for the company to see if they can offer you what you're looking for and if you're a fit for the mission, vision, and culture of the company.

Your Skills Weren't What They Needed

Even though you meet most of their requirements, the employer may have some additional wants not listed in the job description, and you don't have those. Maybe they want people who have the right skills for their future plans.

You Didn't Behave Well

Being passive is certainly not a good idea, but displaying overwhelming behavior is not recommended either. It is good to be enthusiastic but try not to be too eager. Also, try not to pass the thin line between self-confidence and arrogance. Even if you have more skills and know more than the interviewer, you shouldn't act as if you do.

If you make the employer think you are a hard-to-handle person by interrupting constantly, for example, or refusing to answer questions, you're not going to get the job. You can't force your way into the company.

The Position Was Relocated

Sometimes companies will decide to move positions around among their different branches to save money. You may have been a perfectly good candidate, but leadership decided to switch the location of the job and so they started focusing on hiring there instead. There are some downfalls to this type of plan, such as not being able to keep the same team together or possibly losing good employees who don't want to relocate. In the end, it's up to the company leadership to decide if this type of role relocation makes sense for their business model and future plans.

The Company Reorganized or Instituted a Hiring Freeze

Every company has to react to unpredictable situations like economic crises, pandemics, and accidents. That's why companies implement a hiring freeze or reorganize. In the process, they discover that some roles are no longer necessary including the one you were interviewing for.

There Was a Better Candidate

When you receive a rejection, that usually means that there is a better candidate out there for that given job opening. That candidate may have more experience, have been better prepared for the interview, have done better research about the company, or have been able to answer the interviewer's questions more effectively.

Every time you apply for a job, you are competing against others; sometimes it will be just a few people, but other times you will be competing against hundreds or even thousands of others. That's why it's important to work on yourself continuously and improve your knowledge and brand.

FINAL THOUGHTS

There are many other reasons why you might not have been invited back for a second interview, but the most common ones are the ones listed. Some of these things you will not be able to control, like a hiring freeze, but others you can work on, like your interviewing skills or preparation.

Although you may not have been hired yet, don't give up. Use the information you've learned to better prepare for future applications and interviews. You will be successful in the end.

38. How to Cope with Rejection While Job Hunting

You applied for several jobs and even went to a couple of interviews, but you were rejected. This experience can be very disappointing and demoralizing.

There's no point in feeing down even if this happens time and time again. Things happen for a reason and maybe the job just wasn't the right one for you. Try learning something from each and every experience you have, so that you are always improving for future opportunities.

Following are some tips that I always share with people who are looking for a job. I hope they will help you as well. Read them, embrace them, and keep moving forward.

THERE'S NO POINT IN TAKING IT PERSONALLY

When you're rejected, it's easy to feel like you're the only person in the world experiencing it. I like to share the story of billionaire Jack Ma, founder of Alibaba. When he was searching for a job he applied for thirty jobs in his home city. He was rejected by every single one of the employers. He even applied to KFC, was interviewed with twenty-four other people, and then was the only one KFC didn't hire. But Mae didn't take the rejection personally; he continued searching and working on himself. Within a few years, he had become one of the richest people in the world.

My favorite motivational speaker Les Brown[101] said, "Other people's opinion of you does not have to become your reality." So don't take rejection too personally and keep looking. Believe that the right job is out there for you, and you'll find it eventually.

---

[101] https://en.wikipedia.org/wiki/Les_Brown_(speaker)

DON'T SHARE YOUR DISAPPOINTMENT WITH THE WORLD

You might be surprised how many job seekers turn to social media to vent their frustration about the job search or to share that they were rejected or failed an interview. Although this strategy might help them feel better for a brief moment, it will hurt them in the long run. We are living in the digital age, and whatever you say on social media is going to be seen by others, including people who might be looking at your job application in the future.

Using social media to express your frustration can have a negative impact on your job search. You may not be considered for a job if interviewers find your posts. Many companies use application tracking systems that include social media data. If you use the same email for your social media and job applications, there is a chance that your social media posts will be seen by potential employers.

If you feel the urge to share your frustration, talk to your friends, family, or significant other. Don't post about it on social media!

FOCUS ON YOUR QUALITIES AND STRENGTHS

The companies you applied to weren't able to appreciate your skills and qualities. Don't worry: Other companies will be able to see your value. Being aware of your strengths, qualities, abilities, and skills is a great way to get over a rejection episode. Sit down, grab a piece of paper and a pen, and start making a list of all the characteristics that you possess. Remind yourself of your strengths and your achievements instead of dwelling on rejection.

This will help you feel better and improve your ability to navigate future interviews. Your close friends and family are more capable of noticing your good qualities than you are, so ask them for help. If you find a new skill, you can add it to your resume.

It is also relevant at this point to go back and review your job search plan. If you have been adding information to it all along, you will now have a full overview of the companies that liked your profile. Start applying to their competitors.

ACCEPT THE REALITY

As a recruiter, I can tell you that there are so many factors that go into the job search that are out of the candidate's control. You will not be able to influence that the company just lost their biggest client and is in a hiring freeze. You have no control over the fact that their priorities have changed.

You can't find out most of the things that are happening behind the curtain. It would be great if organizations informed you about what is happening. But the fact that most of this is out of your control is the reality. Try to see the situation from the employer's perspective: You probably wouldn't be prioritizing job candidates in your communication.

It just wasn't meant to be. You probably don't like it, but you need to understand that there's no point in feeling sorry for yourself. Your time will come as well and, until then, it's useless to waste energy dwelling on the lack of success.

Chances are good you'll get a much better job with your newfound wisdom and interviewing practice. Concentrate your attention, energy, and effort into creating a better strategy for getting a better job.

ASK FOR FEEDBACK AND MAKE ADJUSTMENTS

If you're like most job seekers, the experience of getting rejected can be pretty discouraging. But instead of beating yourself up or wondering what you did wrong, why not take a proactive approach and request feedback from the recruiter or hiring manager? If you do this right, you'll not only get some valuable insights into why you were rejected, but you'll also reap some helpful advice about what to do differently in future job applications.

Of course it's important to request feedback in a polite and professional way. Simply asking for "feedback" is likely to get you a form response or no response at all. Instead, try something like this: "I really appreciate your time and attention during the application process. I would be very grateful if you could provide me with some specific feedback about why I was not selected for the role so that I can improve my chances in future applications." By being specific and polite, you'll increase your chances of getting the feedback you're looking for.

TAKE A CLOSER LOOK AT YOUR APPROACH

The best advice I got in my life was "Apply what is working, remove what is not." The same advice can apply to a job search. We all do things that fail to yield the desired results, but only a few of us stop for a moment to analyze what isn't working. For example, maybe by analyzing your job search plan you realize that you have been applying only to positions that are several levels above your current position. You revise your plan and aim for the right type of job and get hired.

Revise your plan to get rid of what isn't working. The sooner you realize what's not working out, the quicker you'll head in the right direction.

BE REALISTIC IN YOUR EXPECTATIONS

Sometimes our expectations are disconnected from the reality of what the market is offering or what is possible given our experience. If you were working for a company that gave you unlimited holiday time, it could be unrealistic to expect that perk from every new employer going forward.

Times change and we need to adjust our expectations accordingly. A financial crisis will affect the job market just as a pandemic will. Modify your expectations to fit the current reality.

I still remember one developer I met in 2009. He had finished college and was struggling to find a job. I offered to help him. When we discussed what he was looking for, he said he was only interested in a senior developer role with a senior-level salary.

I checked his LinkedIn profile a few years later and discovered he had spent almost two years looking for a job and in the end had had to settle for a junior developer role. If he had simply adjusted his expectations to fit reality, he would have spent the two years working his way up to a higher salary and likely a promotion.

REMEMBER THAT YOU ARE NOT ALONE

We all experience the same fears and struggles when job hunting. We fear that we'll never find the right job or that the new job will not be good enough.

Don't dwell on past rejections and try to remember the positive aspects of whatever you do: those times when you were invited for an interview, for example. Many people didn't even get that chance and were rejected at the beginning.

Millions of people are searching for new job opportunities and struggling like you, and many of them will be rejected too. You are not alone. The sooner you accept this, the sooner you can move on and move forward.

TAKE A BREAK

Job hunting can be a tiring and thankless process. You can send out dozens of applications and not hear anything back or go on a dozen interviews and not get the job. It's enough to make anyone want to give up. But it's important to remember that finding a job is a job on itself and, like any other job, it requires dedication and hard work.

There will be days when you feel like you're getting nowhere, but it's important to keep going. If you need to take a break, that's okay, but try not to let yourself get too discouraged. The most important thing is to keep your phone on and your email checked, so you don't miss any opportunities that come your way.

FINAL THOUGHTS

There will be times when you feel frustrated and down during your job search. It may happen after you have interviewed multiple times and not received an offer or after you have applied to multiple jobs and not even received a response.

Try to maintain a positive attitude. You know your strengths, qualities, and abilities well by now. Remember that there is a company that will appreciate all of these. You have a lot to offer, so you should feel good about yourself. If you can find ways to improve and learn more, that's even better. Using your spare time for self-development is always a great idea.

To stay motivated during your job search, recite positive mantras. Remind yourself that you'll make it through these tough times and that you'll eventually find the right company that will see the value in you. We're all facing the same fears and issues during our job searches, so don't give up!

If you are struggling to find your dream job remember that it could be just around the corner.

39. How to Negotiate Your Salary

If you've received an offer from a recruiter or company representative, this is great news—it means you're one step closer to getting a new job. Just because you finally received an offer doesn't mean you have to accept it as it is. You may be able to negotiate your salary, if you know what you're worth and have the right arguments for it.

Salary negotiations can be a daunting task. However, if you plan and strategize accordingly, you can come out on top. Following are some tips to help you through the process.

THE REASON TO NEGOTIATE A SALARY

Recruiters and employers often expect candidates to say something about the offer and even to try to negotiate both the salary and offered benefits. Don't feel that you are being disrespectful by not accepting the offer as it stands. You do need to negotiate with common sense, and you have to prepare good arguments for why you think you deserve a higher salary or other benefits that will help you do your job better.

In order to understand what similar positions in your industry pay, you need to conduct some research. You can use job boards, company websites, or even salary surveys to find out what other professionals in your field are earning. Once you have a good understanding of what others are making, you'll see if the job offer is in line.

If you're applying for jobs in different countries, it's important to do your research on how to negotiate a salary in each country before you go in for your interview. Different rules apply in different cultures and you need to adhere to the customs of the country where you will be working.

Bear in mind that many companies will give you an offer that is final. In that event, it is a take-it-or-leave-it deal, and so you can't negotiate.

There are many misconceptions about offers. One is that employers are always trying to give you an offer that is slightly below the average in their industry, as they want to save money in every way they can. Most companies have determined a salary range for the role. They will try to operate within the range, but they could go slightly above it if they found a star candidate.

THE BENEFITS OF NEGOTIATING

The benefits of negotiating your salary are as follows:

- getting paid what you are worth,
- setting a precedent for future negotiations,
- establishing that you know what you are doing and you know your value, and
- feeling greater satisfaction with the new job.

Although negotiating your salary can be an empowering experience, it's not for everyone. Many people avoid it because it can put them in an uncomfortable position. If you feel that it's the right time to negotiate, try it. You may end up with a better pay or benefits package.

You don't need to focus exclusively on salary during negotiations. You can ask for better benefits. Or you can ask if they will offer training or certifications to raise your value on the job market next time you search for a new opportunity.

WHEN IT'S APPROPRIATE TO NEGOTIATE

Even if you're ready to negotiate your salary and prepared a set of arguments for it, doing it at the right time is important. In other words, wait until you receive a pre-offer or job offer to start your negotiations.

If the recruiter or hiring manager tells you that their offer is final, you have very limited space to negotiate a better salary, but you can still try. The best way to proceed is to thank them for the offer and ask for some time to think about it. This will give you time to prepare enough data for your negotiation. You should collect enough supporting data that demonstrate you deserve a higher salary.

When negotiating a job offer, limit the back and forth. Once you've asked for a change and the employer has responded with a counteroffer, consider accepting it. At most, do one more round of negotiating. If you go beyond that, the employer may decide you're not worth the trouble and rescind the offer.

If you have already accepted an offer with one company and a second company makes you an offer with better terms, don't try to negotiate a new offer with the first company. You will only look greedy, and this will not create a good impression. Simply take a bit of time to analyze both offers. If you want to accept the second offer, inform the first company as soon as possible. And reject any other counteroffer you get from them—accepting a new counteroffer will, according to anecdotal evidence, have a negative impact on promotions and raises in the long run.

HOW TO PREPARE FOR A SALARY NEGOTIATION

In theory, you could negotiate every part of your compensation package, including the base salary, a sign-on bonus, other bonuses, restricted stock units (RSUs), stock options, health coverage, and other supports for the job, including a car, a phone, and hardware. However, only a small number of people have that much negotiating power.

What you can negotiate depends on the job location. In the United States, for example, you might be able to negotiate a better health care package, but other countries, like Sweden, have a decentralized universal healthcare system for everyone, so you would be wasting your time asking an employer there for more health care coverage.

Negotiating your salary can be a tense, awkward thing to do, especially if you don't like confrontation or are afraid that the company will withdraw their offer and you might jeopardize your position or come across as greedy. At the same time, you should be being paid what you're worth. As long as you've done your research and come to the table prepared, there's no reason you can't negotiate a higher salary.

Do Your Research

You cannot enter into any salary negotiation if you're not prepared with adequate information. So, if you want to win the negotiation, you will need to be well informed and realistic.

Check the salary trends and typical ranges in your industry. There are a number of sites where you can find more info about salary ranges like Salary.com,[102] PayScale,[103] Glassdoor,[104] and Paylab.[105] See what kind of qualifications, certifications, and extra training one needs to have in order to get the best salary for your particular job.

---

[102] https://www.salary.com/
[103] https://www.payscale.com/
[104] https://www.glassdoor.com/
[105] https://www.paylab.com/

Sometimes companies can't afford to offer high salaries, especially companies that are just starting up. You will also need to consider this factor when negotiating.

Also check to see just how popular the job is and how easy or hard it is to find qualified candidates for that position. If your skill set is something that's hard to find, enter negotiations with greater confidence.

Do not ever negotiate by saying that other companies are offering more or that you saw a particular salary range somewhere. Focus more on how your experience and knowledge can contribute to the company and how you can leverage those to increase the value of your offer. Always demonstrate your value; don't build your negotiation on the idea that somebody else in the same role gets paid more.

Determine Your Worth and What You Can Offer

A company will offer a salary based on the overall value you can bring as an employee. They evaluate your seniority, your knowledge, and your expertise. When you are planning to start your negotiation, you should take into account your education level, your level of experience, your career, the skills and abilities you have, whether you have any experience as a leader, and whether you have any relevant certifications.

When negotiating, it's also okay to ask the interviewing company what the main differences are between junior and senior level positions. This will help you determine where you fit in, what salary you are worth, and how much you should be asking for. Different companies have different salary ranges, so it is important to research the company you are interested in before beginning your salary negotiation.

The salary levels for a particular industry can vary depending on the location. It is especially important to consider what your new location will cost you in terms of salary. For example, if you are relocating for a job, be sure to factor in the cost of living and the average salary in the new location. In addition, you may get paid differently depending on whether you are working remotely or on site.

Prepare Your Arguments

After you have determined your worth and checked the current salary ranges on the market, you should put all your arguments together. To provide a good answer to the question "Why do you deserve a higher salary?", look at your achievements and accomplishments. One thing that always works is to provide real numbers and data that demonstrate your achievements and value.

If you have more experience than what is mentioned by the employer in the job description, now is a good time to bring that up.

If you have to cover different time zones, work overtime, or travel for work, factor in those issues when negotiating your salary. Skills that are in high demand in your industry can lead to a higher salary and better benefits.

If the offer is below the market rate for the role you are trying to get, here is what you can say:

Thank you so much for your offer. It sounds like it would be a perfect fit and the company is something that will grow with me too! My only concern at this point is salary. After doing my market research and based on the skills and experience I am bringing to the role, my expectations are between $X and $Y. What can we do to get me there?

It's no secret that salaries are often negotiable, and yet many of us go into job negotiations woefully unprepared to advocate for ourselves. If you're not sure how to start negotiating your salary, Google is a great place to start.

A simple search for "how to negotiate your salary" will provide you with thousands of results, and although not all of them will be relevant to your specific situation and location, they can provide helpful examples of what to say and how to approach the subject. With a little bit of research, you can be fully prepared to fight for the salary you deserve.

Take Perks and Benefits into Consideration

An employer may not be able to meet the demands of a qualified employee. If this is the case, the employee may instead seek extra perks and benefits as compensation for the lack of money.

Many companies are willing to offer company shares or compensation for the costs you incur working remotely. But you can also negotiate more time off, learning and professional development budgets, health and wellness benefits, childcare, or tech hardware.

If you are based in the United States, you can also negotiate your company's match policy for its 401(k). Depending on the terms of the 401(k) plan, an employer may choose to match your contributions dollar-for-dollar or offer a partial match. Some employers may also make non-matching 401(k) contributions. Matching contributions aren't required by law, and not all employers offer them as part of their 401(k) plans.[106]

Maybe you can negotiate additional vacation days, a flexible working schedule, the possibility to stay at home for work more often, better health insurance, or savings for your retirement plan.

Bear in mind that smaller organizations and startups cannot often match MAMAA[107] company offers. These are the offers the biggest companies can make. A smaller company is betting on you believing in the company's potential growth, mission, or vision.

Write Everything Down

Writing things down will allow you to assess things better after the negotiation, in a calm and quiet environment. This will help you make a wise decision that will benefit your career in the long term.

You can also ask a recruiter to email you the pre-offer details to give you an idea of what the company is offering and to help you to prepare for the negotiation.

Don't Be Afraid to Say No

It can be tough when you go through the job application process and finally get to the negotiation phase, only to find out that the company isn't willing to meet your salary requirements. It's important to weigh the pros and cons of taking a job at that point.

If the salary is the only thing holding you back from an otherwise great opportunity, it may be worth considering. On the other hand, if taking the job would mean significant financial strain or a longer commute, it might not be worth it. Ultimately, it's up to you to decide what factors are most important in a job and whether this particular opportunity meets those criteria.

Use the Power of a Counteroffer

If you are offered a new job, your current employer may try to keep you by offering you a better salary. If this happens, you can use it as leverage in your

---

[106] https://www.forbes.com/advisor/retirement/what-is-401k-match/
[107] MAMAA, stands for Meta, Apple, Microsoft, Amazon, and Google's parent company Alphabet.

negotiation with the new company. Or if you get offered jobs by more than one employer, you can use that leverage.

Be Patient

The recruiter or hiring manager may not be able to get back to you right away with a response to your effort to negotiate. They may need to discuss your request with other people in their company, like the compensation and benefits team or the finance team.

If you have other offers in place, you should inform the company you're negotiating with so they know they need to act quickly.

How to Ask for More Time to Consider a Job Offer

When you receive a job offer, you don't have to accept it right away. If you decide to ask for more time, it's important to be careful about how you ask so that you don't insult the hiring manager or risk losing the offer. If you need more time to make a decision, be sure to ask politely and avoid coming across as pushy or unprofessional.

If the deadline they provide you with doesn't seem like enough time, ask the hiring manager if it's possible for them to give you an extension. But be sure to give a good reason why when you ask for an extension. If your only reason is that you are waiting on other offers, you could create the impression that you are not interested in their job.

FINAL THOUGHTS

Many companies give you a specific time frame in the offer letter or email for accepting the job offer. Typically, they'll give you two to three days. If you want to ask for more time, don't ask for more than a week. If you want to negotiate any part of the compensation package, consider a more conservative time frame.

If you do not reply to the employer's request within the specified time frame, your offer could be rescinded as the employer may think you are not interested in the job. It is important to be clear about your intentions and to show that you are interested in the position.

It is generally frowned upon to do more than one ask during the course of a negotiation. Once you've requested a change and the company has responded, you should either accept that new offer or not. But don't see if you can push the number even higher.

Although negotiating your salary may seem like a daunting task, as long as you are prepared and have data to support your request and arguments, you should be fine.

40. The Counteroffer

A counteroffer happens when you have accepted a new employment offer and your current employer offers you new terms (salary, bonuses, senior role, etc.) to keep you. It can be very flattering to receive a counteroffer from your manager, as it shows that they want you to stay.

Counteroffers are very tempting, especially if they represent what you have wanted all along: the promotion that didn't come for years, the salary raise that you were asking your manager about for months, or ownership of a new project. But accepting a counteroffer is, in most cases, like following a mirage. It looks good, but is it real? Why did it take you telling your employer you were going to leave to get them to recognize your worth? If you want to leave your job, think about why and make a wise decision.

What follows are some of the reasons employers make counteroffers:

- It is cheaper for a company to raise the salary of the employee or promote them than it is to pay the extra costs connected with hiring.
- The employee has the skills they need, and filling the vacancy could take weeks or even months.
- The employer is trying to buy time to find a replacement for the employee.
- The employee is a real asset, and they don't want to lose them.

THE METHODS EMPLOYERS USE

If you had not informed your employer already that you were planning to leave, your sudden notice could cause a certain amount of upheaval. Your employer may want to know what happened, why you want to leave, why you are not happy, and what is the overall problem that made you consider another offer.

If your manager wants to keep you at the company, you should expect some of the following promises:

- New plans for your current role

- Promotion plans for you
- New projects that you will own within their company
- A salary raise (sometimes also connected with a promotion)
- Future considerations

The employer may try to play on your emotional attachments to your current work colleagues and the company. They might appeal to your vanity by saying, "You're too valuable, and we need you." Or "Without you, the team will be incomplete." They might even make a veiled threat: "If you leave, we won't finish the project and we will have to lay off people."

If the employer gives you time to think about the counteroffer or asks for you to delay taking the new job so they have time to prepare a counteroffer, know that they may just be buying time to figure out how to replace you.

CONSIDERING A COUNTEROFFER

Before you give notice, think about your reasons for wanting to change your job. Keep these in mind so when your employer makes a counteroffer, you are clearheaded.

Ask yourself the following questions:

- Does the counteroffer eliminate the reasons you decided to leave?
- If you leave, will your resignation be interpreted as disloyalty?
- Do you have the potential for career progression at your current job, or will the new offer give you a better career option?
- Are you using the new offer as leverage to get more money in your current job? Would you like to earn more money?
- Would you like to climb the hierarchy and get a better position in a company?
- Do you feel bored or feel that the company's culture is unsuitable for you?
- What changes to your career and professional life could bring you the happiness you're lacking?

To make a wise decision, you need to thoroughly assess your current situation and be honest with yourself about your wishes and aspirations. Adding a few numbers to your monthly paycheck or obtaining a more important role can increase your happiness at work, but the effect may not last for too long. At first, accepting a counteroffer may seem exciting, especially if you gained new advantages. But, in time, you may discover that it wasn't enough to make you want to stay.

Counteroffers rarely address the true factors behind what prompted you to decide to leave. Even if you are offered a better salary, promotion, or working conditions, chances are you will go back to feeling the same way about your job because the toxic workplace or micromanaging leader remain.

SHOULD YOU STAY OR SHOULD YOU GO

Many studies have covered the topic of counteroffers. One of the often quoted statistics in the recruitment world is that 80 percent of job seekers who accept a counteroffer go on to leave their job within six months anyway. After twelve months, the number can be as high as 90 percent.

I have been a recruiter for many years, and I've placed a lot of people in jobs in that time. Like any other recruiter, I have had to deal with my share of counteroffers. I was always trying to understand why people change jobs, but I also wanted to know why candidates accept counteroffers.

Over fifteen years, I tracked 127 people who received counteroffers and decided to stay in their current jobs. For every counteroffer made, I allowed one year to see if the companies delivered on their promises and if the candidates remained. Here's what I found:

- Four percent (five people) changed their job within three months.
- Eleven percent (fourteen people) changed their job within six months.
- Nine percent (eleven people) changed their job within nine months.
- Twenty-four percent (thirty-one people) changed their job within a year.
- Fifty-two percent (sixty-six people) stayed longer than a year.

Based on this data, you have a 52 percent chance of staying in your company for more than a year when you accept a counteroffer. This is aligned with data from CEB[108] that shows that 50 percent of employees[109] who accept a counteroffer leave within twelve months.

After three years, I checked if each person was still working for the same company. I found out that 92 percent of the people who had accepted a counteroffer had left their company within thirty-six months.

I stayed in touch with many of those candidates and had the chance to speak with them about their different roles over the years. I asked them why they had left in the end. The majority of them told me that the reasons they left went deep—a promise wasn't fulfilled, there was no clear career path, there was a micromanaging boss— and the issues could not be resolved by throwing money at them.

[108] https://www.sciencetheearth.com/uploads/2/4/6/5/24658156/2016-04-recursoshumanos4.pdf
[109] https://hbr.org/2016/09/why-people-quit-their-jobs

FINAL THOUGHTS

Will a counteroffer address the real problem? Sometimes higher pay is the only reason employees want to change jobs, but this is not often the case. More money will not miraculously make you happier in your job if your manager is still a control freak.

Bear in mind that if you get a counteroffer, you haven't suddenly become a more valuable employee. In most cases, the manager is trying to prevent the disruption of the business or to buy time to arrange for your replacement. If you are using your new job offer as leverage to negotiate a promotion or get a higher salary in your current job, this requires a delicate approach and comes with risks.

Nearly 40 percent of senior executives[110] and HR leaders alike agreed that accepting a counteroffer from a current employer will adversely affect one's career. And 71 percent of senior executives and 67 percent of HR leaders[111] said that superiors in the current company would question the employee's loyalty going forward.

Before you accept a counteroffer, always ask yourself why you were looking for a new job in the first place. Will all those reasons somehow magically resolve if you accept the counteroffer? Probably not!

The truth is it is very rare for a counteroffer to be successful in the long term. Maybe you will be among the 52 percent of people who stayed in their job for longer than a year, or the initial reasons for your wanting to leave may resurface even sooner and you will be faced with starting the job search process all over again.

REASONS NOT TO ACCEPT A COUNTEROFFER

As discussed, the main reason not to accept a counteroffer is that it will not change your current work situation. But there are other reasons as well.

Your Co-workers Will No Longer Trust You

Your manager is not the only one who will feel betrayed when you find another job. As soon as the news spreads across the company, your co-workers and colleagues may display changed attitudes toward you as well.

---

[110] https://hbr.org/2019/01/if-youre-about-to-take-a-new-job-should-you-consider-your-bosss-counteroffer

[111] https://hbr.org/2019/01/if-youre-about-to-take-a-new-job-should-you-consider-your-bosss-counteroffer

They will think that the fact that you looked elsewhere and considered leaving means that you're not committed to the company. They may start to see you as someone who's only working there temporarily, since leaving already was an option for you.

Your colleagues will assume that you tried to get a new job in order to negotiate a raise or better benefits for yourself.

Things May Not Work out as Expected

The prospect of getting better pay, better perks, or even a change of scenery can be very exciting. However, getting these doesn't necessarily mean you'll be any happier. You may be bored by the work, exasperated with your boss, or unfulfilled by your colleagues.

If you are considering taking a counteroffer, it's important to weigh all the potential pros and cons. Although there may be some benefits to staying with your current company, there is a number of risks involved. If you sought a new job because you hadn't been given a promotion, you were likely feeling underappreciated.

Will staying change that, knowing that the only reason you were given a counteroffer is that you were going to leave? In other words, it takes a big potential upheaval before you get what you want at your current job. Is the counteroffer addressing any of the real problems at the root of your wanting to leave?

There are two potentially good reasons for accepting a counteroffer. One is that you work in a highly competitive industry in which counteroffers are the common ways people get raises and promotions. In that case, you're doing what you need to do to advance. The other is if you and your manager have a good and trusting relationship, the employer does not resent you looking for another job, and the counteroffer is made with a recognition that you shouldn't have had to get a raise in that way.

FINAL THOUGHTS

If you are thinking of leaving your job, it is best to refuse any counteroffer your current employer may offer. If you are determined to change the direction of your career, it is best to resign and not accept a counteroffer.

Don't stay in a job you hate. If you're not happy or fulfilled, objectively assess your situation and find the best option. Don't resign because you don't feel appreciated but don't accept a counteroffer simply because it will help you earn more money. Find the real reasons behind wanting to leave a job and see if there are ways to solve the existing problems.

If you are thinking of moving on to a different company, then you should take the new opportunity and forget about any counteroffers.

If you leave, try to leave on good terms. In case you don't like the new job, you may want to return.

41. How to Respond to a Job Offer

Did you apply for multiple jobs at approximately the same time and you don't want to accept an offer until you see what other opportunities arise? After all, you want to find the best job. It can be challenging to handle this matter well so that you're not seen as rude or ungrateful.

Following are the best ways to reply to a job offer.

Carefully Communicate Your Need to Delay Acceptance

You receive an offer from a new company, but you'd like to wait for the counteroffer from your manager or see what offers might come in from other employers as well. You wouldn't be the first person to want to compare all the options. Going for the first offer you get may not be a good idea, especially if it's not from the company you prefer the most.

The following tips will help you communicate your need to delay, without affecting the relationship you established with the potential new employer.

Show Your Enthusiasm

It is important to show an employer that you're enthusiastic about the offered opportunity. No one wants to be considered just a backup. Because you never know if other companies will send you offers and this one could be your first and last, tread carefully. Be sure to thank the employer for the job offer. Say how excited you are to have been chosen. If you are not happy with something in the contract, try to call the recruiter instead of sending an email. Many things could be "lost in translation" when you are discussing terms and conditions via email. The phone is way better tool for complex explanations.

Request a Timeframe for Communicating Your Final Decision

When you receive a job offer, you don't have to provide an answer right away. Instead, see what options you have. Most companies want you to respond immediately, but they understand that changing jobs is not easy especially if you need to consult with your family or significant other.

In most cases, the recruiter will tell you the timeframe for giving your answer, usually a week.

Ask for More Time

Do you need more time to reach a conclusion and make a decision? You can always ask for extra time to make a decision, but I wouldn't ask more than once for an extension.

If you do ask, do it politely and diplomatically so it won't be interpreted as an offense. You have several options for the way to ask. You can be honest and tell them that you need two weeks to discuss it with your family and your current boss. Or you can tell them that your manager is sick or traveling and you need an extra week to reach out to them.

The best option is to be direct and say something like, "It's taken real courage for me to start this job search process because I really want to make sure the next company I go to is one I stay at for a long time. I'd like to have more than a week to think about it. I assure you that once I make a decision I will be 100 percent committed to it."

If you have more offers coming, this extra week will give you time to gently push other companies to hurry up with their offers.

If the employer refuses to give you more time, consider whether the company's offer is worthy of consideration. Will it provide what you want in terms of career advancement?

Request More Information About the Company and Team

You can buy more time by asking for more information about the company. If possible, see if you can obtain a tour of the offices to see where you would be working. This will not only provide better insight regarding a potential workplace but will also provide the additional time needed to check out other offers as well.

Consider meeting with your future team. This will take some time to organize, but it will give you more information about the job and the company culture, which could help you make a decision, and it will buy some extra time for your final decision.

COMPARE JOB OFFERS

You got a job offer and you wonder if it's worth waiting for other offers to arrive. To decide, consider several important details. Think about each company's workplace culture, your paycheck, the balance between your personal and professional life, the time you will spend on the way to and from work, and the benefits. If you find plenty of reasons to wait for another offer, then do it. If the current offer meets all or most of your requirements, then pursue it.

When assessing an offer from a startup, it's important to look at how long it took them to burn through their recent funding and how much money they raised. Sometimes a startup will offer you an insane amount of money but their track record shows that they use up money really quickly. Your next paycheck might depend on the success of the next funding round.

 A company might ask you what kind of salary you got offered by another company. This way they can offer you slightly more in order to win you over. Giving out that kind of information is a bad idea. If your first offer is $80K, your offer from a second company might then be $82K instead of the $90K they usually pay. Get offers from all companies and then start your negotiations.

WHEN A BETTER OFFER COMES ALONG

If you have accepted a job offer from a company and then you get a new job offer from another company with better conditions, what should you do?

It's a good problem to have. But after the excitement dies down, you realize you have to make a tough decision.

Although the decision to back out of a job offer may seem like it only affects you, the long-term consequences could be damaging to your reputation.

Do not act by impulse and take time to think through things well. Following are several options.

What Are the Pros and Cons?

Before you make any big decision, it's always a good idea to sit down and weight the pros and cons. This is true whether you're choosing a new car, picking a college to attend, or choosing a new job. When it comes to making a decision, data is key. By taking the time to create a list of pros and cons, you can ensure that you have all the information you need to make the best choice for yourself.

There are a few different ways to go about creating a pro and con list. One method is simply to write down all of the positive and negative points for each option. Alternatively, you could assign a numeric value to each point, based on how important it is to you. Whichever method you choose, the goal is the same: to get a clear picture of the pros and cons for each side so that you can make an informed decision.

Is It Your Dream Job?

It's a big decision, whether or not to leave your current job for a new one. If you have been at your job for a while, it can be even harder. You may have developed relationships with your co-workers and bosses, and you may be comfortable with the daily routine.

But if a new job offer comes along that represents your dream job, it may be worth considering. Even if you have already accepted another job offer, turning it down in favor of the new one could be the right move. It's a risk, of course, but sometimes taking risks pays off. If you land the dream job, it will all be worth it in the end.

Will the New Job Offer a Better Position and Bigger Paycheck?

When you are offered a job with a better job title and higher paycheck, it may be a great opportunity to grow in your career. Of course, it will come with a new set of responsibilities as well. Think carefully about it. Ask yourself if the scope of the role makes you more competitive in the market. Maybe the job offers the title you've been seeking, but does the title hold up to scrutiny? Will other companies see the title as accurately representing the scope of work?

Will You Be Earning More Money?

It's a sad fact, but we all have to work to make money. And while there are many different motivators that can keep us going day-to-day, ultimately we all want to be earning enough money to live comfortably. That's why, when presented with the opportunity to move to a new job that pays more, it can be tempting to take it.

After all, bills won't pay themselves, and we all have dreams and goals that we want to achieve. However, it's important to remember that more money is not always the best motivation to leave a job. There are many other factors to consider, such as job satisfaction, company culture, and the commute. Weigh all of the options before making a decision and remember that ultimately you need to do what's best for you.

Will Your Quality of Life Increase?

A job should offer more than just money; it should also help you live a better life. It's pointless to earn a lot of money if you never have the time to enjoy it. Will the new job give you more time to spend with family and friends or to enjoy your hobbies and passions? In general, will the job allow you to live a higher quality of life? If the answer is yes, then you have good reasons to take the offer and quit your current job.

What Are the Consequences?

There are consequences to every choice you make. If you choose to keep your current job, you may be unhappy in the long term. But if you leave you may end up developing a bad reputation. The employer may not take the news lightly, so handle the situation with care and diplomacy. This is a tough decision to make, so make sure it is worth the effort. If you play your cards well, you'll get the job you want and avoid upsetting anyone about it.

Does It Seem Too Good to Be True?

When you receive a job offer, it's natural to feel excited and flattered. However, it's important to remember that not all job offers are created equal. If you're presented with an offer that seems too good to be true, it's worth doing your due diligence to see if it might just be the opportunity of a lifetime.

HOW TO INFORM THE COMPANY

When it's time to announce your decision to take a second, better offer, get everything in written form first. Do not withdraw your acceptance of the first offer based solely on a phone call. When you have everything in written form, you can inform the first company about your decision.

If you are trying to get more money and are planning to use the new offer to renegotiate terms and salary with the first company, don't. What could happen is that you might be seen as a greedy person and this will close a door to that company in the future. People will remember what you did, and this will influence your chances in the future for sure.

At this moment there is no place for negotiating. Your offer was already approved, the budget was allocated, and if you try to get a higher salary at this stage from the first company, they most likely will reject your request. And even if they raise your salary, your manager will remember it and this is definitely not a good way to start in a new company and build your career there.

If you made up your mind and are planning to accept the new offer, you should inform the first company and their people. If you can, visit them to tell them. If you can't visit them, try to call the recruiter or the hiring manager and explain the reasons. Don't tell them it's about the money. Instead, tell them that the company has more interesting projects or you will be working with a friend, for example.

After the call, you should also send them an email informing them about your decision so it's official, and thank them for the opportunity and express that you are sorry for the situation. The company spent weeks or months trying to fill this position so, by accepting another offer, you have put them in a difficult situation.

And never wait until a few days before your starting day to inform them; do so as soon as possible.

What to Do When a Better Job Appears During a Probation Period

It can be flattering to receive a job offer from another company after being hired and working for a month or so at your new job. But you have to think very carefully before making a decision.

Try to get past the excitement of getting another offer and put your judgment to work. First of all, be discreet, as the news of a new offer may start a negative whirlpool among your colleagues and boss. Then think about the details well so that, when you make a final decision, it will be a firm one.

If you decide to take the offer and leave the company, don't change your mind again. In any case, you may have to face a wide range of unpleasant consequences, such as burned bridges and bad references.

If you're planning to make a big career change announcement on LinkedIn, remove all previous announcements first to limit the impact on your reputation.

FINAL THOUGHTS

If you are faced with two job offers and one is clearly better than the other, it can be a great problem to have. However, you need to carefully consider all of your options before making a decision. The second offer may look better on the surface (offering a higher salary), but you need to think about the long-term consequences of your choice. How you handle the situation could influence your future chances with the company you are rejecting.

Although it is not always the case, sometimes jobs are not as great as they seem. This is because employers often try to make the job and the company seem more appealing than they really are. Once you start working, you may realize that things are quite different than you expected. If you are unhappy at work, it is usually best to leave instead of continuing to feel miserable.

When you're considering leaving a company you recently joined, always bear in mind that you might cross paths with the people again in the future. That's why it's a good idea to explain to your manager the reason you decided to accept another offer and to be honest about it. There's no easy way around this situation.

42. Quitting Your Job with Grace

Leaving your job and moving on to a new chapter in your life is an exciting prospect. However, even though you may be eager to leave, you should be diplomatic when giving notice. After all, you may need good references at some point, and it's not worth sacrificing them just out of carelessness.

When you've been impacted by layoffs, you may feel the urge to be less diplomatic and tell your boss or colleagues what you really think about them. We've all been in similar situations, and during my career I've seen many cases of people deciding to follow their urges and boldly share their thoughts about their colleagues or leaders.

The relief they feel for a few hours or days may be worth it to them, especially when their colleagues consider them heroes for wanting to do something they've wanted to do for a long time. But my recommendation to you is not to say anything at all, even if your boss was a terrible leader or your colleague made your work environment toxic. You never know when and where your roads will cross again and when your former boss or your ex-colleague will be part of the team in the new company to which you are applying.

Once you've burned that bridge, if your employer is asked for feedback, instead of giving feedback on your performance they will be sharing a story about what you did. People don't want to hire someone who is a troublemaker or could potentially create problems in the workplace.

HOW TO FINISH WITH GRACE

When you are considering whether to leave your job, plan a way to do so on good terms. There are a few things you can do.

Pick a Date

You've been thinking about quitting your job for a while, or maybe you have a better job offer you want to take advantage of. Regardless, you need to decide on the date when you'll make the announcement that you're quitting.

When setting the date, be sure to give your employer the typical notice time for the country where you work. In the United States, this is two weeks, but in other parts of the world this could vary by local laws and types of employment.

To ensure a smooth transition, give yourself enough time to wrap up any projects you're working on before you leave your job. Once you have a departure date in mind, start drafting your resignation letter so you're prepared to hand it in when the time comes.

Set a Meeting with Your Manager and Make Things Official

It is not appropriate to chase your manager down the hallways of the company or take advantage of their lunch break at the cafeteria to let them know that you're quitting your job. This is a serious business that should be managed in a diplomatic and mature manner. Schedule a meeting with your boss, as soon as possible, letting them know that there is something you would like to talk about. Or if you don't need to give notice immediately, you can wait for your one-on-one with your manager.

You will feel nervous no matter how many jobs you have left before, and you may even feel guilty about it. But there's really no point in feeling so because the choice you just made is possibly going to improve your life. You have your reason to leave your current job and that's why you said yes to the other opportunity. You don't owe your manager any explanations about where you will go and why. Your manager is not entitled to such information.

What you do need to say during this conversation is a thank you for all the opportunities you had within the company and the valuable lessons and knowledge you acquired since you started working there. You should be prepared to face counteroffers, like a salary raise, more benefits, or even a promotion and other advantages. But in the end you have to be true to yourself, being aware that you took this step because you see it as the best way to pursue your goals.

Write and Submit the Resignation Letter

You usually have to break the news to your boss first and then hand in the resignation letter to make it official. But just in case your boss requires the letter once they find out what your thoughts are, it's best to have it ready the moment you let them know. When it comes to writing such a letter, no matter how laid-back the company where you work is and how well you get along with your boss, you should always use a formal tone. Look at it as an official act and not as a letter to a friend.

Also avoid providing too much information in the letter; do your best to keep it short and sweet. After all, it is your business what you do afterward, so there's no point in giving out too many details. Just announce to your boss that you'll resign from your current position within the company (state its name), starting with the date you've chosen (don't forget to mention it as well). You can write a second paragraph in which you mention your availability and willingness to help with all the processes that will provide an easier transition.

Resignation letter example:

<YOUR NAME>
<YOUR ADDRESS>
<YOUR CITY,STATE ZIP CODE>

<DATE>

<NAME>
<TITLE>
<ORGANIZATION>
<ADDRESS>
<CITY, STATE ZIP CODE>

Dear < APPROPRIATE SALUTATION> <LAST NAME>,

I would like to inform you that I am resigning from my position as <OFFICIAL JOB TITLE> for <NAME OF COMPANY> effective <DATE>.

Thank you very much for the opportunities for personal and professional development that you have provided me during the last <NUMBER OF YEARS>. I have enjoyed working for <NAME OF COMPANY> and appreciate the support provided me during my tenure.

If I can be of any help during this transition, please let me know. I wish the company continued success, and I hope to stay in touch in the future.

Sincerely,
<YOUR SIGNATURE>
<YOUR TYPED NAME>

This is just one of many examples of a resignation letter. If you need to find other templates, just type, "resignation letter example" or "resignation letter template" in Google and you will find many other options.

If you are looking for a resignation letter in your language, just type the phrase in your native language.

Do the Exit Interview

An exit interview is the last interview you will have in the company you are leaving. For some people, this can be a stressful moment. For others, this is the time to tell the HR representative all the bad things that happened to them in the company.

The HR representative or the company owner will ask you questions like, "What are your main reasons for leaving?" "What company are you joining?" "What improvements would have caused you to stay with us?"

Even if you think your criticisms could help you improve the corporate culture, keep in mind that your feedback from the interview could be shared with your manager after you leave. This last interview could close the doors when you want to return one day.

An exit interview is the last impression you'll leave your employer with. That's why it's important to be a professional and not let your emotions ruin your future chances.

Get Ready to Leave the Company

By this point, there are only a few days left until you step out of your office for good. Use this time to take care of unfinished business, to distribute among your colleagues the projects you won't be able to finish, to provide any useful information your colleagues may need about certain transactions and clients, and to brief them about everything that needs to be finished. In other words, you need to get them ready to fill your position until the company finds someone else for the job.

Knowing that you will soon have nothing to do with the company any longer, you may be tempted to start procrastinating at work and wasting time instead of continuing to do your job. If you want to quit your job with grace, the best way to do it is to keep on being the same reliable employee the company enjoyed. After all, working will make time fly by quickly, so you'll be out of there before you know it.

Also, on your last day at work, don't forget to send an email to all of your colleagues telling them that it has been great working with them and that you'd love to stay in touch with them. Encourage them to reach you on your LinkedIn profile or via another social network account you may use. And because not everyone is on Facebook or LinkedIn, you can also add your private phone number and private email so they can reach you easily.

My recommendation is to send the goodbye message to your private email address and BCC all your colleagues you want to reach. They could be on holiday or sick, so when they read the message you will be already gone. But when they return and write you will be able to get their message even though you no longer have access to company email.

You can also ask your colleagues or your boss (if you are leaving the company on good terms) for a recommendation on LinkedIn. If they say yes to your request, send them two or three options for a letter. People are busy and if you provide several examples, it might save them time.

It is not easy to leave a job with tact and grace if it is a bad job, but making a good impression even as you prepare your exit from the company may pay off someday. You never know when you might need a recommendation from your former boss or colleagues to land a dream job.

There is one secret that recruiters will not tell you or confirm, but some hiring managers reach out to their peers in the company where you work to check your references before they move forward with the offer. Through this informal request, they are looking for any red flags they might have missed. This practice is considered illegal in some countries, as it could have serious impact on your career.

FINAL THOUGHTS

Over the years, I've heard plenty of stories about people who have unintentionally damaged their careers by quitting their jobs in a less-than-graceful manner. In most cases, these individuals had good intentions but didn't realize the potential repercussions of their actions.

For example, one person I knew was so eager to leave her job that she didn't bother to give her two weeks' notice. As a result, she ended up burning bridges and further damaging her already shaky professional reputation.

Another acquaintance quit his job by sending an angry email to his boss. Not only did this get him blacklisted from future opportunities at that company, but it also made it difficult for him to find a new job since potential employers were worried about his frame of mind.

In contrast, people who quit their jobs gracefully tend to have an easier time moving on to new opportunities. They often maintain positive relationships with their former colleagues and supervisors, which can be helpful when networking for new jobs. Additionally, quitting gracefully shows that you're able to handle difficult situations in a professional manner - something that will reflect well on you in the long run. So next time you're considering quitting your job, make sure you do it the right way.

43. Career Coaches

We've all been there. You're stuck in a job you hate, with no prospects for advancement. Or you're unemployed and feeling lost, with no idea what to do next. When you're facing a career crisis, it can be helpful to talk to someone who's been there before. That's where a career coach comes in.

A career coach is someone who specializes in helping people find their way professionally. They can help you assess your skills and interests, figure out what kind of job would be a good fit for you, and develop a plan for pursuing your dream career. If you're feeling stuck in your career, consider reaching out to a career coach for help.

WHAT DOES A CAREER COACH DO

People often seek advice from career coaches when they are unclear about their next steps or when they want to prepare for a job interview and raise their chances of success. A career coach can help you develop a plan for your future, identify opportunities, and make the most of your skills and talents. They can also help you understand your career goals, make a plan for reaching them, and even determine if they are what you really want.

Coaches can also help you with your self-esteem during a job search. You may be one of the most skilled professionals in your field, but if you don't know how to present yourself during an interview you probably won't get the job you want. A career coach can help you practice your interviewing skills until they match your other professional abilities.

They may also provide guidance on how to network, find jobs, and develop a professional profile.

A Career Coach Helps You Create a Career Plan

After talking to you and assessing your current career status, a career coach can come up with a plan that is personalized for your needs and future goals. The coach can also help you find the right job and make sure that it is a good fit for your skills and personality.

A Coach Will Help You Change Direction

If you're feeling anxious or stressed about your job, a career coach will provide support, empower you to make decisions that are best for your career, and help you find the courage to pursue your desired career. You may even need to change the direction you're heading in, and a coach can help you see that need and then help you take steps to make the change.

A Coach Can Help You Explore Career Options

When you talk with friends and family members about your career, they usually tell you that you're doing just fine and not to worry. A career coach, on the other hand, isn't going to minimize your concerns or tell you what they think you want to hear. Instead, a career coach will listen carefully and then give you their best objective feedback.

A Coach Will Position You to Be Ready for Opportunities

A career coach can help you make a major career change that will make you feel more fulfilled and happier. If you don't know how to make this happen on your own, your coach will help you set a plan to achieve your goal.

A Coach Will Support You in the Job Search Process

You may have sent out resumes but not received any favorable responses. This can be very frustrating and disappointing and may even lower your self-esteem. A career coach can assess your strategies and offer advice on what to do differently to improve your chances of success.

But how can a career coach help you during an interview and to get the job you want? Having a career coach on your side means that you'll have the chance to practice and prepare for interviews. With the help of a career coach, you will get to experience every possible scenario for an interview, so you'll be calm and convincing when the moment comes. The coach can also help improve your communication skills.

WHEN DO YOU NEED CAREER COACHING?

There are specific times when getting help from a career coach is especially beneficial. Most people seek career coaching during their job search or when they need to progress in their current career. Coaches can help with specific goals, providing guidance for how to approach and pursue them.

But coaching can also help with more general work-related issues, such as morale and mood. A career coach will support you, especially when you don't feel support from the other people around you.

FINAL THOUGHTS

If you are struggling during interviews, consistently making it to the first interview but never the second, or never landing an interview in the first place, consider hiring a career coach.

You can benefit from the support of a career coach even if you have a job that you do not want to leave. I was once in a difficult situation at work. I felt stuck and hopeless. I wasn't happy with my job performance, and going to work every day was a painful experience. I didn't want to quit because I loved my co-workers, but I just couldn't see any progress.

That was when I found a career coach to help me realize what was going on and understand how to overcome it. The career coach helped me identify the blocks that were preventing me from being successful at work. After several months of working with the coach, I became more productive and happier at my job. When my boss saw how I had improved, he promoted me.

The main benefit of having a coach is that you don't have to go through the challenging time alone. Because the coach is on the journey with you, you feel accountable to them and you're more likely to follow through on your commitments. Because the coach is working closely with you, you can get objective feedback on what you're doing. They serve as a sounding board for your ideas, and they may have new ideas and suggestions for ways to overcome the obstacles that you face.

44. Why Constant Learning Is Critical to Your Career

It is important to work continuously on acquiring new skills and knowledge in order to have a successful career. As new technology influences our jobs, you will need to develop new skills for mastering that technology. Smart professionals never get comfortable with the status quo; they are always trying to expand their knowledge and learn new skills. This attitude makes them better prepared for what is coming because the future belongs to people who can adapt.

No matter what career stage you are in, it is important to continue learning as much as you can. Stay up to date on technology and the breakthroughs in your industry and don't miss out on opportunities to improve your skills and knowledge.

THE IMPORTANCE OF CONTINUED LEARNING

Learning keeps your mind active and engaged; learning new things boosts your creativity and productivity.

No matter how great your skills are, they will eventually be superseded by new skills. Work processes constantly change and improve, and you need to keep pace with those changes.

Many companies prefer candidates who demonstrate that they are still learning and open to new ideas. This is because they know those people will be more coachable and adaptable.

FOSTERING ONGOING LEARNING

Most companies provide learning workshops and trainings. In addition, you can find online courses, certification programs, and opportunities for skill development in most industries. Your ongoing curiosity about your field and your desire to keep up and stay in the forefront will lead you to new books and articles on topics related to your profession.

REASONS TO EMBRACE CONSTANT LEARNING

Your diploma is important but so is your ability to stay current on industry trends and understand why they matter. Employers appreciate employees who never stop learning and who integrate constant learning into their work culture. Following are more reasons to embrace constant learning.

Constant Learning Is in High Demand by Employers

Two candidates apply for the position. One is confident that he doesn't need to learn because he already knows what he needs to know. The other is willing to learn continuously, even if she possesses the required set of skills.

Which candidate do you think is more likely to be given the job if they are both equally qualified? The candidate who is willing to learn. Being confident in your abilities is important, but being willing to learn is what will set you apart from the competition.

Constant Learning Promotes Happiness and Fulfillment

Don't you feel better when you learn something new? Learning new things makes us feel happier and gives our lives more meaning. Plus, learning is good for our brains and memory.

Constant Learning Helps Advance Careers

We all have career goals and desires. Reaching those goals becomes much harder when we stop learning. When you're not learning, you're not growing, and if you're not growing you're not getting closer to achieving your goals.

Thanks to technology, the opportunities to learn are endless. You don't have to go to a classroom to learn new things; you can find opportunities everywhere.

Sites like Udemy,[112] Domestika,[113] and Coursera[114] can teach you everything you need in your current job or gain knowledge that will prepare you for a new role.

---

[112] https://www.udemy.com/
[113] https://www.domestika.org/
[114] https://www.coursera.org/

FINAL THOUGHTS

The skills required for a recruiter have changed significantly since I started working as one. Now, in order to be successful in this role, you need to be able to use storytelling, inbound and outbound marketing, psychology, data scraping, data analysis, sourcing, email marketing, and basic programming, none of which was required when I first started.

This is just one example of how the job scope can change significantly over time and over the span of a single career. This is why it is important to continue learning new skills and knowledge.

You may even find that the new knowledge you acquire transforms you in ways that lead you to a new career altogether. For example, you may be working as a finance manager but then fall in love with social media and decide to move into marketing instead. These types of career changes will become even more common in the future, especially as new types of jobs emerge and others become obsolete. For example, social media manager is a career that didn't exist twenty years ago, and personal computers and dictation software have made the once important career of typist or data entry clerk almost obsolete.

45. Epilogue

Denzel Washington[115] once said, "If you died tonight, your employer would advertise to fill your job role by the end of the month. But your loved ones, chosen family and friends, would miss you forever. Don't get too busy making a living that you forget to work on making a life."

Your job is important, but it's not your entire life. At the end of the day, your loved ones are the ones who matter most. Don't get so caught up in work that you forget to spend time with the people who mean the most to you.

Don't let work consume you to the point where you forget what's really important. Work to make a living, but don't forget to work on making a life as well. That's what will matter most in the end.

Looking for a job can be tough. There's a lot of competition out there, and it can be hard to stand out from the crowd. That's why it's important to network and expand your LinkedIn network, even if you're not actively looking for a job. Often, it's not what you know, but who you know that matters most. Networking is essential for finding a job!

Get to know as many people as possible, and don't be afraid to ask for help. Stay positive throughout your job search, and eventually you'll find the perfect position. Who knows? Maybe one of your LinkedIn connections will be the key to landing your dream job.

Although job hunting can be difficult, it doesn't have to be painful. Don't be discouraged if you don't hear back after your amazing interview or if you're told you're a runner-up. You never know when an employer will reach out with another offer. Remember: A no is just a no for now. With the right job search plan and this book by your side, you can land your dream job in no time.

Although it may be tempting, taking the first job opportunity that comes your way is hardly ever a good idea. If something doesn't feel right, don't talk yourself into it. A lot of things look great on paper, but the reality is often different.

A job is a big commitment, and it has to feel right in your gut.

---

[115] https://en.wikipedia.org/wiki/Denzel_Washington

Don't ever become too attached to any organization, company, person, place, or project. If you want to attach to something, find a purpose in life, your mission, your calling and stick to that.

I believe that knowledge is power, and I want to empower as many people as possible to find their dream jobs. The world is changing rapidly, and it can be tough to keep up. I hope that the information that you find on **www.jobsearch.guide**[116] will help you stay ahead of the curve and land the jobs you really want.

If you have a minute to spare, I would really appreciate a short review on Amazon, Goodreads, or the site where you bought the book. You can write a short positive post on social media (LinkedIn, Twitter, Instagram, Facebook) about this book using this hashtag: #JobSearchGuide.

Five-star reviews and positive feedback from readers like you make a huge difference in helping others find this book. Many thanks for considering my request.

Good luck with your job search!

Jan

---

[116] https://jobsearch.guide/